"Bishop Sampson has developed a creative use of King's principles, using his high moral standard to suggest best practices for business. He raises some prudent ideas worth our consideration."

—Rep. John Lewis (D-GA)

"Bishop Rodney Sampson is at once incisive, inspiring, and thought-provoking. *Kingonomics* is a superb book that provides unique and compelling insights into the principles of collaborative leadership and the strategies for economic success, based on the life of Dr. Martin Luther King Jr., as applied to today's business environment. Guaranteed to be a truly rewarding experience for all readers, regardless of background. Highly recommended!"

—Andre Bisasor,
Founder, Harvard Extension Service & Leadership Society;
President, Institute for Negotiation Leadership & Diplomacy

"*Kingonomics*...expands our view of currency and gives us a new paradigm on expected returns."

—Henry Hardin,
CEO and President, SCI Companies

"With *Kingonomics*, Bishop Sampson has successfully blended together Dr. King's practical and philosophical approach to economic self-sufficiency. His clear, crisp, and compelling approach is a must-read for people wanting to gain knowledge and to virtually guarantee results."

—Alan W. Urech,
Principal, Stoney River Capital Partners LLC;
Sr. Vice President, 200 Peachtree

"*Kingonomics* is a powerful experience for each person who turns the pages. The right course of action for our economy!"

—Derrick Miles, CEO,
The Milestone Brand; Author, *Superhuman Performance:
Using Your Gifts to Perform at Extraordinary Levels*

"Bishop Rodney Sampson is a student of life and has mastered many insights into the behavior of mankind; he is observed as a spiritual minister and a business advisor to many persons. *Kingonomics* translates many of the teachings of Dr. Martin Luther King Jr. and makes them applicable by individuals in this world as they participate in the struggle for economic recognition, inclusion, and reward. No science better illustrates the consequences of our actions more than economics. By teaching these lessons with the precepts grounded in our spiritual faith, Bishop Sampson helps clarify our opportunities and responsibilities in 'Ceasar's world' around us. I highly recommend this book to learn more about how to find economic success that is in sync with your spiritual self."

—Charles H. Green, Executive Director,
Small Business Finance Institute; Author, *Get Financing Now*

"Rodney Sampson did an amazing job of educating me about the insights and issues that Dr. Martin Luther King Jr. presided over. The book is an easy read for the historian, educator, businessperson, or layperson who wants to understand more about the depth and breadth of the turmoil our country went through during the 1960s. As I read *Kingonomics*, the words on the page became transformative and made me take a deeper look at where we are today and how important Dr. King's work was to the success of assimilating cultures, education, and financial opportunities to all people today. Wow, the book is great!"

—Rick Singer,
CEO and Master Coach, The Key Worldwide

"Bishop Rodney Sampson's *Kingonomics* combines the principles taught by the late Dr. Martin Luther King Jr. and what Sampson has learned as a tremendously successful entrepreneur to produce twelve 'currencies' or strategies that, when practiced, will almost inevitably generate success. Read this book and remove the words 'failure' and 'impossible' from your vocabulary."

—Bishop Charles Edward Blake Sr.,
Presiding Bishop, Church of God in Christ (Los Angeles)

"On *tomorrow*, many will reflect and say that Bishop Rodney Sampson was a prolific thinker ahead of his time; *today*, I say, according to 2 Chronicles 20:20, 'believe in the LORD your God, so shall ye be established; believe his prophets, so shall ye prosper.' *Kingonomics* captures a philosophical framework that, if embraced today, will impact your tomorrow and generations to come."

—Bishop Allen T.D. Wiggins, Senior Pastor,
The Hope Church; Executive Director,
The Village of Orlando

"Bishop Rodney Sampson has embodied the manifestation of Dr. Martin Luther King Jr.'s economic philosophies in his timely, prophetic book, *Kingonomics*. Beyond the book, I know firsthand that Bishop Sampson works tirelessly to manifest sound economic- and educational-based causes that benefit all of humanity. *Kingonomics* is a great investment."

—Bishop Paul S. Morton Sr.,
Presiding Bishop, Full Gospel Baptist Church Fellowship, International;
Senior Pastor, Changing A Generation Full Gospel Baptist Church;
Author, *Changing Forward: Experiencing God's Ultimate Power*

"Sampson reminds us that Dr. King's message is as relevant today, if not more so, than it was forty-five years ago."

—Dr. Robert R. Jennings, President, Lincoln University

| RODNEY SAMPSON |

KINGONOMICS

TWELVE INNOVATIVE CURRENCIES FOR
TRANSFORMING YOUR BUSINESS AND YOUR LIFE
INSPIRED BY
Dr. Martin Luther King Jr.

BenBella
BENBELLA BOOKS, INC.
DALLAS, TEXAS

BenBella Books, Inc.
10300 N. Central Expressway, Suite 400
Dallas, TX 75231
www.benbellabooks.com
Send feedback to feedback@benbellabooks.com

Printed in the United States of America
10 9 8 7 6 5 4 3 2 1

Library of Congress Cataloging-in-Publication Data is available for this title.
978-1-936661-08-4

Editing by Cortney Strube
Copyediting by Francesca Drago
Proofreading by Laura Cherkas and Kimberly Marini
Indexing by Clive Pyne
Cover design by Faceout Studio
Text design and composition by Elyse Strongin, Neuwirth & Associates, Inc.
Printed by Berryville Graphics, Inc.

Distributed by Perseus Distribution
(www.perseusdistribution.com)

To place orders through Perseus Distribution:
Tel: (800) 343-4499
Fax: (800) 351-5073
E-mail: orderentry@perseusbooks.com

To my children,
and to the children of everyone who embraces *Kingonomics*

| CONTENTS |

| FOREWORD |

Most people, including economists and the general public alike, would agree that the economic crash in 2008 set off the worst recession since the Great Depression of the 1930s. These are certainly the worst economic conditions that most Americans have experienced in the twenty-first century.

The economic situation for African Americans and Hispanics, those with the highest unemployment and poverty rates, is more profound than at any other time in modern history. On almost all indicators, white Americans have fared better than most minority groups, but they too have felt a pinch from the disparities in the economy even when there has been some economic growth.

As William Julius Wilson, the Lewis P. and Linda L. Geyser University Professor at Harvard University, pointed out in his article on "Being Poor, Black and American: The Impact of Political, Economic and Cultural Forces," public attention to the plight of poor, black Americans began to wane through the second half of the 1990s and into the early years of the twenty-first century. Wilson makes the point, and rightfully so, that there has been scant media attention to the problem of concentrated urban poverty neighborhoods in which a high percentage of the residents fall beneath the federally designated poverty line and little or no discussion, such as what Dr. Martin Luther King, Jr. did, has been engaged by mainstream political leaders or civil rights activists.

Dr. Rodney Sampson is to be commended for focusing on and reminding us of Dr. King's real purpose, certainly in the final years of his life: the inequities suffered by minority and underserved people whose civil and human rights were ignored and unrealized as part of the American Dream. Through this book, Sampson puts into perspective Dr. King's concerns and the major focus of his work. If digested, this volume can provide a backdrop for what must be a continued focus if the nation—and ultimately the world—is to advance. While most people are seeking to understand the still lagging economic situation, and devise a means by which they can stay afloat, Sampson points out that we must thrive, not just survive, which is the basic premise for which Dr. King fought.

There must be a continued call for labor leaders, civil rights organizations, and others to unite and demand that political leaders and others stand up for and defend human dignity. Sampson reminds us of Dr. King's stance on poverty and its devastating effects on America. Dr. King proposed that poverty is not a consequence of a lack of education restricting job opportunities; nor is it a consequence of poor housing that stifles home life, leads to fragile family relationships, and distorts personality development; rather, it is an evil that must be abolished through guaranteeing a decent wage and income to all individuals. Indeed, Sampson reminds us that Dr. King's message is as relevant today, if not more so, than it was forty-five years ago.

Dr. Robert R. Jennings
President
Lincoln University, Pennsylvania

| INTRODUCTION |

THE ECONOMIC RULES MUST CHANGE

Many believe that what ultimately led to the death of Martin Luther King, Jr. was his pursuit of his "divine purpose": to tackle the social and political inequalities that were affecting minority and underserved communities in America and around the world. For it was in the process of championing this cause that his voice was forever silenced.

While most of us are well aware of Dr. King's sweeping dream of equality and freedom for all, many do not realize just how keenly focused he was on *economic* issues, especially in his later years. Without economic opportunities, King often noted, the pursuit of happiness extolled in our Declaration of Independence was impossible.

Dr. King spent the last months of his life fighting for the collective bargaining rights of underpaid workers and planning a march in their honor. At the time of his death there was still a great deal he wanted to do for the underserved and underrepresented, and he had become deeply concerned about giving them the solid footing they needed in order to realize *lasting* success. King was very concerned that the very civil rights and social liberties he'd been fighting for had little real chance of taking hold. Why? Because no provision was being made for economic liberties. Many of the people who were gaining new freedoms did not have access to the same financial resources and infrastructure that majority citizens enjoyed, making them unable to fully utilize the new liberties they were supposedly gaining. In fact, many of those liberties still don't truly exist for all Americans.

King was acutely aware that without change in the economic rules, none of the other changes he envisioned would have a fighting chance in the long term. Dr. King's final book, *Where Do We Go from Here*, was dedicated to this very issue. In its pages, he spoke candidly about the non-blacks in America who were supporting the modern-day civil rights movement. He pointed out that while these individuals were "on board" with blacks gaining recognition as human beings (rather than "coons" and "beasts," as they were commonly regarded), their support quickly waned when these same freedom fighters asked for equal opportunity in the education and business arenas. Many white supporters were quoted as saying things like, "These things take time, Dr. King!" and "Your community is asking for too much too soon." Historically, the entrenched majority population has always been extremely resistant to granting blacks access to the same economic resources—both subtle and obvious—that they themselves rely upon for success.

> *Historically, the entrenched majority population has always been extremely resistant to granting blacks access to the same economic resources—both subtle and obvious—that they themselves rely upon for success.*

If one looks at the federal legislation that was passed in the United States during the century following the emancipation of slaves in the South, it is readily apparent that not one piece of federally mandated legislation dealt with equal access to jobs or capital to launch viable businesses. In fact, much of what *seemed* like legislative progress was actually instituted in the form of presidential executive orders rather than progressive laws. Yes, there were *some* federal laws that "mandated" fairness in education, commerce, and voting, but legislation without enforcement, proper funding, and the cooperation of individuals, corporations, and state governments produced no real impact on the day-to-day lives of the very citizens the legislation was created to aid.

In 1954, for instance, the landmark Supreme Court ruling in *Brown v. Board of Education* essentially declared segregation illegal. Though it specifically targeted education, it had much broader implications, putting an end, "in theory," to segregation in transportation, public buildings, and businesses. The ruling, however, did not provide for equal access to jobs in the same establishments where people of color were now allowed to shop! In reality, there was a decline in black wealth and business because there was no reciprocity of ownership in the mainstream marketplace. Business ownership was largely a one-way street. Banks and shop owners were required to *accept money* from persons of color—no hardship there!—but they were not required to give them jobs or business loans.

And while the Civil Rights Act of 1964 was extremely important, it covered only federal and state governments and "some public places." It did not extend to Wall Street, nor did it include the human resources departments at publicly and privately held companies, venture capital firms, banks, and most universities. Hence, historically black colleges and universities (HBCUs) were created to educate the majority of persons of color in America. More than one hundred of these institutions persist to this day.

Affirmative Action was also a missed opportunity for inequities to be meaningfully resolved. What many who complain loudly about Affirmative Action fail to realize is that this policy, which "began" with President Franklin D. Roosevelt's New Deal legislation, historically benefited mostly *white females* in America. Roosevelt's main goal in promoting the New Deal was to keep the Democratic Party together; minorities actually gained very little from it, at least in its early decades. Although the New Deal was not specifically intended to benefit women, by the end of World War II in 1945, 19 million women, mostly whites and mixed immigrants, were working outside the home because our men were fighting a war.[1] This was at a time when, according to the U.S. Census Bureau, *the entire black population* of America was only 13 million.

The New Deal's affirmative action programs actually targeted un-employed white males as a positive (or "affirmative") effort to get them back to work and boost the economy after the Great Depression. Again, though, with so many white men at war and unemployment dropping to almost nothing, *white women* were given millions of skilled and unskilled jobs. (Though this was in no way a "women's movement," such as the one to follow in the 1960s, which was spurred, ironically, by Dr. King's Civil Rights Movement and which finally included both black and Jewish women.) With 55 percent of government jobs reclassified by Roosevelt in the 1940s, single white women were hired first, and then married white women, who acted as placeholders for white men until they returned from the war. From the women's suffrage movement (which mobilized largely because the 15th Amendment of 1870 had given black *men* the right to vote—only temporarily, it turned out), through the New Deal of the 1940s, and later through the gains of the women's rights movement that emerged in the 1960s, white women have historically been granted rights before black men and women. *Black women*, possessing the "double whammy" of both gender and skin color, have usually been the last ones invited to the table. It was Sojourner Truth who, in 1851, questioned, "Ain't I a woman, too?" A hundred years after emancipation of slaves in the Southern United States, black females were not part of the women's suffrage movement. In the WWII era, when white women were filling defense-related jobs, black women were clerks, textile workers, or domestic workers without pensions. They were not included in the Social Security Act of 1935, nor were they even counted as "women." Even as late as the 1960s and beyond, when black women got jobs, they were mostly low-paying domestic jobs that no one else wanted—still without Social Security benefits.

Although policies such as Executive Order 8802 (also known as the Fair Employment Act), which called for an end to discrimination in the defense industry, were supposed to prompt "sweeping" changes for black *men*, there was no enforcement of that order, either. The U.S. military was not desegregated until 1948. Before the Great Depression and even today, black men are often "last hired, first fired" or completely shut out of the private sector. They still have to settle for a lower pay scale and lower wages, though this unwritten, unspoken "policy" is now carried out in more subtle ways.

It's also important to note that even the whites that *joined Dr. King's cause* typically fared better than the blacks they were trying to support. Many of these people were Jews who had been oppressed not only in this country but also in Europe during World War II. However, because of certain U.S. laws that worked specifically against blacks, those with white skin were better positioned to navigate society's written and unwritten rules and thereby benefit economically from the changes for which Dr. King fought than were the blacks for whom King was primarily fighting.

Dr. King's economic work was cut out for him. He was not just fighting for jobs and fair pay, but for the recognition of an entire community's humanity. For before equal wages and opportunity could be gained, blacks first had to be considered men and women! Otherwise, they wouldn't even count. So King focused much of his early attention on issues of basic dignity and fairness; causes around which he could more plausibly rally popular support.

Alas, though, when you are the one holding the door open for everyone else, you can't always get in the room before it becomes too crowded. Someone must be left outside. Just as Moses led the Israelites to the edge of the Promised Land but never took them *in*, so, too, did Dr. King get his followers to the edge of *their* Promised Land. His primary role, we might say, was to point us in the right direction and move us closer. Though he may not have taken us all the way to the goal he envisioned before his young life was cut short, he definitely escalated the conversation and left directions by which we could find our way. It's those directions—derived from the ideas and recommendations he laid out in his writings and speeches and expounded through my interpretation of those messages—that form the essential philosophy discussed throughout the pages of this book. I call that philosophy *Kingonomics.*

We Need a New Foundation

Since Dr. King's death, America and the world have most certainly flourished, but we have also seen enormous strains on the economy and on society, with the wealthy becoming wealthier, the poor becoming poorer, and the middle class struggling. Why is that? Well, I'll give you one good, simple answer—though it may not be the answer an economist would give. The foundation upon which much of our nation's wealth was built was one of greed and selfishness. Consequently, I feel, it was just a matter of time before it started to crumble. And crumble it has. In fact, three industries (real estate, banking, and insurance)—all originally built in part with free slave labor and unjust economic policies—have been severely challenged during our nation's recent Great Recession. All of these industries required government bailouts to save them, and their journeys to full recovery still seem like long and uncertain ones.

Greed and selfishness were the basis of our nation's wealth? Yes, of course! Chattel slavery, an American economic institution, helped build these industries. Slavery provided the government and the private sector with *unfree* free labor for hundreds of years. Imagine building entire cities and industries without having to pay the massive labor costs required. In most business ventures, as you probably know, human resources are by far the greatest costs. Remove these from your profit and loss statement and just watch your EBITDA (earnings before interest, taxes, depreciation, and amortization) soar. The use of chattel slavery in America was based entirely on greed, selfishness, and hate. Though many economists today tout greed as a healthy driving force in business, I beg to differ. Greed caused entire generations of American citizens to turn a blind eye to one of the most horrific, large-scale injustices ever inflicted on a people. Greed is not a foundation built to last. We need to build a better foundation if we want a future we can proudly hand off to our children.

As a bishop in the Lord's church, I teach and believe in the universal law of sowing and reaping: you reap what you sow in this world. Hosea 8:7 says, "They sow the wind and reap the whirlwind." Proverbs 11:25 notes, "A generous man will prosper; he who refreshes others will himself be refreshed." Other faiths teach this concept as well. Hinduism and Buddhism, for example, espouse karma, the belief that "what goes around comes around." In other words, we all suffer the consequences of our actions. How we treat others is how we will eventually be treated. Bottom line: universal law is universal law. The consequences of law can be made worse (or better) depending on our willingness to address and correct our behavior.

America made such an effort to correct its ways during the Reconstruction, following Lincoln's emancipation of the slaves in the South. These years saw a period of growth and upward mobility for our most disenfranchised citizens and for our nation as an economic and civil whole. For the first time in American history, blacks were beginning, slowly but surely, to experience economic opportunity and a political voice of representation. Black men were actually given the right to vote via the 15th Amendment.

After Reconstruction, however, the pendulum swung back the other way. There came a new period of "Deconstruction" and disenfranchisement, enforced via the "Black Codes" and Jim Crow laws. These new, mean-spirited laws, and the violence, murder, and intimidation that came along with them, were designed solely to defeat the gains that the hardworking (called "lazy" by the masses) former slaves were making in politics, business, and society. To grasp the extreme damping effect of these laws, look at the number of black officials elected in South Carolina within the first decade after emancipation: 190, which was nearly half of total elected seats. Then take a glimpse at the same statistic twenty years later: zero. In Reconstructed Mississippi, there were 112 black state elected officials and even two U.S. senators. Within twenty years, there were none—all because of the new legislation and practiced intimidation and violence by whites against blacks.

The Union had agreed to grant all freed slaves "forty acres and a mule" for their contribution to building the foundation of America's wealth. Unfortunately, only a very few ever received it because the grant wasn't enforced after President Lincoln's assassination. The winds of hate were blowing anew across the fertile fields of our economic and social policy, and a whirlwind of systemic poverty was the result.

Fast-forward a century and a half. Today's uneven distribution of wealth in America—in 2010, the total wealth of blacks amounted to approximately $4,400 on average, $5,500 for Hispanics, and approximately $110,000 for whites, according to Pew Research Center, which defines wealth as home and land ownership, stocks and bonds, businesses, investments, and life insurance policies[2]—is a direct result of two things: (1) our collective failure to enforce federal and state economic legislation, and (2) our unwillingness to extend basic economic dignity, knowledge, and access to all of humankind. Today, our nation's unemployment, illiteracy, and crime rates, not to mention our prison industry, have ballooned to disastrous proportions and our nation's Standard & Poor's triple-A credit rating was downgraded in 2011 for the first time in history. No human with a moral conscience and an accurate understanding of American history can deny that an economic correction must occur in order to "right past wrongs." We must empower our most disenfranchised and abused citizens to "catch up" and compete on an even playing field with fair rules and treatment. I truly believe that if we take this courageous moral step, we will, by the universal law of reaping and sowing, set our nation once again on a trajectory to become the greatest nation on the face of planet Earth.

But here's the most important point: regardless of what policies the government may or may not enforce to help correct imbalances, we can all seize the reins of change ourselves. We can do that, first and foremost, by jettisoning greed as our main business model. Each and every one of us, regardless of race or economic background, can adopt *collaboration* as the new driving force of the twenty-first century. That is how we can change the world.

Age of Collaboration

King was not a businessman in the traditional sense, but he was certainly entrepreneurial in spirit. He had the drive, innovation, and risk-taking nature of an entrepreneur. He also deeply understood the value of collaboration, not just as a social tool but as a business principle. King imagined a world where people worked together both for the common good and for mutual gain. This vision stands in stark contrast to the profiles of greed we've seen of late from Wall Street and boardrooms across the country. Selfishness, not collaboration, often helms the current economy. And it has harmed us all.

One of the main challenges in rebuilding our economy is to re-orient our "me"-focused society. The majority of businesspeople are still primarily looking out for Number One. After all, this is the business model they were taught in business school. But having a me-first attitude is like trying to navigate solo without instruments—you severely limit what you can accomplish. It doesn't have to be that way. That's why, throughout this book, I stress King's message of collaboration, community, and championing a collective cause. If you build anything—a business, a family, a personal life—around a collaborative cause, it can connect you with like-minded people. And when you're connected with like-minded people, you are much more likely to transform your life and business in positive ways.

Conversely, when you choose to live an isolated life, your exposure to transformative opportunities and causes is limited. Your ignorance, biases, hang-ups, and internal insecurities go unchallenged and box you in. Although some spiritual and physical challenges may be endured in isolation, it is through collaboration that creative new solutions are discovered. The greatest business ideas and models are those that solve the challenges of society and meet the needs of its citizens. You simply can't see such solutions when working in a vacuum. Whether it is balancing our federal budget, decreasing our nation's wealth gap, or creating democracy and economic freedom in Africa, collaboration is the crucial ingredient for our economic future. Cooperation, not competition, is the new business model. The great news is that we now have astonishing tools for making it happen.

> *The greatest business ideas and models are those that solve the challenges of society and meet the needs of its citizens.*

Dr. King wasn't thinking of Facebook when he famously envisioned a world in which the descendants of both slaves and their "owners" could live and work together in peace, but digital social networking, engagement, and construction is certainly a significant way in which his vision is already being realized. People of different races and cultures come together every day on Facebook, Twitter, YouTube, LinkedIn, and other online communities to socialize, do business, exchange and debate ideas, and work toward change. Autocratic dictatorships in North Africa and the Middle East were toppled as a result of organized efforts through social media. Barack Obama, the forty-fourth president of the United States, was elected in huge part because volunteers and donors leveraged social media to recruit millions of new voters and break campaign fundraising records. The technological means we now have for connecting with others are well beyond anything King could have imagined in his day, yet his principles of collaboration and cooperation apply just as much now as they did five decades ago. The question is, can we evolve past our differences and come together, collaboratively, to sustain our world—today and in the future? I believe we can and will.

The Currencies of *Kingonomics*

The *opportunities* to collaborate and cooperate are virtually boundless today. But to join together in an innovative, entrepreneurial, and mutually beneficial way—foreign territory to most—will require a sound set of information, resources, and perspectives to navigate our journey. I refer to these intangible assets as *currencies*. And these currencies are exactly what *Kingonomics* prescribes. The Twelve Currencies of *Kingonomics* that this book will explore were "minted" by distilling central ideas from the life and works of Dr. King and combining them with real-life experiences from my life and the lives of other successful and collaboratively minded twenty-first century individuals. The result is a set of guidelines by which I believe you can realize your full economic (and personal) potential. *Kingonomics* is, in my humble opinion, the way Dr. King would have shepherded us through this tumultuous decade and beyond, had he lived a long and healthy life.

It is my hope that the twelve vital currencies introduced in this book will lead to collaborative solutions to our most vexing challenges, on both a collective and personal level. I truly believe King's ideas lay down a marvelous path that anyone, regardless of race, creed, gender, or religion, can follow to fulfill his or her true potential.

And here's a crucial point to understand: I believe it is *in the realm of free enterprise* that these ideas have the best chance of taking root.

In King's day, he looked to religion and politics as vehicles for creating unity. Today, religion and politics have become more of a catalyst for division and individualism than collaboration and community. Yet, through *entrepreneurship*, I believe there is hope. Today, we must use the business arena to foster the collaboration required for the creation of a sustainable society. Why the business arena? Well, interestingly enough, people seem to put their differences and biases aside when there is an opportunity to make a mutual dollar. Have you ever noticed that? I firmly believe that as more people collaborate to build mutual wealth, our differences will cease to divide us. Instead those very differences will provide creative marketing opportunities and exciting new solutions to problems.

Toward that end, it is my hope that the intangible currencies outlined in *Kingonomics* will eventually lead to *tangible* currencies that produce new companies, joint ventures, partnerships, jobs, revenue, and wealth.

Let's join hands and begin this adventure together.

THE TWELVE CURRENCIES

Growing up in Atlanta, Georgia, I naturally acquired a certain consciousness about such legendary natives as former U.S. Ambassador to the United Nations Andrew Young, American Civil Rights Movement leader and U.S. Representative John Lewis, and, of course, Dr. Martin Luther King, Jr. In fact, it would have been impossible to attend Frederick Douglass High School, walking distance from Dr. Martin Luther King Jr. Drive, without being exposed to King's words. As the child of a dedicated single mother who considered it important for me to appreciate my heritage, I gleaned much of the contextual knowledge of my youth from the writings of Dr. King. As I got older, I became increasingly fascinated by these writings and began to memorize his speeches from beginning to end.

Like many people born today in America, I came from humble economic roots. My family was not poor, but we certainly struggled financially. Yet innovation and entrepreneurship were always in my DNA. At a very young age, I began to show my first creative and entrepreneurial tendencies: I played the piano, organ, and keyboard on a contract basis at churches throughout Atlanta. The majority of people in my community were black like me, largely because of housing and lending policies that kept my mother and grandparents locked into homogeneous neighborhoods. So my entire worldview was black. It wasn't until the age of eighteen, when I enrolled at Tulane University in New Orleans, that I experienced my first truly diverse environment outside of casual social interaction. For the first time in my life, I was attending classes, studying, and socializing with Anglos, Jews, Asians, and Hispanics as well as blacks. It was the first time I had ever collaborated with more people who *didn't* look like me than with those who did. This was a revelation to me. It caused me to substantially broaden my perspectives of the world and the opportunities it afforded. Since that time, I have always viewed multicultural collaboration as a rich garden of possibilities.

In fact, now that I'm forty years old, multicultural collaboration has become my way of life. Today I do business with people on four continents. (And because I can never forget my roots, I strive to become involved in ventures that ultimately, in some way, give back to people who are facing daunting economic challenges.) My mantra, if you will, is that you have to connect with the heart before you extend the hand. I learned this directly from Dr. John C. Maxwell, who has sold more than 19 million books about leadership and trained millions in his Million Leaders Mandate initiative throughout the world.

But here's the important point: I would never have *met* Dr. Maxwell, nor had the amazing good fortune to live MLK's dream of working successfully in a connected, collaborative way with thousands of global citizens in numerous nations, had I not learned the twelve valuable *currencies* of *Kingonomics* at a young age. It has taken me some years to hone these currencies into teachable principles, but I have practiced them for many years. And it is through practicing these currencies that I have achieved business and personal success.

Currency Defined

The term *currency* is normally thought of, or simply defined as, money or cash—a tangible substance that can be earned, saved, exchanged, invested, spent, carried around in our pockets, or sewn up inside a mattress. In reality, money is only an external manifestation of currency in action. Yet currency is also intangible. It is a function of our values, actions, beliefs, and relationships. Currencies are patterns of thought and behavior in which we invest our energies. Currencies, as I define them, have much more value than money, though if we practice them diligently, we will attract plenty of the latter.

I'll explain how that works as the book unfolds. For now, I'd like to briefly introduce you to the twelve currencies that form the core of *Kingonomics*. Again, they have served as the foundation of all of the success and fulfillment I have experienced in my lifetime, and they are all derived from the words, ideas, and actions of Dr. Martin Luther King, Jr. He invested heavily in the principles demonstrated in these twelve currencies and I encourage you to do the same.

The Twelve Currencies

1. **The Currency of Service.** Dr. King called for an end to the era of "self-seeking" and the beginning of the era of service. Service-mindedness is a fundamental currency of *Kingonomics* and a key to doing business in the globally connected world of the twenty-first century. We must better serve not only our clients and customers but humanity itself. New technologies, including social media, offer us real-time windows to the dire problems much of the world's population faces daily. We can no longer turn our backs on the natural calamities that are occurring worldwide, nor on the desperate needs and dramatic disparities in material wealth that plague our planet. We must answer the call to service.

Businesses are beginning to move out of the profit-at-all-costs model of the twentieth century and coming to realize that service must be at the core of their organizations' cultures. Many of us are discovering that selfishness, the currency of greed, is not all it was cracked up to be in business school. Service must be the new motif. But here's the fascinating part. When we think of our business primarily as *offering a service* and secondarily as generating a profit, an interesting thing happens: profit comes to us as never before!

This goes back to the universal principle of reaping and sowing: the more we focus on others, the more currency circles back to us, both tangible and intangible. When our goal is to genuinely and respectfully serve others—our customers, our employees, our shareholders, our board members, and our communities—those same people reward us with their support, business, and ongoing investment. We also get the intangible benefit of feeling, with each transaction, that we have made a *deposit* into society rather than a withdrawal.

It is in depositing, not withdrawing, that our true power lies.

2. The Currency of Connectivity. We all like to think we can make it on our own, but "no man is an island unto himself." Solitude can be a gift when contemplating life's deepest questions, yes, but too much isolation can be a curse.

Dr. King was, above all, a champion of connectivity. By that I mean he was always looking to build community—physically, spiritually, mentally, emotionally, and economically. He believed that we could accomplish more together than we could apart, and he made his life a living example of this principle. The power of many minds and hearts working together is exponentially greater than that of many minds working separately. Now that the world is electronically connected in ways that King could never have imagined, it is the time to *use* the power of this great connectivity engine in order to find radical new ways to mutually support one another in business and life, and to form strategic partnerships at a whole new level.

Connectivity, not me-against-the-world individualism, is the new business model of the twenty-first century.

3. The Currency of Reciprocity. Dr. King warned of the perils of being financial "takers" without giving back to those who provide our wealth opportunities. He repeatedly warned against the kind of capitalism that extracts profits from disadvantaged countries and communities but does nothing to improve the economic conditions in those places.

Reciprocity—giving back to those who buy our products and services, supply us with materials and manpower, or otherwise support us—is good for business because it creates positive business relationships and a lasting, expanding market energized by goodwill and mutual gain. Reciprocity does not just mean tossing our supporters and customers a bone now and then. It means providing them with genuine business opportunities so that they may play a meaningful role in the market they are helping to create. Reciprocity is crucial in both domestic and international business.

4. **The Currency of Positivity.** It is well known that Dr. King was inspired by the nonviolent, nonaggressive strategies of Mahatma Gandhi. In fact, King is the American leader best known for using nonviolent civil disobedience as a vehicle for social change. When he was gunned down in Memphis on that fateful April night in 1968, he was there to support the garbagemen's strike in a peaceful manner. His positive philosophy of nonaggression and nonconflict, if embraced by businesspeople, can have deep ramifications in the world of commerce.

Business in the new era must adopt a fundamentally creative and strength-based approach as opposed to a reactive and negative one. It's time to move away from the competition-driven business model of the twentieth century and adopt a new, more cooperative approach. The Currency of Positivity means we no longer focus the bulk of our energy on one-sided and aggressive takeover tactics. We seek to collaborate and partner with other people and business entities to drive the new economy. We use most of our energy to *leverage our strengths*, while forming partnerships to mitigate our weaknesses. We are no longer obsessed with defeating the competition. We aim, instead, to be the best *we* can be while embracing competition as positive and necessary. Positivity means focusing on the *value we are adding to the world* more than the rewards we are wringing from it. When we do this, we all gain more than we do when we are gain-focused.

5. **The Currency of Personal Responsibility.** Another way that King and Gandhi were in sync was expressed through Gandhi's famous advice to "*be* the change you wish to see in the world." Both King and Gandhi knew that change does not happen from the top down. Instead, the followers must lead by the choices they make every day; then the leaders will follow.

In the world of commerce, both as consumers and merchants, we, too, must *be* whatever change we want to see in the marketplace. Do we want to see more honesty, goodwill, and generosity in our business community? Then we must be more honest and generous in all of our dealings. We cannot rely on our government or business leaders to make any changes we are not willing to make ourselves. Just as those who have been systematically *in*cluded at the table of opportunity have a personal responsibility to change the world from the top down, those who have been systematically *ex*cluded, for whatever reason, have the added responsibility (and privilege) of changing the world from the bottom up.

6. The Currency of Self-Image. Shakespeare advised, "To thine own self be true." But who *is* "thine own self"? It's not one's ego, as we so often see in business circles. Nor is it the set of limited beliefs that have been implanted in us by those who, for their own reasons, might insist on regarding us as inferior or flawed. It is something deeper and more spiritual.

It is extremely important that we all take the time to know *who we really are*—including our beliefs, our values, our tastes, our skills—and that we form a positive, loving relationship with our inner selves. Only then can we present an *exterior* image to the world and to the business community that serves both ourselves and humanity at large.

Dr. King was a deeply spiritual man who believed that people have deep and abiding worth, no matter whom they are or where they come from. But many of us were raised in a culture—or in families and neighborhoods—that put chains of shame upon us. As a result, we have come to believe we have no worth. We lack confidence and belief in ourselves. As a result we have been afraid to discover who we are, at our deepest core. And so, the image we project to the world, through our actions, our speech, and even our physical appearance, is at odds with the excellent beings we truly are inside.

The Currency of Self-Image means believing in who we are and putting forth an image into the world that congruently and accurately reflects our highest version of ourselves. In this way we dispel the majority of the interpersonal barriers that get in the way of good business and connectivity.

7. The Currency of Diversity. King was a huge advocate of stepping outside of our comfort zones and our familiar spheres of influence, especially in business. Oftentimes, we close ourselves off to our ideal path by putting on blinders born of prejudice and habit. When we need advice, we talk to the people with whom we are most comfortable. And who are those people? Why, people who look, talk, and act just like us, of course!

We *must*, however, diversify our decision-making process by purposefully seeking out those who aren't of our same ethnicity, religion, gender, or social backgrounds. Through this eye-opening process, we learn new truths and are exposed to the wide range of values, perspectives, and effective practices that drive our global economy. The future of commerce lies with those who are willing to follow King's advice and look to new faces and places for opportunity. We certainly don't need to be best friends with everyone on the planet, but we do need to develop enough respect and curiosity toward people unlike ourselves to allow ourselves to explore new opportunities of mutual self-interest.

8. The Currency of Character and Dignity. King believed that an economic system built on suspicion and distrust fosters negativity, fear, and excessive self-protectiveness. A business atmosphere of *trust*, however, promotes creativity, mutual support, and the sharing of ideas, to the benefit of all. Trust is all about character.

Character, one's moral or ethical integrity, is one of our most precious business currencies of all, and we must earn it, spend it, and invest it wisely at every opportunity. Everywhere we invest this currency, it eventually pays dividends. And I do mean everywhere. When we ourselves become absolutely trustworthy and exemplary—doing the right thing at all times, even when no one is looking—an amazing thing happens. The world around us transforms. Trust begets trust. Character begets character. Investing the Currency of Character and Dignity builds long-term stability in both our businesses and personal lives.

9. The Currency of Dreaming. As King's life attested, we cannot afford to become embittered, apathetic, or defeated by the obstacles society often throws in our paths. Rather, we must remain (or become) dreamers—big dreamers—infusing all of our business decisions with belief in the dream of opportunity for all. Without vision, business becomes a hollow exercise, leading nowhere. "Profit for profit's sake" is too small a dream to drive businesses of the new era.

All of our actions and decisions must be positive and intentional. We must each write our own internal "I Have a Dream" speech, not only for our businesses but for our lives and the world as well. And then we must advance toward those dreams forcefully and with purpose.

10. The Currency of Openness and Transparency. King was intensely aware of the economic exclusion that often occurs, especially for minorities, when business takes place behind closed doors. The white, male "old boy network," for example, often looks only within itself for new business partners, investors, suppliers, and vendors. The closed doors of the "American business club" have done a great deal of harm, some of it unconscious and unintentional, to those thirsting to gain entrance and play vital roles in the economy.

The new era of business *must* be one of openness and transparency. As the new business owners and operators of the twenty-first century, we must serve as living examples of transparency by reaching out to all kinds of people in an open, fully accountable way. We must demonstrate how openness and inclusion result in *better* decision-making and *better* market penetration. We must show that transparency is good for business.

Openness and transparency must pervade our business *relationships* as well. We must learn to plainly and honestly discuss taboo topics such as race, economic class, sexuality, and religion. We must learn to openly acknowledge our differences, with honesty, grace, respect, and even humor, as we continue to explore our commonality.

11. The Currency of Creativity and Innovation. Innovation, one of the most vital currencies of *Kingonomics*, is intimately tied to several other currencies, such as diversity, openness, and courage. As Dr. King was well aware, innovation occurs only when we open our minds to new ideas, new desires, new markets, and new technologies. And that, my friends, only occurs when we fearlessly step out of our comfort zones and embrace others of diverse cultures, races, ages, genders, and educational backgrounds.

Innovation will be the lynchpin of success in the new Collaborative Era. Gone are the days of stable, giant corporations that can survive by doing business the same way, decade after decade. Today's businesses, large or small, must be nimble and responsive to quickly changing demands in the market. The need to innovate must spur us on to new levels of collaboration, for it is only by working closely with those *unlike ourselves* that stale and tired thinking is cracked open and discarded.

Businesses are learning that including more people in the creative process results in a greater pool of truly innovative ideas. The truck driver may be better informed about some things than the CEO is and may have the next "big idea" that changes the way the company does business.

12. The Currency of Courage. Lastly, there is no avoiding King's message of love. Every human transaction, at its deepest level, boils down to a choice between fear and love. King believed unabashedly in the power of love. To act with love is to act with courage. It is to refuse to allow fear to dictate our actions and decisions.

How does this message apply in the harsh world of enterprise? The underlying thinking of "traditional" business is: I must protect what's mine or someone else will take my piece of the pie. This is a fear-based approach. As you'll soon discover, however, the whole model of a "pie" is off base. There is not a limited "pie" over which we must all fight in order to get our fair share; rather, there is a living, dynamic "ocean" of opportunity that steadily increases in size as we continue to work together, fearlessly, to create mutual success.

As long as we proceed in fear, our opportunities will be constricted by conflict, competition, and defensiveness. If we can learn to embed love within our business transactions, we will courageously unleash a surplus of creative energy that we can use to build not only our own companies but also the *entire industries* in which we do business.

That's the short version of the Twelve Currencies of *Kingonomics*. Let's take a closer look at each of them.

THE CURRENCY OF SERVICE

In his famous speech "Drum Major Instinct," Dr. Martin Luther King, Jr., spoke about a new standard of greatness that Jesus Christ had set for mankind. It was a greatness rooted in humility, kindness, and service. King pointed out that, like Jesus's, *our* greatness will be revealed not through our academic and scientific achievement, but through our ability and willingness to *serve*. How do you react when you read those words? In our society, we often think of prizes, accolades, accomplishments, wealth, status, and other concrete signs of achievement as the primary measures of greatness. And we all want to be great, whether we openly acknowledge it or not. Most of us believe we achieve greatness by shooting to the proverbial top, by working to *surpass* others, not serve them. Yet King's message tells us that to serve others is the measure of greatness.

> *Most of us believe we achieve greatness by shooting to the proverbial top, by working to surpass others, not serve them. Yet King's message tells us that to serve others is the measure of greatness.*

But serve them how?

The Currency of Service flips common business logic on its head. It says you are the greatest when you are the least. You are great when you are putting the needs of others first. King believed that we achieve our fullest human potential only through generosity and altruism, not through the darkness and ignorance of selfishness.

In other words, we must always practice an unselfish concern for the welfare of others to truly thrive; a business paradox, perhaps, but a crucial truth.

Ask almost anyone you meet today the simple question, "What are you doing for others?" and the answer is usually the same: "Not enough." But plenty of noteworthy businesspeople out there are doing *more* than enough. For example, Mark Zuckerberg, founder of Facebook, was the world's second-youngest billionaire at the tender age of twenty-six (his partner, eight days his junior, was technically the youngest), with a net worth estimated at $6.9 billion. He recently donated $100 million to help improve the long-troubled school system of Newark, New Jersey. This is a shining example of service in a community that desperately needs it, and a perfect demonstration of "giving back" from one who has been blessed to be in a position to do so.

Do you think his altruism has hurt him as a businessperson or helped him?

Although Zuckerberg is an example of giving on a grand scale, as business leaders and entrepreneurs, we can do our part on the scale at which we're working. We simply can't afford to be selfish any longer. Our culture is plagued by greed and, regardless of what some economists claim, greed is irrational, shortsighted, and bad for everyone, including the greedy person. We truly do reap what we sow—individually and collectively. For evidence, look no further than our most recent recession. It was created by pure, unadulterated greed; unbridled *taking* at the expense of others. When we give unselfishly, however, both the receiver and the giver reap immense benefits. Yes, even in cold, hard dollars. It is amazing to me that more businesses have not discovered this principle. *Service helps everyone involved in the transaction: both the served and the server.* Pure selfishness, on the other hand, ultimately harms both parties.

How many of the most devastating problems the world is currently facing might not even exist if we had just embraced King's message of *becoming great by serving one another*? Well, the good news is that it's not too late to start. To be successful entrepreneurs and business leaders, we must stop being distracted by ego and start serving with humility. We must realize early on in our careers that it's not all about us. Rather, it's all about the other person. This is good news for business, too, because that "other person" may one day become our customer or client.

When we adopt a constant mentality of service, we begin to attract a following that will remain faithful to us throughout our careers. Unselfishness, in the end, is better for business than all the greed in the world.

Service-Mindedness Builds Business Relationships

Service and volunteerism can be great tools for connecting diverse types of people. Service-mindedness leads to the building of authentic and meaningful relationships, both in business and in personal life. *Self*-service, on the other hand, kills the very relationships that are essential to a thriving business.

Because many start-up entrepreneurs lack the relationships necessary to give their businesses traction, volunteerism and service can provide a perfect starting platform by which to meet new people in a meaningful way. It's possible your first investor might come from the board of the nonprofit agency for which you volunteer!

Right now, my Opportunity Community Development Corporation enables me to connect with some very successful, high-net-worth individuals and institutions that share my ideals about the wealth gap in America. Our uniting passion is to "facilitate the creation of wealth in underserved communities via innovation, economic dignity, advocacy, education and opportunity-based lending, investing, and granting." But during the course of our service-oriented work together, the topic of business inevitably comes up in conversation and mutual opportunities are explored. Business relationships naturally develop.

There's no more personal and effective way to show your "true colors" than by volunteering. And best of all, anyone can serve in this manner. Volunteering can literally open doors. Perhaps, for example, there is a trade show you'd like to attend but you can't afford the entrance fee. What better way to get on the inside track and meet the movers and shakers who are participating in, or even *running*, the event than by serving as a volunteer?

Or perhaps you might consider joining the board of a nonprofit organization whose cause you are passionate about. In so doing, the opportunities to meet others with similar interests—with whom you can network and collaborate—will abound. I know of one woman, for instance, who went through a home ownership program and became so excited by its effectiveness that she decided to volunteer with the organization, even through a difficult stint of unemployment. Today she is its office manager.

I can't stress enough the importance of serving your way up! Service is a way to not only showcase your skills but demonstrate to the world that you are a person with values, commitment, and integrity. These are the very qualities that business owners often seek.

Of course, it is very difficult to demonstrate your integrity to a person who can't see such character because of preconceived notions about race, age, gender, sexual identity, or religion. But the best way to fight your way through these preconceptions is by unselfishly volunteering. Often it is observing kindness in one person that enables others to challenge their prejudices about that person's entire "group." I once heard a story, for example, about an elderly woman who was quite homophobic. Her car broke down in a dangerous-looking neighborhood and the man who stopped to help her was openly gay. He spent an hour of his day to ensure her car was towed and give her a ride home. They got to know each other a little and she liked him a great deal. He treated her with such unselfish compassion that she was forced to abandon her prejudices about homosexuals in general. Now the two exchange gifts every Christmas and meet for coffee a few times a year.

Whenever you perform service, you have the opportunity to smash prejudice and build relationships. And those relationships often lead back to business in surprising ways.

Make a Deposit into Society

I firmly believe that we, as humans, each have a calling greater than ourselves. If goodwill is your intention, it will invariably multiply itself, creating more and more of the same. If your primary goal, however, is only to increase the bottom line and fill your own pockets, then you are driven by what I call a "taker's energy." And, as the laws of nature dictate, "like begets like." We naturally attract people who are similar to us; who project the same values and tendencies. Takers attract takers and givers attract givers. Negative thoughts and actions attract negative outcomes and results. Positive thoughts and actions attract positive outcomes and results. It's quite simple.

Let's return to the universal law of sowing and reaping. When you focus on supporting the needs of others, the universe responds by taking care of you. Why? Because you're taking care of others. On a strictly biological basis, you are *helping* the species rather than *harming* it.

If you are a giver of life, service, and goodwill, you will tend to reap good things. On the contrary, if you are a taker and your life is all about what *you* want and need, the opposite will eventually occur. I stand firmly behind this spiritual and experiential conviction. Of course, bad things do happen to good people. But people of unselfish goodwill tend to bounce back and ultimately triumph over challenges. We can't look at a person's life and say, "What good did being unselfish do her? She got cancer anyway!" This is a shortsighted point of view. Instead of judging a person's life by one or two moments, negative or positive, we should look at the grand story told by *all* of his or her moments strung together. People who serve others tend to have greater, more inspiring, and more successful stories in the long run because they are ultimately helped and served *by* others.

I can tell you, from personal experience, that when I was able to move my colossal ego out of the way in my business life and begin thinking of service instead, good things started happening for me. Several years ago, for example, I began a very promising business venture with spiritual applications. During this egotistical period of my life, I believed I was irreplaceable, even in my own business. Because of this, I was blinded by the attention I received from the marketplace;

I was constantly being called upon to speak and give interviews about "cutting edge" ideas. But my partners—and some of my employees—developed animosity toward me because of this attention. Yes, perhaps this was a demonstration of their own insecurities, but my inability to perceive their feelings also prevented me from opening a dialogue that might have improved the climate. Though I was a "giver" and did project a positive attitude, I also had the unnecessary handicap of ego, which prevented me from serving as effectively as I could have. Getting fired was the best thing that ever happened to me. It forced me to re-commit myself to service over ego.

Although I couldn't see it at the time, being ousted from the company positioned me to move forward with many other exciting, service-based ideas and innovations. In fact, if I had not been removed, I probably never would have worked with Mel Gibson on *The Passion of the Christ*, partnered with Dr. John Maxwell's organization in Namibia to train more than thirty thousand leaders, advised foreign heads of state in Africa, or received the high honor of being consecrated a bishop in the Lord's Church. So, in the end, my former business partners' "evil" intentions were transformed into a greater good that has served thousands of people.

Sometimes the simplest truths come late. I woke up one day and realized that when I focused mainly on helping others, I, too, was greatly helped in the process. Always, in every case. This principle works exactly the same way for businesses as it does for individuals. I hope you arrive at this realization for yourself sooner rather than later.

Service Has a Boomerang Effect

I have leveraged the Currency of Service on a number of occasions in my life and I'd like to share a couple of examples of how it has played out. Under Dr. John C. Maxwell's leadership training program, EQUIP, I served six months per year for three years, at my own expense, in Namibia, Africa. My visits to Windhoek, Namibia, as a leader were quite special, and I have internalized each encounter I had the privilege of experiencing there.

My efforts were far from easy, however. They entailed major inconveniences, including enduring a more than twenty-four-hour flight; spending weeks at a time away from my family; and living for long periods of time entirely out of my comfort zone, eating strange food and observing odd customs.

But I believed in the cause and I was following my passion to serve.

In addition to the moral rewards I derived from the experience, my economic investment has paid off ten- to fifteenfold because of the amount of business I did in Africa. While in Namibia, I had the opportunity to meet, advise, network with, and receive advice from top political, faith-based, and private-sector leaders. Because of my willingness to serve people in Namibia by teaching, training, and coaching them about how to become better leaders, long-lasting relationships were established. My positive acts of service placed me in a strategic position to forge many ongoing business connections. To this day I receive opportunities from Namibia, ranging from speaking offers to a variety of viable investment opportunities.

Another example of the boomerang effect occurred when a fellow bishop heard positive reports of my service in Africa and, as a direct result, referred me to a position as advisor to the head of state of an African nation that was seeking to increase its U.S.-based relations. The reason I was in the consciousness of this bishop was because of my well-known service and investment in the African continent. His recommendation resulted in a very lucrative business contract.

I also have standing collaborative agreements with two cultural kingdoms in Uganda. And because they are supporters of my goods, services, and products, I have assured them that I am making specific plans to invest back into their communities. (And this is a key point: we must economically support the communities with whom we do business! We'll discuss this in more detail in Chapter Four, but I couldn't resist mentioning it here.)

Another example of service opening doors of opportunity was when, as an undergraduate at Tulane University, I cofounded an organization called Tulane Men Against Rape, which was in response to the increased incidence of on-campus date rape. The organization offered advocacy and facilitated counseling and intervention. The ultimate reward in this case, of course, was the satisfaction that I, along with the others involved, derived from helping to create a safer, more enlightened campus environment and community. One fraternity brother, however, got more tangible benefits: when the program was later funded, he received a full-time contract position.

When our goal is to genuinely serve our customers, employees, and communities, they reward us with their support and business. (This is due to the Law of Reciprocity, discussed in Chapter Four.) After all, who do *you* prefer to give your business to—someone who has unselfishly treated you well or someone who has treated *himself* well at your expense?

Service First, Profit Second

I always advise entrepreneurs to think of their businesses as providing a service first and generating a profit second. Sound strange? It's not strange at all when you think about how business works.

I have talked about service in terms of "serving humanity" in a charitable sort of way, but service has an even more immediate meaning in business. It also means good old-fashioned *customer* service to make your customer happy. If you always keep your business focused on how well clients and customers are served rather than on the mechanisms used to increase profits, you will never have to *worry* about profits. Too often, our business-school mentality has us jumping through hoops to increase our quarterly margins while we ignore the most basic questions: Are we *serving our customers* in the absolute best way possible? Are we treating them, in every aspect of our business, exactly the way we would want to be treated? Are we serving them with full respect for their time, needs, tastes, values, and happiness?

The goal of business is not only to market our products and get them into customers' hands, but to turn our customers into raving, joyous fans. Far too many businesspeople forget that all-important goal. They fall into the trap of thinking that the world somehow *owes* them business. They look at potential customers as little more than profit centers to be tapped. They don't take the extra step needed to turn their customer base into a fan club that will advertise their product free of charge. Great, customer-centric *service* is the best way to turn customers from passive consumers into active *advocates*.

One fact of commerce has not changed since the day the very first goat was exchanged for the very first barrel of wheat. That is, the best advertisement you will ever get is a happy customer. Word of mouth—whether in person, by phone, or over the Internet—is the single best way to build a business. It always has been and it always will be. When a real, live, noncompensated customer raves about the service he or she received at your business, it does more good than all the Google AdWords you can buy and clever tweets you can tweet. In fact, with the growth of social networks that now assign customer ratings to every product and service under the sun, word of mouth is more important than ever. One bad review from one mistreated customer and your entire *global sales* can suffer. Simply put, you want customers saying good things about your product and company. You do this by serving them well. Some simple steps for serving customers well are the following:

1. Take the time to find out who your customers are and what they need. You can't serve people if you don't know anything about who they are. Take the time and effort to respectfully learn about the lives, needs, and desires of your potential clients and customers. (See also Chapter Three.)

2. Create a solution that truly serves the customer. Develop products and services in response to real needs of real people, rather than creating a product first and then thinking about how you can sell it to customers. Make every product or service a solution to a need.

3. Deliver your solution with respect, humility, and an eagerness to constantly improve. As you deliver your product or service, always ask your customers/clients if there is anything they need that you are not providing exactly as they want it. Observe them every step of the way and look for signs of confusion, resentment, or annoyance. Make the improvement of service a constant, ongoing goal.

4. Deliver more than you promise. Always find a way to provide an additional service that was not expected. This simple act of offering extra can do more to turn your customers into raving fans than anything else. I recently talked to a friend, for instance, who'd been furniture shopping and had narrowed his choices down to two stores. One of the stores presented its delivery policies as if they were an inflexible edict, handed down from the corporate gods. The other store asked him when *his* most convenient delivery time would be and offered to take away his old furniture free of charge. This extra service, needless to say, convinced my friend to buy at that store.

Focus on serving the needs and wants of your particular customers and your business can't go wrong. For example, if you provide a software tool and your main customers are computer game programmers, then you should be aware that these folks tend to work long and late hours. Therefore, they will want access to support and documentation around the clock. A toll-free support line that operates from 9:00 a.m. to 6:00 p.m. would not best serve your particular customer. On the other hand, if you provide a friendly, warm, and understanding support person at 3 a.m., you will please your users.

Serving clients and customers requires putting yourself in their shoes and considering their (1) needs, (2) wants, (3) expectations, and (4) appreciation for extras.

What do customers *need*? What basic things must be done to get the product into your customers' hands and make it work as promised? If your product is a computer printer, for example, then you must give your customer an easy way to buy supplies such as ink cartridges and special paper. Your customer *needs* these supplies in order to operate the printer. Your customer must also be able to hook up the printer and use it effectively with modern computers and operating systems. These are basic requirements to make the product functional. It's surprising how often even this simple step is overlooked. How many times, for instance, have you found yourself scratching your head and cursing because of poorly written assembly instructions that prevented you from using a product?

What do customers *want*? In addition to getting the product or service to function, there are many additional things the customer or client *wants*, such as the ability to purchase the product easily and receive and use it quickly. Customers want to buy and use products or services in a hassle-free way. Generally speaking, the harder you make them work to get your product or service, the less interested they are. Always make the *customer's* ease and convenience—not your own—your priority. It never fails to amaze me how many businesses flip this around.

What do customers *expect*? Always consider how customers' *expectations* have grown and changed over the years within your target market. For example, if most of your competitors accept credit cards and are open evening hours, then the reality is that this is what customers will *expect*. Operating a cash-only restaurant or a convenience store that closes at 7:00 p.m. puts you at odds with customers' expectations and will cost you a great deal of business.

What will surprise your customers? Finally, what kind of extras can you provide to make your business special in your customers' minds? You've considered their expectations; now think of something they might *not* expect. At Christmastime, for example, one gift store I know gives each customer a small Christmas ornament with each purchase. This never fails to produce a smile on customers' faces. What can you do to make each of your clients or customers walk away from the transaction smiling? Provide something *unexpected* but really *appreciated*—a thank-you note and coupon, a surprise gift, or just an unexpectedly high level of service.

Be service-minded not only toward charity but also toward the people who make your business tick: your clients and customers.

It Is All About Investing and Reinvesting

Service-mindedness is all about investment—depositing and withdrawing. And though withdrawing, or reaping dividends, may be the most enjoyable part of the process, you can't withdraw until you have invested. Can you imagine trying to withdraw $10,000 from the bank if you hadn't first made a deposit? Therefore, before you or your business can make withdrawals, you must first invest in others, yourself, and your community. I advise people who want to start a business to spend at least twelve months depositing before attempting any kind of withdrawal.

For that first year, focus on building relationships, investing, and saving. Don't ask anyone to buy anything yet. See if you can bring value to 250 people for a year, so that when it's time for you to sell your company's products or services, you can hopefully convert a good percentage of those people into new customers. Even if you pick up only 10 percent (twenty-five) of these 250 people as clients, that's a very good basis from which to launch your operation. Let's say those twenty-five clients refer you to two people each. Now you have seventy-five potential clients! By contrast, most new business-people jump in and start pitching and selling to people they don't know, stifling the success of the venture before they even get started. If you take the time to get to know people and to serve them in some way, you will learn about their needs, wants, and desires; this will allow you to thoughtfully market and sell to them once your business is launched.

Now here's an example of how *not* to conduct business. At least once a week, someone who is a part of a network marketing company contacts me via Facebook. As a courtesy, I respond to this individual's message, and what often immediately follows is a pitch about a multibillion-dollar industry and how it will make me a boatload of money if I get involved with it. This just screams "wrong approach" for several reasons. First of all, the marketer doesn't know me from Will Smith. Second, the marketer hasn't taken the time to ask me about *my* interests, business focus, and desires. (Mind you, a simple review of my Facebook profile and a Google search would have revealed most of this.) And third, the marketer has zero concern about how my investment in his company will impact *my* personal purpose and destiny. It's all about him and what he is selling, whereas involvement in my nonprofit, investment in my crowdfund for entrepreneurs, or simply inquiries about my interests and needs would be less of a waste of time.

Ideally, after a year of serving others—by giving them a helping hand, volunteering for a cause they support, or making connections that secure them a contract or new job, for example—you'll be able to pick up the phone and say, "Hey, I just started this new enterprise and I want your support." You've already made an investment, so how can they say no? They may not buy your product or service directly, but they may introduce you to people who will! The point is that they will actively *want* to help and support you.

Service Provides a Route to Passion

Service offers other benefits as well. There may be no better way to zero in on your life's passion than by volunteering. Through unpaid service, you often find your true calling in life. Volunteering helps you learn about those things that are rewarding to you even without a paycheck.

Service was certainly the route by which I found *my* passion. Thanks to the goals of my family, my career path—physician—had already been more or less set by the time I was in the sixth grade. So I vigorously pursued the appropriate academic and professional courses. However, during my three and a half years in medical school, I also became very active in community affairs, speaking at youth days and a wide variety of conferences about the value of giving back. The more I volunteered in this way, the more passionate I became about the subjects I spoke about, and about speaking and leadership in general. Just one semester away from receiving my MD degree, I decided to change the course of my life. I made the shift toward pursuing my true calling: social entrepreneurship.

Even after all of those years of dedication to medicine, I finally understood that, for me, medicine was not my true purpose and I was pursuing this career primarily to please others. I discovered that I could best fulfill my purpose through entrepreneurial and cause-based pursuits. By pursuing my passion as a volunteer, I found my true calling. By serving, I was served.

Dr. King, too, discovered his purpose early in life through the passionate service of others.

Make the Shift

While Dr. King was busy working to ensure economic equality, he was surprised to learn that the very people who were trying to *deny* this equality were lacking it themselves. As he pointed out in his speech "Drum Major Instinct," King came to realize that many of the white sheriffs and police officers to whom he spoke during a prison visit were not making much more money than blacks in similar positions. He had always thought the white workers were fighting to protect their wealth, but in reality, they didn't have any wealth at all; they were just fighting to survive. And it's very difficult to serve others when you are living with a survival mindset. Survival-mindedness makes us hostile, suspicious, and self-protective. It closes us down rather than opening us up.

So how do we get around this? The surest way to outgrow a survival mindset is to flip the switch: start thinking of our businesses and job efforts primarily as *offering a service to help others* and secondarily as a means for generating profit. The moment we make this mental shift away from trying to survive paycheck to paycheck, and begin to think in terms of the service we are offering to others, interesting things happen: Possibilities expand. We become fully purposeful and alive. We never "work" another day in our life! We begin maximizing our time and energy as never before. Our perspectives on the mundane responsibilities of doing our jobs take on a new light. Business starts to soar, profits increase, and shareholders and investors are delighted! All because of a simple but profound shift in attitude: service first, profit second.

To sum up: volunteer, align yourself with like-minded people, make deposits before withdrawals, put your customers' needs first, and serve the communities with whom you do business. An important thing to remember, though, is don't serve with a quid pro quo in mind. Don't *expect* something of equal value in return. Give generously and sincerely, *expecting* nothing in return. For that's when true magic happens. In the words of Dr. King, ask yourself on daily basis, "How have I served my fellow man today?" This isn't lofty advice that only the saints among us can follow. It is the soundest business advice you'll ever receive.

3

THE CURRENCY OF CONNECTIVITY

One rainy Saturday afternoon, my wife and I decided to watch TV together. We flipped through the channels and landed on a scene from the 1992 comedy film *My Cousin Vinny*. We didn't plan to keep watching, but scene after scene drew us in and before we knew it we were watching the closing credits. Oddly enough, this broadly comical movie contained a theme relevant to this chapter. If you've seen it, you'll recall that Vinny (actor Joe Pesci) is an inexperienced New York attorney who must travel to Alabama to free his wrongly accused cousin of murder charges. It's his first court case and he really wants to win it on his own. That's what his *ego* demands. But he keeps finding himself forced to rely on help from others, particularly his fiancée, Lisa (actress Marisa Tomei). In the end, he wins the case but doesn't feel too great about it. As he and Lisa ride off into the sunset, Lisa asks a sulking Vinny, "So what's your problem?"

"My problem is I wanted to win my first case without any help from anybody," he replies.

"Well, I guess that plan's moot," she says, then adds in mock horror, "You know, this could be a sign of things to come. You win all your cases, but with somebody else's help, right? You win case after case, and then afterwards you have to go up to somebody and you have to say, 'Thank you.' Oh my God, what a [bleep]ing nightmare!" As the credits roll, both Vinny and the audience are reminded that needing others is not a loss but a victory.

We live in a country where rugged individualism has always been hailed as a sign of strength. Images of the lone pioneer, clearing trees from his land and fending off bear attacks, are an integral part of the American psyche. And indeed, the rugged individualist was a sensible model for an era when most of the world was separated by distance and lack of communications technology. But the world has changed and I believe we have entered a new period: the age of collaboration. In this new era, we will continue to celebrate the strength of the individual but will also recognize our collective strength and our deeper need to connect with other people. The idea of relying on other people will be seen no longer as a sign of weakness, but as wisdom. In fact, we will begin to recognize that, as the old song goes, "People who need people are the luckiest people in the world."

An odd thought, isn't it? That *needing* people makes you lucky? But indeed it does, according to the second currency of *Kingonomics*—connectivity—because if you don't *need* people, you won't seek out their company, their advice, their input, or their collaboration. You'll fall into the trap of thinking you really *are* self-sufficient—that it's a sign of strength to do everything on your own. This is no longer a wise position, if it ever was. The currency of human connectedness is absolutely critical for success in today's globally wired, economically interdependent world.

In *My Cousin Vinny*, the main character needed people all along, but refused to recognize it till the end. *Realization*, however, is an extremely important step for us all. For it is only through *understanding the importance* of the Currency of Connectivity—*knowing* that we need people and being prepared to do something about it—that we can truly experience the "luck" promised in the song lyric.

The time has come for us, as businesspeople, to acknowledge that we do indeed need to connect to other human beings. Particularly, we need to connect with those of nationalities, geographies, and cultures different from our own. Why? Because it is only by connecting and collaborating with people unlike us that we gain the global perspective required for success in the twenty-first century. Regional and individual isolation no longer make sense in a Web-driven world where new markets are being penetrated every day.

Collaboration Is the Key

The majority of great human achievements could not be accomplished without collaborative efforts. Just look at the making of the movie *My Cousin Vinny*. In order to make it work, many famous actors, all with their own egos and needs, had to work together seamlessly to make a balanced and believable story. Of course, they did not accomplish this alone. In addition to a large cast, there were scores of people behind the scenes: producer; writer; director; casting agent; set, costume, and lighting designers; set builders; key grips; and publicists, among many others.

Or look at the field of professional sports. Not one player ever won the World Series or an NBA championship by himself—not even Michael Jordan. A sports team succeeds as a result of the diverse and complementary skills of its players, not because one person has all the answers. A business is no different. Together we are greater than the sum of our parts.

Diverse *skills* are not the only reason to collaborate, however; diverse *backgrounds* also bring us a host of values, perspectives, knowledge, and tastes that we simply cannot learn from people who are just like us. Again, let's look to the movies. The smash summer hit of 2011, *Pirates of the Caribbean: On Stranger Tides*, was made by a cast and crew that reads like a microcosm of the United Nations. Geoffrey Rush is Australian. Penélope Cruz and Àstrid Bergès-Frisbey are from Spain. Judy Dench is British, Johnny Depp is American, and Yuki Matsuzaki is Japanese. The cinematographer, Dariusz Wolski, comes from Poland. The list goes on and on. Many cutting-edge technology companies today employ engineers and executives from China, Brazil, India, Russia, and the United States working together side by side. Collaborate with someone from a different nation and culture and you gain not only the benefits of that *individual's* perspective but access to a whole new *world* of ideas, knowledge, and attitudes. That's because each of us brings a world with us—a world of tastes, values, knowledge, and cultural preferences—and this world contains a hidden wealth of untapped resources. Each time you decide to hire or partner with someone from another nation, faith, or culture, you are able to tap into an existence unlike your own.

Connection Already Exists

As Dr. Martin Luther King, Jr. noted in his speech "Why Jesus Called a Man a Fool," we are indirectly interacting with people who are different from ourselves all the time, just by using the products, technologies, and services that are readily available to us. In fact, when you think about it, it is virtually impossible to do anything on a daily basis without the involvement of people from other nations, cultures, races, and religions. Every necessity and luxury you indulge in has the imprint and intelligence of someone who doesn't necessarily look, think, or act like you. Though you may choose to exercise your God-given right to disassociate yourself from those who don't reflect what you see in the mirror, it doesn't mean that you are not, in some very important ways, dependent upon them. To believe otherwise is pure self-delusion and foolishness, Dr. King taught.

You've heard the expression, "No man is an island unto himself," derived from one of the written meditations of seventeenth-century poet John Donne, but I prefer a quote from philosopher William James: "We are like islands in the sea, separate on the surface but connected in the deep."

So, in a sense, every person *is* an island. That is, we pretend to be self-contained and separate. We "populate" our little island with its own culture, language, and architecture, but underneath it all, we are part of a greater structure that connects and unites us. We can either recognize that connection and use it to maximum advantage, or we can ignore it.

Isolation Kills

Human beings don't typically do well when isolated from others, which is why solitary confinement is usually considered to be the worst form of punishment. Yes, there are the rare Thoreau types who thrive, for a period of time, by living remotely from society, but for many of us, complete isolation can lead to our downfalls.

One of the most talented film directors of our time, Steven Spielberg, continues to take the opposite approach—constantly seeking out other people for shared success. His partnership with writer and director George Lucas and his Lucasfilm production company spawned the blockbuster Indiana Jones series and helped catapult Spielberg to the superstardom he enjoys today. Spielberg collaborated successfully with so many stars, producers, and composers that when he was ready to bring the true story of *Schindler's List* to the big screen, multiple studio heads fought with one another to produce the film, even though it hardly appeared to be blockbuster material.

Spielberg went on to win an Academy Award for his direction of the film. He then used this recognition to build new connections in the nonprofit world. Donating his portion of the profits from *Schindler's List*, he created the Righteous Persons Foundation, an organization dedicated to strengthening the Jewish community and preserving the memory of the Holocaust, and has become an ardent supporter of Holocaust survivors. Spielberg now works with numerous other charities as he continues to develop new connections from old connections, expanding ever-outward in a growing web. In spite of his enormous talent, he is the first to admit that none of his achievements could have been accomplished by him alone. He is a model of connectivity.

Connectivity Is Innate

I believe the principle of connectivity is encoded in our DNA. Just look at the way the human body works. In order to fight disease, catch a baseball, or play a guitar solo, literally trillions of cells of different types must communicate, coordinate, and work together toward a common goal. Each cell has an individual life of its own, yet each is plugged into the bigger job of keeping the whole body alive, healthy, and creative. The amount of intercellular collaboration required to do something as simple as picking up a pencil is absolutely staggering. It dwarfs anything the most powerful supercomputers can do. Yet such connectivity happens seamlessly and effortlessly.

If, on the other hand, our cells argued among themselves or became egotistical about their own particular roles—the blood cells, for example, wanting more recognition, oxygen, and nutrients than the muscle cells—nothing would ever get done. Chaos would result. Cancer, in fact, *is* what happens when cells begin to behave selfishly, without concern for the whole body.

Healthy bodies know all about connectivity and collaboration on a cellular level, yet we often fail as a species to create powerful connections and relationships with others of our kind. I believe this stifles progress and innovation in the arts, in science, in business, and in politics. So did Dr. King. It was one of his most passionate premises.

The Currency of Connectivity is absolutely essential to maximizing our productivity, especially when it comes to our professional careers and entrepreneurial pursuits. Business, by its very nature, does not take place in a vacuum. It is a collective effort. Those who make connectivity an essential business currency gain the vital advantage of learning more about the real needs of their customers and clients than those who think they know it all themselves. On the other hand, without forging deep connections all we can do is *imagine* what our customers want. And such imaginings are usually off base because they're built on an extremely limited frame of reference.

Leaders who are plugged into connectivity are smart enough to enrich their *internal* teams as well, by bringing a wide range of perspectives and values to the decision-making process. They forge a genuine bond of connection with everyone on their team. They create a workplace where the human connection comes first and the business connection comes second. When people feel honored for their basic humanity and feel a sense of genuine connection with their employers and team members, productivity skyrockets. This has been shown over and over. In Tom Rath's book *Vital Friends: The People*

You Can't Afford to Live Without, he claims that his team's research shows that people who have a best friend at work are *seven times more likely* to be engaged on the job. Companies that encourage genuine connections among their employees tend to have teams that bond like family members and remain committed and loyal.

As Dr. King pointed out in his "Why Jesus Called a Man a Fool" speech, you are *already* connected to the whole world through the products you use and the services you employ. You are also connected through the music you listen to, the movies you watch, and the sports games you enjoy. So why not make *conscious and deliberate* use of connectivity so that you can reap the same advantages many highly successful teams, companies, and artists have enjoyed over the years?

Global humanity is our true "body," and each of us is one of its cells. If we don't collaborate, we truly fail to fulfill our ultimate purpose on Earth.

What Is Collaboration?

Connectivity, as I use the word, means any meaningful exchange between two human beings. Collaboration takes connectivity to a new level. To collaborate effectively, we must incorporate the following seven elements:

1. **Human recognition.** All stakeholders involved must recognize one another's genuine needs, along with their inherent human value.
2. **Respect.** Recognition of others must be performed with mutual respect, even when there are major differences in philosophy, culture, values, language, and appearance.
3. **Conversation.** A dialogue must then occur; a listening-heavy conversation about the challenges and opportunities for all stakeholders involved.
4. **Cooperation.** The stakeholders must then agree to cooperate in a mutually beneficial way.

5. **Negotiation.** Win-win terms for mutual benefits and contributions must be negotiated.
6. **Agreement.** The results of these negotiations must be *recorded* in some sort of formal agreement.
7. **Real-world execution.** The deliverables of the agreement must be executed for mutually favorable outcomes and objectives, thus creating a tangible manifestation of the collaboration.

Collaboration cannot exist without a genuine, heartfelt intent to connect on a human level. We must do a better job of reaching out to one another across the globe, turning differences into strengths. Those who forge the most connections in the new millennium will be those who succeed.

Connection Heals

Connectivity is also one of the greatest healing forces on our planet. Communion with other people who are dealing with challenges similar to our own has been shown to play a vital role in overcoming physical, mental, emotional, spiritual, and financial hurdles. The Currency of Connectivity was certainly in play when two alcoholics, Bill Wilson and Dr. Robert Smith (aka "Dr. Bob"), joined forces to create Alcoholics Anonymous (AA), an organization that, over the course of seventy years, has saved millions of lives from alcohol addiction by the simple act of connecting one alcoholic with another.

The collaboration began in 1935. Wilson (later known as "Bill W.") was struggling with an addiction that was threatening to take over his life completely. He was on the verge of ruining a promising career on Wall Street and his marriage was heading down a similar path. He was trying to stay sober on his own, but wasn't finding sustained success.

During a failed business trip, Wilson was tempted to drink to "drown his sorrows," but part of him also desperately wanted to stay sober. He was a man at war with himself. He suddenly had the remarkable realization that in order to avoid picking up the bottle he needed to *help someone else* who was struggling with alcohol. By phoning local churches, he was directed to another alcoholic by the name of Dr. Bob Smith. The two forged a connection and, long story short, Wilson eventually moved into the home of Dr. Bob and his wife, Anne. The idea was that they would mutually support one another in living a sober life. After some success with this joint venture (which included the addition of a spiritual dimension), the men took their message of connectivity and mutual support on the road and shared it with others. Bill W. allowed other alcoholics to live in his home without paying rent and board, even though this caused some serious problems with his wife and household. The organization known as AA grew from these early experiences. Some of the success stories told by these previously hopeless and helpless individuals have been the stuff of miracles.

AA has grown in size and popularity from just over one hundred members in 1939 to literally millions worldwide, in large part because two "remarkably unremarkable" men understood the immense power of connectivity. The secret? One person helping another. The organization connected with a segment of the population that had been virtually written off and, in so doing, radically changed the course of their desperate lives and those of their families, for good. The alcoholics who live sober lives thanks to AA are the first to admit that they could not have done it alone. AA's treatment model of attending frequent group meetings, keeping connected to a sponsor, and following a twelve-step program now serves as the basis for helping people with numerous other addictive behaviors.

Connectivity heals.

Connect to the Wider Network of Society

Although solitude can be a gift when contemplating life's deepest questions, too much isolation is an impediment to growth. In the vast majority of cases, when an individual is cut off from others, his mental and physical health deteriorates. However, it is not only *individuals* who pay a price when isolated from the rest of humanity;

whole groups of people can suffer consequences that are neither healthy nor evolutionary. Ghettos, where the Jews in Europe under Hitler's reign were forced to live in poverty and isolation, pinched off residents from the mainstream of humanity and created a great deal of stress and misery for them. Slaves in America's early days were forbidden from leaving their plantations or interacting with others, thus forcibly keeping them ill-informed, uneducated, and unable to organize collectively. This held back a people's collective growth for decades to come. Similarly, in our modern "ghettos" (as they are called, although people are not literally *forced* to live there), isolation can also prove to be highly detrimental. Few would disagree that people "stuck" in these living environments with little opportunity to interact with other people and places tend to lead lives that are impoverished in many ways, including economically.

People of all socioeconomic backgrounds can live in self-imposed exile. Isolation is often a mindset rather than a physical place. You can be in a "ghetto" of your own making while living in Beverly Hills, Palm Beach, or Manhattan's Upper East Side if you prevent yourself from forging deeper and wider connections with humanity at large. And you can be just as impoverished in your own way as an inner-city teen with no resources. The mental ghetto is a hideous place to live in one's consciousness; it is lonely, repetitive, stale, and stunted, even if it includes horse stables and golf.

Thousands of businesses have failed in recent decades because they have adopted a ghetto mentality of their own. By this I mean they have ignored the wider world at their fingertips and insisted on playing by the same old rules, with the same old products and services, the same old business partners, and the same old types of internal team members. Because they have not availed themselves of the connective ideas, practices, and technologies of the modern era, they have fallen out of touch with progress and their ideas, products, and ways of doing business no longer have relevancy.

Even when isolation is not actively harmful, it can certainly be "nonevolutionary." When we encounter tribes of indigenous people, for instance, that have not had contact with others for centuries, we typically find that they have not changed or evolved, culturally, very much over the years. Though they may preserve some rich heritage and tribal rituals, typically they are not great innovators on the world stage.

Connection Builds Business Relationships

Dr. John Maxwell taught me that the success or failure of anything we do in life is totally dependent on the relationships we have or do not have. It is often said that it's not *what* you know, but *who* you know. If this is the case, then how do we meet the investors, advisors, partners, employees, and customers necessary to create a successful business venture? And how do we engage these people in collaboration? Well, for starters, profitable engagement with others requires enthusiasm, self-confidence, good communication skills, patience, honesty, and recognition of other people's values. But even more than this, it hinges on an attitude of *bringing value to other people*. That is the essence of true connection. When we approach others with the intention of offering them positive benefits, we build a network of great connections very quickly. On the other hand, when we approach people from a basis of advancing our own needs, we repel them.

> *The success or failure of anything we do in life is totally dependent on the relationships we have or do not have.*

Neediness is, by nature, a repellent force. It discourages connectivity. Think about it. How do you feel when a stranger makes a beeline for you on the street with his hand out, or when an overly eager salesperson "attacks" you the moment you walk into an electronics store? You immediately pull back, either physically or internally. It's a natural reaction.

Many of us have also known what it's like to have a needy friend or to spend time with a needy individual. We soon begin to find their energy clingy and off-putting; before long we start letting their phone calls slip to voice mail. We don't have the energy to deal with them.

But when someone approaches us with the intention of serving *our* needs, the doors of connectivity fly open. Remember this principle every time you approach someone with business on your mind.

It takes time and effort to *learn* about other people's needs, and this can't be accomplished with a one-sided conversation. Give-and-take is necessary. I've learned that if it's mutually very difficult to talk with a certain person, then it's probably a waste of your precious time to attempt a true connection with him or her. This is a conclusion that can often be drawn fairly early on in the relationship. If a person doesn't take the time to engage you in a courteous dialogue, listen to who you are as a person, and share something about him- or herself with you, then he or she probably isn't going to take the time to hear about your business opportunities. Don't try to force connectivity.

Personally, I try to allow business relationships to develop organically and strive to build influence with a person, regardless of whether or not we ever actually do business together. I do this primarily by listening—carefully and without preconceptions—which helps me figure out how I can encourage the speaker, through my insight and experiences, to achieve his or her highest destiny. Often this involves providing a referral or introduction that can help advance the individual's cause. Before I can "sell" to someone, I have to connect with him or her in a genuine, human way. I have to know how I can bring value to a person.

Every business success, in fact, requires that we connect with people—customers and clients. If we all knew how to connect with customers who will purchase what our business offers, then growing a business would be very easy. But for most of us, connecting with others is a challenge. Perhaps this is because most of our business efforts are focused on selling, rather than reaching out with our hearts, minds, and ears.

We must reverse that trend and learn to connect *first* if we want to know who might be truly interested in us and what we have to offer. It is often remarked that "people buy people," not things. In other words, if people genuinely *like* you, they will want to support your business, especially when they receive value from it. This is true of the hiring process as well: people tend to hire job candidates with whom they feel a personal connection. In fact, many executive coaches and consultants today focus predominantly on helping their clients become more likable.

Replace the Traditional Sales Model

Unfortunately, millions of inhabitants of this planet are marketing great products and services but fail to sell them because they forge no authentic connections with potential customers. Salespeople can often repel potential customers. (Again, think about your own response. How do you feel when you pick up the phone and get verbally pounced upon by a telemarketer who can't even pronounce your name, much less show an interest in your needs and desires?) Much of this misguided behavior stems from the traditional sales mentality, which is completely focused on the need to make *our* sales quotas, as opposed to learning about and assisting with what *others* need, regardless of whether or not this leads us directly to a business transaction. Those who base their behaviors on the *client's* needs, on the other hand, build long-term connections that eventually serve *their own businesses* much better than aggressive sales techniques.

For example, I spoke to a woman recently who went into a retail store looking for a certain product. The salesperson took the time to really listen to her needs and, as a result, recommended a very different product, and one that was sold only at a competitor's store. The woman gratefully went to the competition to buy that one product, but she has since returned to the original retail store dozens of times. Why? Because it proved to her that it had her best interests at heart. It was willing to lose a short-term sale in order to create more value in *her* life. Consequently, it gained a customer for life.

Influence Energizes Collaboration

Dr. John Maxwell says, "Leadership is influence . . . nothing more, nothing less." I broaden this to say, "*Collaboration* is influence . . . nothing more, nothing less." Influence is the ability to create change in people. Influence will take you farther than money ever will, and it can open doors that traditional resources can't. It will also give you the leverage to create change, even when your strategies and systems fail.

Dr. King was a world-class influencer. He moved people to action. Influence can rally people together around a collective cause, and that cause can be your business's products and services. Remember this: people *want* to be influenced by you or they wouldn't be walking into your shop, talking to you on the phone, or reading your company's brochure. Influence flows from knowing how to (1) inspire respect, (2) demonstrate expertise, (3) determine what you want to accomplish, (4) project confidence when pursuing your goals, (5) communicate your desires with clarity and passion, and (6) present a call to action that resonates with people. But influence only happens after a genuine connection is made. Some basis of commonality must first be established. Trying to influence someone you know nothing about is like trying to feed a hamburger to a vegetarian. It's not going to work.

How do you develop influence? Help others, make contributions to your community, demonstrate integrity, serve as an example, show respect, connect with others, and offer value to others instead of trying to meet sales quotas. You do *not* develop influence by cold-calling strangers, lecturing people, using aggressive sales techniques, or treating people as if their function in life is to fulfill *your* business needs.

Synergy Redefined

Synergy was the buzzword of the last decade. Leaders, politicians, and businesspeople discovered that the power of many minds and hearts working together was greater than that of many minds working separately. Through synergism, many exciting partnerships were formed.

Yet many of these relationships were not *symbiotic*, or collaborative, in nature and thus they have not endured. I believe the coming age of collaboration will be more symbiotic than synergistic.

What do I mean by this? *Symbiosis* is a scientific term referring to the habitual "cooperation" that can occur between organisms of different species. Although the term, in science, can include *parasitic* relationships, wherein one organism takes disproportionately from another, I use the term to mean a mutually dependent relationship that is beneficial to both parties.

Examples of symbiosis abound in nature. For example, many species of plants depend on insects, such as bees, to pollinate them, while the insects depend on those same plants for food. The plants produce brightly colored flowers with inviting scents to attract the bees; the bees then carry the pollen from the stamens of one flower to the stigma of another. In the process, the bee is fed while the plants' vital reproductive materials are exchanged. Neither species could survive for long without the other.

Another example is the Egyptian plover birds that feed on the bits of meat stuck between the teeth of crocodiles. The crocs dutifully open their mouths and patiently allow the birds to feed without trying to swallow them. Why? Because the crocs get a free teeth cleaning, sparing them pain and tooth loss, while the birds get a free meal!

Let us take a lesson from nature and avail ourselves of the endless opportunities for symbiotic relationships that exist in the business world. Let's connect with others with whom we can form mutually beneficial relationships that also support the common good. For example:

- Company A's waste products provide eco-friendly fuel or packaging materials for Company B. In the process, both companies save money *and* help the environment.

- Company A opens a discount gym on the premises of Company B. Company B provides Company A with all of its customers while reaping the benefit of having healthier, more energetic employees. Additionally, time, money, and energy are saved for all.

- Company A funds some of the research and development costs for Company B to create healthier ingredients for snack foods. Company A gets to be the first to bring a healthier snack product to market, Company B receives financial support, and the world gets to lower its cholesterol level!

As with above examples, think in terms of symbiosis as *you* connect with potential business partners. Is it a give-and-take situation, or is it all take? The best relationships are those that are mutually satisfying and that neither party would want to live without. Almost any business relationship that provides mutual benefits while helping make the world a better place is a healthy, symbiotic one.

Embrace Technology, Don't Hide From It

The world is now electronically connected in ways that Dr. King never could have imagined. Social networking has been forever integrated into our way of living. Let's now *use* the enormous strength of the great connectivity machine we have created to find exciting new ways to mutually support one another in business, to connect with customers new and old, and to form strategic partnerships at a whole new level.

Connecting electronically is already happening every day via social networking communities such as LinkedIn, Facebook, and Twitter. But we've seen only the very tip of the iceberg. As technology continues to get better at providing custom solutions to individual consumers, smart businesspeople will *leverage* that technology to connect with their target markets. For example, the day will soon be upon us when television becomes fully interactive, with advertisers able to target *individual consumers* based on their age, tastes, gender, shopping preferences, and value systems. How will you use such technology to build connections?

As Emily Nagle Green points out in her book, *Anywhere: How Global Connectivity Is Revolutionizing the Way We Do Business*, there is no longer a separation between our work lives, our home lives, and our social lives, thanks to the prevalence of smart mobile devices that keep us networked at all times. How much longer are you going to ignore these new connective tissues and insist on doing business in the outdated, isolated, and primitive ways?

Can you think up a creative new iPhone app that will help consumers make sharper, more enjoyable social decisions while simultaneously leading them to your business? Can you think of a LinkedIn business group that you can help, for free, by offering your online expertise (while simultaneously promoting your consulting business)? Can you write an iPad- or Kindle-friendly e-book and give it away to potential customers via an e-mail campaign?

What are you waiting for? Use technology to connect and collaborate!

If, as the familiar African proverb suggests, "it takes a village to raise a child," then it takes people and connectivity to build a business in the twenty-first century. It's as simple and straightforward as that. But even if we don't embrace connectivity in business, we need to embrace it in our lives. Otherwise we become like blood cells isolated in a petri dish, living only for ourselves and no longer performing our crucial role in the "body of humanity." Are you ready to discover what you and your business are capable of achieving when you think of yourself no longer as an isolated competitor but as a vital part of a whole? Are you ready to answer the call of connectivity?

THE CURRENCY OF RECIPROCITY

I n the sermon "Rediscovering Lost Values," delivered in 1954, Dr. Martin Luther King, Jr. lamented the fact that despite all the scientific leaps we have made to bring the world together as a "neighborhood," we have not yet succeeded in making it a "brotherhood." All of the genius of science, it seems, is designed to *extract* value from the world, but we have not yet developed the "moral genius" to *contribute* value in return.

It is often said that there are two types of people on the planet: givers and takers. Givers are dedicated to providing value *to* other people. Takers are always trying to acquire value *from* other people. It's my experience, though, that most people don't fall neatly into one group or the other; most of us are made up of a little of both. And that's a good thing. You see, we need to have a little bit of giver and a little bit of taker in us. The ideal middle ground, in both business and society, is a system of both giving and taking for all parties involved.

Why both? Well, too much taking is obviously not a good thing— that's how criminals, exploiters, and political tyrants operate. They care only about what they can extract from a system, whether that system is the environment, the economy, their families, the government, or society as a whole. They chop down trees, metaphorically speaking, but don't plant new ones.

But too much giving is not a good thing, either. Although giving is generally a wonderful thing, people who constantly provide benefit for others without getting anything in return eventually become angry, bitter, burned-out, or despondent. A system of *mutuality* is crucial for a healthy business climate to exist.

Reciprocity is the currency by which mutuality thrives. Reciprocity means balancing what you receive from a system with what you reinvest back into it. It also means the act of giving back that which you have been fortunate enough to receive.

Reinvest in the Community

If you are an entrepreneur, *Kingonomics* strongly suggests you make a habit of reinvesting a portion of the profits from your business back into the community or population in which you operate. This reciprocity is necessary for the community to grow and stabilize, and for its members to become healthier, more vital participants in your industry. Your consumers must have some ownership, some stake, some financial power in the market you're selling in. Otherwise, with no mutual stake or interest, your clients' loyalties will be based simply upon their arbitrary decisions to consume your product and service, and can be easily attracted away by your competitors. True economic power is built through a conscious, inclusive effort to form mutual relationships with your customer community; if you fail to do this, that community may eventually turn away from you.

Nobel Peace Prize winner Muhammad Yunus understands the importance of empowering consumers and workers to play more vital roles in the economy. Through his Grameen Bank, he has provided millions of dollars in "microcredit" business loans to people too poor to qualify for standard bank loans. As a result, many craftspeople and small farmers around the globe are lifting themselves out of poverty by becoming vital participants in marketplaces as entrepreneurs, when they were formerly only consumers.

Most people on the planet are net consumers, rather than net producers, and they largely consume nonappreciating assets. A nonappreciating asset is one that does not increase in value over time. Examples are cars, furniture, or computer equipment. Yet, it is the accumulation of *appreciating* assets that creates jobs and builds communities. Examples of appreciating assets might be a house, a stock portfolio, or a profitable business. It is very good for your business if your client or customer base possesses appreciating assets, particularly thriving businesses. In this way, they can create a growing, dynamic market for your products and services. As profit-sharing participants in the marketplace, they can eventually become your suppliers, your strategic partners, and your vendors as well. As they grow, you will grow, too (provided you are an honest, fair, and value-adding businessperson). Everyone is happy and mutually fulfilled on such a two-way street.

Reciprocity is about reinvesting ideas, innovation, money, and assets directly into local or global communities and causes that feed, or are fed by, your business. The principle is simple: wherever dollars are created and generated in a community or population—whether it's a physical community, a virtual community, a cultural/ethnic community, or a customer base—a percentage of those dollars should be reinvested into the same communities they came out of in some way. This is the essence of reciprocity. Particular attention should be paid to local communities where your business presence is felt. This doesn't mean companies ought not invest or donate overseas—for example, in underserved and developing nations; it just means that a strong, local focus should also exist. Through this balance, opportunities for collaboration between local and global causes can be created.

> *The principle is simple: wherever dollars are created and generated in a community or population—whether it's a physical community, a virtual community, a cultural/ethnic community, or a customer base—a percentage of those dollars should be reinvested into the same communities they came out of in some way. This is the essence of reciprocity.*

As an example, my work in business and the nonprofit sector often puts me in touch with pastors and leaders in predominantly black churches. What I have learned is that, quite often, collections received from parishioners in these churches are allocated to contractors outside of the black community to build churches and other facilities. This phenomenon is so widespread that I often urge these leaders to understand that collecting donations from poor and middle-class African-American communities to erect churches that are predominantly financed and built by companies and individuals outside of their communities is a terrible drain of the community's financial power and wealth. There is no reciprocity in such a deal, particularly when most banking institutions are not compliant with the Community Reinvestment Act of 1977, which encourages banking institutions to assist in meeting the needs of borrowers in all segments of their target communities, including the low-income and underserved. This noncompliance goes unchecked because members of the community often do not have enough information to take the banks to task. Therefore, lending to churches becomes a taking-only initiative; money is taken from the African-American community but rarely reinvested there by the lending institutions.

I have never seen this kind of practice in Jewish or Muslim communities. Have you ever heard of a Jewish synagogue being financed by Muslims or Christians? Globally, I don't take issue with an organization spending its hard-earned dollars with any reputable bank or business it chooses. A religious institution is certainly *free* to partner with any vendor it thinks will do an excellent job, regardless of race, creed, sex, or political affiliation of its owners, shareholders, or employees. But I believe it has an obligation to do so thoughtfully, with a keen eye toward reciprocity and reinvestment first. It should ask itself who is benefiting, both directly and indirectly, from the dollars being collected and spent. We can't expect to see reciprocity extended *to* our global communities on a larger external scale until there is reciprocity *within* our own local organizations and communities.

We'll discuss this concept a bit later in the chapter. For now, let's look a little more closely at how reciprocity works.

Service Triggers Reciprocation

The currencies of *Kingonomics* are intricately interwoven. The Currency of Service plays a strong role in reciprocity. How? Well, when we receive an act of service from someone, we feel impelled to reciprocate. In the same way, when we *give* an act of service, the recipient wants to reciprocate with us. This is known as the Law of Reciprocity. It is a very powerful principle, both in business and society.

In the business world, trust is built not by what you say or promise, but rather by what you deliver. When seeking to form key reciprocal relationships that can help grow your business, first ask yourself, "What can I bring to the table?" It doesn't have to be a ten-thousand-dollar referral or a concrete business benefit of any kind. Simply demonstrate to others that you are genuinely willing to serve them in some way. Prime the pump of the Law of Reciprocity.

> *In the business world, trust is built not by what you say or promise, but rather by what you deliver.*

When I meet someone new, for example, I almost always ask, "What can I do to help you right now?" The person might just need a quarter for the parking meter or a ride to the grocery store. You will be surprised by how fast people want to reciprocate if you simply extend them a favor. If they see you taking consistent, unselfish action to create value for them, not just in their businesses but in their lives, they will trust you and send business your way whenever the opportunity presents itself.

Building Business Through Reciprocity

Robert B. Cialdini, a professor of marketing and psychology at Arizona State University, writes about the rules of reciprocation and their place in human culture in his book, *Influence: The Psychology of Persuasion.* He explains the sense of reciprocal obligation we feel when someone does us a favor. "The rule says that we should try to repay, in kind, what another person has provided for us. If a . . . man sends us a birthday present, we should remember his birthday with a gift of our own; if a couple invites us to a party, we should be sure to invite them to one of our own."[1]

Cialdini cites a number of examples of reciprocity in action. He notes, for one, a university professor who decided to send Christmas cards to a number of people with whom he was not personally acquainted. In response, he was inundated with cards from total strangers. In another example, he mentions that the country of Ethiopia made a $5,000 donation to Mexico after an earthquake rocked the latter country in 1985. What is remarkable about this story is that, at the time of this donation, Ethiopia was in a state of economic ruin, drought, and warfare. The country didn't have a dime to spare. Cialdini became curious about this and did some research. He learned that fifty years earlier, Mexico had sent aid to Ethiopia following its invasion by Italy. Reciprocity reached back half a century to prompt Ethiopia to help out.

Cialdini also examined the Hare Krishnas, a religious sect that used to raise money by begging, dancing, and chanting on city streets. Many passersby would cross the street in order to avoid the robed, head-shaven, finger cymbal–playing devotees.

One day, however, the Hare Krishna organization decided to change its approach and embrace the Currency of Reciprocity. Its members started giving gifts such as flowers or books to pedestrians *before* asking for a donation in return. "The unsuspecting passerby who suddenly finds a flower pressed into his hands or pinned to his jacket is under no circumstances allowed to give it back, even if he asserts that he does not want it. 'No, it is our gift to you,' says the solicitor, refusing to accept it. Only after the Krishna member has thus brought the force of the reciprocation to bear is the target asked to provide a contribution to the society." Soon, the public's reaction toward them changed. According to Cialdini, "The benefactor-before-beggar strategy has been wildly successful for the Hare Krishna Society, producing large-scale economic gains and funding the ownership of temples, businesses, houses, and property in 321 centers in the United States and overseas."[2]

We often see this same "implied reciprocation" strategy used by charities that mail us "free" greeting cards, mailing labels, or even coins, knowing that many of us will feel compelled to return the favor.

Though this kind of strategy can seem rather transparent, it is still very useful to think about how you can trigger the Law of Reciprocity, which is a very powerful principle that should not be ignored, in your business. Giving first, however, is an idea that takes some getting used to. It seems to run against the very grain of traditional businesses. Many business owners, particularly those with information-intensive products and services, may fear that if they give their core offerings away, they will lose potential income. My experience has been the opposite. I have found that being generous is the way to go. You won't "land" every prospect, and, yes, you will occasionally give away something of value that you could have charged money for, but for the most part, clients and customers are vastly more predisposed to doing business with someone who has given them something of value.

It's all right to make sure your client/customer understands that what you are doing for him is beyond the call of duty. You don't want the client to take the gift for granted, nor assume that he or she is automatically "entitled" to it. It is only when people are fully aware that you are doing them a favor that they feel a responsibility to reciprocate. On the other hand, that doesn't mean you should set up a quid pro quo expectation—you scratch my back, I'll scratch yours—nor should you feel you are *owed* a returned favor. (And you certainly should never demand one.) It means that you somehow need to make it clear that what you're offering is a gesture of goodwill and generosity. That's all. Find a nice way to let the client know that your information, time, and service have value. But don't force the issue.

Also, of course, be careful not to give away the whole store for nothing. For instance, you might offer the prospective client some free advice about improving his or her business, using your special expertise to demonstrate why certain changes would make sense. But you don't need to share every detail as to how these changes could be implemented. For that, the prospect will need to purchase your full consulting services.

Be generous with your expertise without rendering your paid services irrelevant. Keep in mind that the amount of free time, information, and energy you give away should always be proportionate to the size of the sale or contract you are seeking. A web designer trying to land a $15,000 corporate contract, for example, might be willing to create a functional mockup of the website for the prospective client, along with some custom-designed art and text samples. But, obviously, a local baker who wants to build a simple website for $250 would not receive a similar amount of free work.

It's All About the Long View

The bottom line here is that it's all about building long-term relationships, not just seeking one-off sales transactions. Don't be perturbed if your customer doesn't purchase your product or reciprocate right away. If you lay the right groundwork, your generosity *will* pay off in the end. The Law of Reciprocity ensures that giving usually triggers a response, though that response can sometimes occur much later.

I recently spoke to a screenwriter, for instance, who offered an up-and-coming young producer some free written advice on a screenplay he was trying to produce. The writer's advice was thoughtful, thorough, and well written. It solved a thorny script problem the producer was grappling with. Several *years* later, when that same producer was looking for a writer to pen a script for a well-funded studio movie, whom do you think he called? Gratitude for that small chunk of free advice came back to the writer in the form of a five-figure writing contract, plus a wealth of great industry contacts.

Always remember that, as the airlines often say, customers do have choices. If your competition is generous with information and you are not, the customer is probably going to go with the provider or supplier that has given him something of value. So adopt the spirit of giving as your standard approach and watch the Law of Reciprocity kick into high gear for you and your business.

Remember that not every act of giving will be reciprocated in the precise manner you might have in mind. If you enter an encounter thinking that offering a business referral will net you a referral of equal value in return, you are confusing a relationship with a transaction. It's not that cut-and-dried. True reciprocity hinges on giving *without the expectation* of an immediate return or a specific return. Simply adopt the habit of adding value whenever there is an opportunity to do so. The reciprocation that eventually occurs can often come in much grander ways than you even imagined. I can't tell you how many times I have seen small business favors, given generously, returned tenfold, a hundredfold, or even a thousandfold by the recipient.

Reciprocity is a powerful currency.

East Versus West

As I often point out, it helps to examine other cultures to gain a wider perspective on business practices. There are lessons we can learn about reciprocity, for example, by studying China. Those who have done business in China have probably noticed that it takes longer to establish a business relationship there than it does in America. This is in part because of the deep kind of reciprocity that is ingrained in Chinese business and culture.

While Americans tend to maintain a distinct separation between their personal and professional lives, the Chinese traditionally build much more intimate relationships with their business associates. In a 2006 article on the Columbia Business School website titled "Trust and Reciprocity in Chinese Business Networks," Professor Michael Morris of Columbia University is quoted as saying, "In China, if you're going to do business with someone you start by forging a personal, effective bond. You exchange gifts, have a series of meals together, and you may be invited to meet their family. The personal bond paves the way toward a working relationship."[3]

Morris has been studying comparative business cultures since the 1990s. According to his team's studies, this commingling of one's personal and business networks has deep ripple effects in both spheres. As with many things, the Chinese tend to take the long view and are less concerned with immediate results. A business favor, for example, might be "returned" in one's social sphere, and vice versa, and it might take a long time to develop. There is less of a defined sense of "favor A equals returned favor B." Rather, there is a trust in the principle of "what goes around comes around." The deeply embedded type of reciprocity that the Chinese practice probably has a subtler and more profound effect on behavior than the American version of reciprocity, in which we tend to separate how we act in business from how we act with friends and family and generally expect favors to be returned in kind.

One study Morris was involved in looked directly at the way businesspeople in both cultures do favors for one another. Americans, it turned out, are much more likely to do business favors for people when they can see the clear possibility of a favorable payback. In China, however, there is a greater tendency to do favors even when there is no clear sense that the other person can or will be able to return the favor. Part of the reason for this, Morris suggests, is connected to the Chinese concept of *face.*

We sometimes hear about people in Asian cultures being extremely concerned about the idea of "saving face." In the West, many of us tend to interpret this as excessive concern over public image or an obsession with avoiding shame. For instance, we have all heard tales, many of them undoubtedly apocryphal, about students, soldiers, or businesspeople committing suicide rather than bringing shame on their families, nations, or employers. We Westerners scratch our heads in wonder at such behavior. But the true Asian concept of "face" goes beyond the superficial concept of shame. Yes, "saving face" *can* be a negative, shame-based motivator, but it can also be a very positive one.

The concept of face also includes the degree of honor and respect one generates for oneself among family, friends, neighbors, and business associates. Much of one's face is based upon the amount of good one is perceived as doing. "This system of face," says Morris, "functions much like a credit rating. If you have helped a lot of the others, you'll be seen as high in face, and this makes it very hard for people to say no when you do ask for something."⁴ Your face thus functions as a subtle sort of currency. The more you have, the more likely people will be to help you when you are in need or when you are looking for business opportunities. Conversely, if you have done little to offer assistance to others in your neighborhood or workplace, your face value will be lower and others will not feel as compelled to help you when you ask for it.

The point of looking at the Chinese approach is to reinforce the idea that although reciprocity is a vital currency, it's not a dollar-for-dollar exchange. You have to trust in it and invest in it as a general principle, but you can't expect direct and concrete returns on every favor you do. Rather, you would do well to think a bit more like Chinese businesspeople: become the *kind of businessperson* and the *kind of human being* with whom people naturally want to reciprocate. And eventually, that is exactly what they will do. Over the course of a lifetime, this long-term attitude will bring much more success than short-term, "I did you a favor, now you pay me back" kind of thinking.

Reciprocity at Every Level

Remember that practicing the Currency of Reciprocity doesn't necessarily have to be an overly time-consuming or expensive exercise. There are many cost-efficient ways to provide value for a wide group of customers, especially in our age of digital media.

For example, I recently spoke with Jim, the owner of a contracting business who e-mails out a free monthly newsletter to his present and prospective customers, which is full of helpful tips about how to do home repairs yourself. At first blush, this would seem counterintuitive. After all, if you're helping your home-repair customers become better do-it-yourselfers, they're going to need *your* services less and less. Right? Many of Jim's friends and competitors, in fact, chide him about this very thing and tell him he's shooting himself in the foot. However, Jim's experience has been quite the opposite. He has seen an upswing in his business that he attributes to the newsletter. Like the Chinese businesspeople described above, he takes the long view and focuses on building "face" and providing value. As a result, Jim's customer community not only recognizes him as a generous sharer but also as an expert who knows his trade so well, he can teach others how to do it. As a result of his perceived expertise, people frequently turn to him when they need the kinds of contracting services he provides.

Giving Back: The Ultimate Form of Reciprocity

One of the highest goals of *Kingonomics* is to create a world in which businesses routinely *give back* as a part of their business plans. Giving back is the ultimate form of reciprocity. I believe—and I think Dr. King would have agreed with me—that every business that has experienced any kind of success should show gratitude for that success by making reciprocal gestures in the communities that support it (and wherever else its help is needed).

If businesses learn to take their obligation to reinvest or "give back" seriously, I can easily envision a future where much of the current work of charitable organizations would be done by businesses as part of their Corporate Social Responsibility charters. Business/charity partnerships would also be more effective because local reinvestments would be made with business know-how, based upon the charitable organization's reputation in the community. Businesses would not do *all* the work of charities, however, but would become resources for charities with causes that are aligned with their own social responsibility mandates. By partnering with independent charities or their own charity foundations, businesses could thus solve problems *they're already good at solving*. Multinational corporation Procter & Gamble, for example, uses its expertise to create commercial water-filtration systems via its Children's Safe Drinking Water Program to help relieve the shortage of clean drinking water in developing nations (where, according to its 2011 annual report, 35 percent of its net sales are generated). After all, who better to clean up water than the water-cleaning experts?

Corporate social responsibility (CSR) is growing. Here are a few more examples of companies that use the strengths they have developed in business to give back to their customers and communities in targeted ways.

Bove's Café in Burlington, Vermont, "conquers hunger" on a daily basis by providing quality Italian food to its customers. So when Bove's decided to give back to the community, it opted to help those in financial need. By teaming up with Shaw's Supermarkets, it was able to make a substantial donation of food and money to the Chittenden Emergency Food Shelf. Although Bove's had been donating to this charity for years, partnering with Shaw's allowed it to expand its service so that it could offer nutritious products to those in need. Bove's gave back by doing what it knows how to do best: feeding people great food.[5]

Greenshops.com, a "collective" of eco-friendly retailers in Bakersfield, California, has developed an organic relationship with its local community. It sells a line of picture frames made from old fence boards and junk lumber donated by area residents and businesses. In addition to keeping building materials out of the local landfill, the company adds value to the community by giving jobs to adults with disabilities through an organization called BARC. Greenshop employees also donate their time to clean up graffiti and plant trees locally. Again, these efforts are a natural extension of the company's vision and core merchandise.[6]

Don Wilson describes his particular brand of "reinvesting in his community" in a post on BusinessNewsDaily.com. "I'm the proprietor of Wilson's Soap Co. in Philadelphia. It's a handmade process and generates a lot of end pieces, etc. Instead of rebatching them, I watch Craigslist for people looking for donations and have sought out some of the local homeless shelters. In the past year I've donated 1,000 bars of soap, all of which were local donations except for 200 which were sent to Haiti."[7]

Reciprocity involves giving back not only to local causes and communities but also to global ones, especially for companies with international markets. L'Occitane, for example, makes a famous hand cream that has sold quite successfully worldwide. So when the company decided to reciprocate on a large scale, it launched the L'Occitane Foundation, which dedicates itself to the following three main goals:

1. To support Braille packaging and blindness-prevention programs in Burkina Faso and Bangladesh.

2. To support economic cooperatives run by women who make the shea butter that is a valuable component of its skin creams. (It supports the cooperative businesses of eleven thousand women in the African nation of Burkina Faso.)

3. To preserve the environment through the promotion of botanical knowledge.[8] (The Foundation's reciprocity is based on reinvesting not only in areas where it acquires some of its resources but also where it can best apply its business expertise and corporate vision.)

Of course, we shouldn't overlook the value of good old-fashioned cash. It is appropriate for those who are good at making and managing money to give back in a financial way. For example, Christopher Cooper-Hohn manages one of England's largest hedge funds. He funnels a substantial percentage of the fund's profits to the Children's Investment Fund Foundation, a charity that tries to better the lives of children in numerous ways. Wealthy businessman Eli Broad and his wife, Edythe, have created philanthropic organizations with assets of $2.1 billion and donated to everything from arts foundations to genome research, in areas underfunded by other charities.[9]

If you are a businessperson or entrepreneur, I urge you, today, to start thinking about the skills your business possesses and how they might help a cause or charity. Are you willing to donate a small percentage of your business's time, resources, and expertise to giving back to the community and the world? If you have accumulated any kind of fortune, then I believe your answer should be yes. Don't worry, though, your generous reciprocity won't really cost you in the long run. As the law of sowing and reaping dictates, your giving will give back to *you* in greater ways than you can imagine.

Lessons in the Art of Giving Back

Giving back is not always as simple as it sounds. Though it is relatively easy to write a check, it is harder to give back in a way that "keeps on giving." This requires effort and creativity. As with any business decision, you should practice giving back in such a way that your efforts will produce the biggest bang for the buck. It turns out there is a real craft to giving well.

Many MBA students nationwide are now acquiring the professional tools necessary to do just that. It is becoming more and more common for business schools to offer courses on philanthropy. But this is not just "crack open the checkbook" philanthropy. According to the article "Lessons in the Art of Giving" in the July 18, 2010 online issue of *Financial Times*, "The purpose of these courses is to teach MBA students how to have a strategic edge in their giving. This is accomplished by, among other things, conducting site visits to nonprofit organizations, tracking social and operational metrics, and measuring the impact of their charitable contributions."[10]

Not exactly ideas we typically associate with charity. That's because we tend to think of business and charity as two opposing impulses. Charity is usually thought to be motivated by the heart. It flows from a compassionate desire to share our money, skills, or belongings with others. Charity does not follow quid pro quo rules. It doesn't usually ask for anything in return. It does not watch the bottom line. It is not analytical, critical, or demanding. It believes giving is its own reward.

The business impulse, on the other hand, flows more from the head. It *is* critical and analytical. It wants to make sure it is getting the greatest ROI (return on investment) possible. It doesn't want its contributions to be squandered in inefficiency or blatantly misused. It wants its money and material donations to accomplish as much good as they can.

The philanthropist of the future will have to learn to straddle the fence between these two opposing impulses and strive to be both a "saint" and a businessperson. In an economy that is likely to remain tight, the heart and the head must join hands to ensure that charity resources perform as well as business investments.

In the aforementioned article, Kristen McCormack, who teaches a course on practicing philanthropy at Boston University's School of Management, is quoted as saying, "At some point in their lives, most of these students will either be a corporate donor or an individual donor and my class teaches them how to do philanthropy effectively. Most general MBAs that I've taught marvel that there is this world out there that they never thought existed, and they are surprised by how hard it is to give away money."[11] McCormack tries to teach students the real, working mindset one needs to be a philanthropist today. "People tend to think, 'Philanthropy: that's easy. You have a lot of money, and you give it away.' But to do philanthropy well, you have to understand social problems and what is at the root of them, you have to be able to take in a lot of information and evaluate what an organization is doing, and you have to make hard choices. Donors have a lot of challenges and I want students to understand their perspective . . . They have to say 'no' a lot more often than they say 'yes.' And there are hard choices: Do you give to a start-up or to a group with a proven track record?"[12] She also adds that her class breaks "the myth that you have to be rich to be a philanthropist."[13]

Giving back is less about how much money you give and more about how you strategically deploy it. You have to learn to *leverage* your giving, whether it's on a large scale or a small one, so that it can make its greatest impact.

We Can't Rely on Reciprocity from Others

This brings me back, indirectly, to a point I made earlier in the chapter. I said that we have to learn to practice reciprocity effectively on a small scale within our own communities and organizations before we can expect to benefit from it ourselves on a large, external scale. Let's take a little closer look at this idea.

What do I mean by reciprocity on a large, external scale? Well, one example of that would be the concept of reparations, the idea that government or other institutions should formally "repay" a segment of the population that has been unfairly exploited in the past, such as

Native Americans or African Americans. The short-lived "forty acres and a mule" policy following the Emancipation Proclamation was intended to be one such form of mass reciprocity. Freed slaves were to be compensated (reciprocated) for the sweat equity they put into the building of our nation's infrastructure and wealth. Of course, as I mentioned earlier, this initiative didn't really pan out after President Lincoln's assassination.

Today, many people still clamor for large-scale reparations programs that would benefit black communities in America. But let's face it, the debate over African-American reparations isn't going to be resolved anytime in the foreseeable future. Although that type of large-scale reciprocity certainly seems more than justifiable to me, I, for one, am not holding my breath waiting for it to happen. Are you? The point is that whether you're in favor of reparations or not, there's really very little you or I can do to make it happen anyway. However, I believe that one thing we *can* do is take responsibility for the way we spend our own dollars. We can, in effect, create our *own* reciprocity rather than wait for it to be given to us. We can do this by spending our money in ways that will actively benefit our own communities and families.

One way to approach this, in my opinion, is to change the way we donate money. For example, a good percentage of the donations we currently give to our religious institutions (many of which are not practicing reciprocity, as I pointed out earlier) could be leveraged more efficiently by supporting higher education, innovative skill development, small business creation, and new jobs. According to polls conducted by the Barna Group and Pew Research Center published in 2011, approximately 23 million of America's 40 million blacks attend church regularly. If we apply Italian economist Vilfredo Pareto's 20/80 rule, (which states that 20 percent of any given group usually contributes 80 percent of its value), then 20 percent of this group, or about 5 million individuals, subsidize the nearly $70 billion in mortgage principal and $210 billion in compounded and accumulated interest over time that churches currently carry. That's nearly a quarter of a trillion dollars that will be leaving the black community in the current and next generation and will have to be paid for by our children and grandchildren. Meanwhile, we face the daunting task of preparing nearly 3 million black children under the age of five[14] to attend college in the future (which they *must* do in order to have even a remote chance of competing in the marketplace). Maybe we should reallocate some of our giving and pool our resources, acquire the debt from current lenders, charge a much lower interest rate to the churches, and reallocate the savings to viable investments, community and economic development, housing, and education—especially education.

Let me break down why this should matter to everyone, not just those of us directly affected. According to Bureau of Justice statistics published in 2003, 68 percent of state prison inmates did not receive a high school diploma.[15] And people with less education commit more crimes than those with more education. That's a widely recognized, statistical fact. Although lack of education may be an encouraging trend for those who make money by investing in publicly traded prisons and in our privatized penal system, which makes its money by awarding contracts and extracting free labor, it is definitely harmful for not only those communities where education levels are lowest but also for our nation as a whole.

Lives are being destroyed because of lack of education, and it is our responsibility to spend our money in ways that can help correct the problem. Until more black Americans start owning financial institutions such as banks and investment funds, we must leverage our own charitable giving to create more balance. Perhaps one day, reciprocity *will* come to those of us who have been historically exploited, in the form of large-scale reparations programs. Perhaps banks will begin to refinance existing church mortgages to reflect modern-day lending and investment practices (today, interest rates are at an all-time low, yet most churches can't get refinancing even though many of their banks received bailout money) and approve qualified vendors of color to construct houses of worship and learning. Perhaps one day there will be an *expectation* that all businesses and institutions should reinvest in the communities from which they extract their dollars. But until that day, we have to make reciprocity *happen for us* by spending our business and charity dollars in ways that come back to our own families and communities. This is true for any group that has suffered exclusion.

But remember, we must also be reciprocators ourselves and extend mutual benefits to economically challenged people with whom we do business around the globe, be they suppliers, vendors, customers, or employees. We must do our parts to allow everyone to play in the ownership and profit-sharing game.

Reciprocity, whether on the small scale of an individual giving business back to someone who has helped him, or the grand scale of a corporation investing millions in the global communities that provide its customer base, is one of the most crucial currencies of *Kingonomics*.

CHAPTER 5

THE CURRENCY OF POSITIVITY

W e've all met them—those agents of doom and gloom whose very presence seems to speak of impending disaster. You can spot them coming a mile away by the gray cloud that seems to hover over their heads and the resentful expressions on their faces. You just know that when they open their mouths, they will report injustices they have suffered or express needs that are not being properly fulfilled by others. Whether they were born that way or simply learned to operate on negative energy, these "Eeyores" of the world never seem to have anything positive to add to a situation. They are perpetually victimized, angry, fearful, or resentful. Their efforts are always on the taking, obstructing, blaming, and disrupting side. Worse still, they are usually more than willing to bring others down to their own depths of negativity and dissatisfaction.

We've all met the opposite, too—those people who seem to "light up a room" the moment they walk in. They exude a buoyant kind of energy that is all about giving and contributing. They are the kind of people we are drawn to at parties and want on our teams. These folks operate on an "adding" rather than "subtracting" wavelength and are always seeking ways to strengthen a team, make a better product, or improve a service. No matter what happens to them, they see the proverbial cup as half full. They are quick to offer a word of praise and encouragement to others. They are creative forces rather than destructive ones.

Dr. Martin Luther King, Jr. was one such remarkable individual. The notion of "We Shall Overcome" was integral to the spirit of his work, as evidenced in nearly all of his speeches and writings. No matter how many defeats and setbacks he experienced, no matter how much hatred and prejudice he encountered, no matter how many legal and political roadblocks were thrown in his path, King refused to allow his spirit to be broken. To his dying day, he remained a shining model of optimism and positivity.

So what about you? Be honest. Does your demeanor scream, "Why do terrible things always happen to me?" Or do people actually perk up when you enter a room? It's not hard to gauge. Just pay attention to facial expressions and body postures. Do coworkers turn toward you and open up with a smile or do they turn away and close down? Do people have a tendency to appear from nowhere and gather around you, or do they disappear and head back to their desks when you enter the scene?

Which type of person do you think is more likely to experience business success in today's transparent, interconnected, people-driven world?

It's All in Our Thoughts

The way we affect others flows directly from the thoughts we choose to entertain. We can entertain fearful, resentful, negative thoughts or we can entertain creative, positive, value-adding thoughts. It's really that simple. We control our positivity/negativity quotient by the thoughts we choose to energize. I've heard this phenomenon described in many different ways. Some say it's like two dogs; the one you feed the most (positivity or negativity) will grow stronger and triumph over the other one. The choice of which dog to feed, though, is totally in *our* hands. It is this choice that effectively determines the kind of life we lead.

Thoughts are extremely powerful because they trigger emotions. Negative, fearful, and angry thoughts produce negative emotions, which feed into more negative thoughts, which feed into more negative emotions in a constant downward spiral. We've all had bad days when everything feels like a catastrophe and seems to go wrong. That's because negativity contains a self-perpetuating mechanism; it feeds on itself and produces more and more of the same. Repeated negative emotions lead to negative moods. Repeated positive emotions lead to positive moods.

> *Thoughts are extremely powerful because they trigger emotions. Negative, fearful, and angry thoughts produce negative emotions, which feed into more negative thoughts, which feed into more negative emotions in a constant downward spiral.*

Your habitual moods, either positive or negative, then lead to what we might call your general attitude about life. And unless you are a great actor, the attitude you carry internally is reflected in your outer appearance and behavior. It powerfully affects the people around you, such as employees, partners, investors, and customers. Negativity is bad for business; positivity is good.

The Physics of Positive and Negative

When we talk about positive and negative energy, it helps to think in terms of physics. In the world of physics, negative energy is the energy of taking/absorbing/receiving; positive energy is the energy of emitting/charging/filling. Think of a car battery. The negative pole *accepts* a charge, while the positive pole *gives out* a charge. Or think of a pump. One end pulls in water through suction. We'll call that the negative end. The other (positive) end emits water.

In nature and in physics, both types of energy are needed. In the world of human enterprise, both types of energy are also needed, but we need to pay close attention to whether we are a "net-positive" or "net-negative" person. Do we give more than we take? Do we contribute more than we demand? Do we build up more than we tear down?

The type of attitude you carry—either positive or negative—depends, again, on the habitual thoughts you choose to entertain. You have total control of the situation. You can choose which dog to feed. Positive attitudes have an enhancing or "contributing" effect on every situation you enter into. They invigorate not only you but the people around you. Negative attitudes have a sapping or draining effect on people and situations. They are like the suction end of the pump: always pulling something away. That "something" can be energy, assets, enthusiasm, or resources. Aside from making *you* feel gloomy and pessimistic, negative thoughts can turn a party into a funeral and optimism into dread at the drop of a hat. A positive attitude attracts while a negative attitude repels. Plain and simple.

Some examples of draining, negative attitudes, behaviors, and feelings are

- cynicism,
- apathy,
- hopelessness,
- fault-finding,
- victimization,
- neediness,
- problem-focusing,
- fearfulness,
- arrogance,
- lack of enthusiasm,
- unresponsiveness,
- entitlement,
- complaining,
- anger,
- jealousy,
- backbiting,
- pettiness,
- one-upmanship,

- dishonesty,
- resentment, and
- lethargy.

Some examples of contributing, positive attitudes, behaviors, and feelings are

- cooperation,
- humor,
- problem-solving,
- creativity,
- motivation,
- high energy,
- generosity,
- helpfulness,
- encouragement,
- leadership,
- inspiration,
- supportiveness,
- contribution-mindedness,
- willingness to serve,
- striving for excellence,
- compassion,
- humility, and
- personal responsibility.

Which set of attitudes do you suppose produces vibrant, effective organizations? The Currency of Positivity is not just a "feel-good" proposition; it provides the very fuel on which successful human enterprise operates. That's why Dr. King—who embodied the second list as few human beings ever have—constantly worked to *inspire* his fellow man in a positive way, rather than lapse into anger and criticism. Yes, he could be angry in the face of injustice, and yes, he could be critical in the face of apathy, but he took great care to be a net-positive leader, because he knew that only through positivity would his cause be energized.

Benefits of Positivity

We all have much to gain from the Currency of Positivity on every level of life—physical, mental, emotional, and spiritual. Numerous studies in medicine and positive psychology, such as the one recently conducted by Dr. Mary E. Charlson, professor of integrative medicine at Weill Cornell Medical College,[1] have shown that a positive attitude promotes habits that lead to better health and longer life. One reason positivity is good for us may be that keeping a positive attitude helps us handle stress, bad news, and challenges in a more productive manner. Some other obvious benefits to positivity are the following:

- It allows you to see opportunities where others can't.
- It *adds* value, while negativity strips it away.
- It bolsters creativity and productivity.
- It helps you bounce back quickly from injuries, illnesses, and setbacks.
- It inspires others around you.
- It attracts others to your leadership.
- It *feels* good.
- It changes your brain chemistry.
- It gives you hope and optimism, which tend to produce better real-world results.
- It strengthens relationships.
- It serves as an antidote to worry and stress.
- It lets you see *strengths* in yourself and others, rather than just flaws and weaknesses.

Positive communications lead to happy lives and happy relationships. Psychologist John Gottman asserts the "magic ratio" that keeps marriages together is 5:1. That is, when discussing a disagreement, successful partners offer one another five positive comments for every negative one. In one of his studies, he observed seven hundred newlywed couples for fifteen minutes each, and, based solely on counting the number of negative versus positive comments, was able to predict, with 94 percent accuracy, which couples would divorce within ten years.[2]

Look honestly at *your* personal and business relationships. What ratio do *you* use?

Of course, there is a time and place for negative feelings and comments, too. It would be crazy to react to financial ruin, the death of a loved one, or a troubling health diagnosis with a smile and a dance step. An angry outburst may occasionally be the only effective way to get needed attention from someone. After all, even Jesus Christ was known to lose his temper when he saw the moneychangers doing business at the temple. So feeling sad, angry, or gloomy is not wrong, but *dwelling* there for long is not healthy. Becoming habitual in our anger and resentment is poisonous to the human spirit, no matter how justified our outrage might be. One of the most powerful living lessons Dr. King gave us was his resilient, positive attitude and willingness to keep fighting with positive energy and enthusiasm even after the most disheartening setbacks.

Hope Floats

As a candidate, President Barack Obama used the word *hope* repeatedly in his speeches and writings, and for good reason. Hope is an attitude that not only alters our moods but enables us to envision brighter futures. Hope is a self-fulfilling prophecy; it creates its own positive results, just as fear creates its own negative results.

Hope and fear literally change the way our bodies work. Fear can increase adrenaline, turn our stomachs more acidic, make our muscles rigid, and contribute strongly to the addictive consumption of drugs, alcohol, and unhealthy foods. Hope does the opposite. According to a recent article by Irene Lane on Examiner.com, "The Mayo Clinic recently reported on the correlation between hopeful thinking and stress management. Researchers found that hopeful thinkers 'cope better with stressful situations, which reduces the harmful effects of stress on (the) body.' Hopeful thinkers experienced better general health in the form of longer life spans and lower rates of cardiovascular disease, as well as greater achievement, increased determination, and lower rates of depression."[3] Hope naturally feels good, which makes us more prone to take good care of ourselves through exercise and healthy habits.

Fear causes us to shut down. When we do this, pessimism creeps into our words, thoughts, and actions, and drives our decisions, creating negative outcomes. This negativity spills over into our relationships with our children, friends, neighbors, and coworkers, making everyone feel less safe and secure. Hope opens us up, nurtures our relationships, and makes our teammates and families feel safe and optimistic. Hope spurs us to dig down and pull out our deepest strengths and creative talents, while fear makes us rely on familiar behavior patterns, even if they haven't worked for us in the past.

Hope and energy are intimately connected. I recently saw a snippet of the talk show *No Huddle* on the NFL network. The show featured four personalities from the football world discussing football-related topics in an unscripted way. Michael Irvin, a key member of the Dallas Cowboys' Super Bowl–winning teams of the early 1990s, said something that caught my ear. The panel was discussing whether it was time to give high-profile college draftee Tim Tebow a shot at the starting-quarterback position for the Denver Broncos. Irvin was in favor of the change because he thought it would give the team new hope for winning. Though I can't recall his exact words, he said something like, "The amount of energy a team expends is directly proportional to the amount of hope it feels about winning a championship." He went on to explain that it is just human nature to hold back on our energy levels when we don't perceive any real hope for victory. Conversely, even a glimmer of hope can infuse a surprisingly high energy level into a team and trigger it to accomplish amazing things.

Hope is an unusual emotion in that it isn't derived from outer circumstances as other emotions are. Feelings of happiness, for example, often arise when our needs are met and we're feeling safe and satisfied, while sadness often occurs in the presence of misfortune, injury, or death. Feelings of hope, on the other hand, arise when precisely the opposite emotion might seem the most logical response. Hope comes into play when things are going poorly or there's uncertainty, doubt, bleakness, or bad fortune on our plates. We might even say that hope is an unreasonably optimistic reaction to dire circumstances.

It may be unreasonable, but it's also vitally important to a successful life and business.

Hope allows us to back up from the trees and see the whole forest—the forest of possibility. It lets us consider options and outcomes that are not currently evident to our senses. Hope is the mechanism by which dreams are empowered and bold new enterprises are mounted. Hope is a decidedly human enterprise; it allows us to steer toward a positive, *imagined* future rather than the one the evidence may be pointing to.

> *Hope is the mechanism by which dreams are empowered and bold new enterprises are mounted. Hope is a decidedly human enterprise; it allows us to steer toward a positive,* imagined *future rather than the one the evidence may be pointing to.*

Belief in a better future is what keeps us going. It is the antidote to worry, fear, and despair. Worry, we might say, is the exact opposite of hope. Worry spurs us to envision everything that could possibly go wrong in a given situation. It shows us panoplies of imagined catastrophes. These scary visions can quickly overwhelm our emotions, shutting down our creative minds with fresh waves of fear. Without hope, the dire imaginings produced by worry and despair might cause us to collapse. Hope is the engine by which we build better lives for ourselves, our families, our team members, and our nation.

In fact, we can even say with some scientific accuracy that hope makes us smart while fear makes us stupid.

Will Marré, author of *Save the World and Still Be Home for Dinner*, refers to the research of Dr. Robert Kinsel Smith to shed some light on how this works. Each of us, it seems, is capable of employing several different modes of thinking, such as reason, common sense, and intuition, to solve problems. When we employ reason, for instance, we consider which choice makes the most *logical* sense. When we employ common sense, or situational thinking, we consider which course of action is *likely to have the best results* in a real-world context. Intuition, on the other hand, is a gut sense. When we employ intuition, we ask ourselves which choice *feels* best. There are many variations of these thinking modes, as well. Each of us has particular modes we rely on more than others. It is only by using a rich assortment of thinking modes that we make our wisest decisions.[4]

But here's the key point: we can only *use* all of our thinking capacities when we are feeling relaxed and in a generally positive frame of mind. Whenever we are overcome by fear, adrenaline kicks in, our thinking closes down, and we begin to rely on only our most familiar or primitive modes of thinking. We go into fight, flight, or freeze mode. In the presence of fear, therefore, we make poorer, less-informed decisions.

How often have you seen a retail store, for example, react fearfully to a drop-off in business by reducing the number of hours it stays open? Rather than look for creative ways to draw in new customers, it resorts to a defensive, essentially negative strategy. The reduction of business hours then results in even fewer customers, which results in even shorter hours, and before long the store is out of business.

Hope is the antidote for this kind of thinking. Hope allows us to be more creative by opening up all of our thinking capacities.

As human beings, we face enormous challenges at this point in our collective history. Without hope, we don't stand a chance of rising to these occasions. *With* hope, however, we can look our challenges in the eye and accomplish any goals we envision. Fear literally makes us stupid. So it is wise to choose hope instead.

Positivity in Business

Positivity, I hope you're starting to see, is not just a personal, "feel-good" choice; it is a business choice as well.

The attitude you project has massive ripple effects across your business. For example, when you're looking for affiliates, suppliers, or employees, a positive attitude will attract success-minded people to you. When you are positive and passionate about the products and services you offer, that passion will be contagious with others. A positive outlook about your industry will net you many invitations to speak at business gatherings and participate in symposiums, seminars, dinners, and policy-making meetings.

A positive attitude will also powerfully color the *methods* you use for operating your business. If you go about your day with the mentality that you *can* accomplish your goals and take care of whatever problems come your way, then you and your team will see obstacles as creative challenges, not brick walls, and you will find your way around them rather than allow yourself to be defeated by them. Positivity also empowers you to set a great living example of how you want your customers to be treated.

Your marketing efforts, too, will benefit from a positive attitude. You will take a creative, value-adding approach as opposed to a negative tack that relies on *defending* your products or badmouthing the competition. You will be motivated to promote your strengths rather than point out the other guy's weaknesses.

As researchers such as Barbara Fredrickson, author of the book *Positivity*, continue to learn more about how we achieve optimal functioning in the workplace, the term *positivity* has finally begun to capture the interest of business leaders. What we're discovering about positive emotions at work is essential knowledge for anyone who wants to lead organizations to higher performance. We must realize that both negative and positive emotions drive business results, each in their own way. Negative emotions limit our thoughts and behaviors, which can *occasionally* help us to act more decisively in times of stress or crisis. But it is positivity that broadens our outlook, opens us up to new solutions and ideas, and brings more possibilities into view. Positivity should be our daily operating mode, with negativity used only on rare occasions, as needed.

One of the most powerful business questions you can routinely ask yourself is, What are we doing in the workplace, specifically, to increase our positivity quotient? Does your organization, for example, hire executive coaches to help develop emotionally intelligent, positively oriented leaders? Does it offer incentive programs that encourage employees to contribute creative ideas? Does it reward exceptional team members with celebrations and awards? Does it work hard to create a physical and emotional atmosphere that is pleasant, attractive, and even fun? Does it fire up its team members with goals that are both challenging and achievable? Does it constantly reinforce those goals with positive "we can" rituals? Does it bring in inspirational speakers? Does it publish inspiring stories on its website or in its company newsletter? Does it post signs with inspiring messages?

If not, then you need to go back to the drawing board and think of some lasting and meaningful ways you can create positivity. Don't worry about *fighting* existing negative energy; that will only reinforce it. Focus all your attention on creating a new sense of the positive. If you do that, negativity will fall away naturally and your business will blossom as a result.

Here are some things a positive attitude can accomplish in the workplace:

- **Reduce stress.** Laughter, cooperation, and positive energy are the best antidote for the crippling levels of stress that can sometimes infect a team, especially during long and challenging projects.

- **Reduce absenteeism and lead to greater productivity.** People *want* to come to a positive, appealing workplace instead of one they dread. Employees will be less likely to avoid work (e.g., take sick days) or slack off on the job.

- **Improve customer relations.** Positivity is infectious. Your customers will want to do more business with your company if you feed them positive energy with every interaction, instead of repelling them with neediness, surliness, or a sense of business entitlement.

- **Improve motivation and encourage peak performance.** A positive work environment increases sales and motivates your team to do a better job. Remember, hope *creates* energy. Lack of hope cancels it.

- **Make teamwork more effective.** When negative attitudes of suspicion and intrateam competitiveness pervade the workplace, it is virtually impossible to form effective teams. But when everyone feels as if they're working positively toward the same goals, teamwork soars.

- **Improve decision-making.** When team members make decisions from a place of fear, they shut down their highest-thinking capacities and resort to primitive, so-called lizard-brain functioning that originates in the limbic system and is all about fight, flight, or freeze. Positivity, however, unleashes creativity and allows for innovative strategies to emerge.

- **Enable risk-taking.** Only when a positive belief system dominates your management team will your company feel empowered to take the risks that are sometimes necessary for growing a business. In an atmosphere of negativity and fear, on the other hand, risks are avoided at all costs.

- **Make it more fun.** Work should be a source of enjoyment, not misery. When we maintain a positive attitude on the job, we no longer feel the need to collapse on the sofa at the end of every workday. Work becomes rewarding instead of something to escape and "recover" from.

Productivity and Positive Management Behavior

Throughout the course of history, it seems, there has been an excessive reliance on negative management techniques to generate results in organized enterprises. Belittlement, threats of nonpayment or job termination, harsh and unreasonable demands, even physical abuse have been used to "motivate" workers to be more productive. Just as parents were taught "spare the rod, spoil the child," managers were led to believe that if they showed any lenience toward workers, the latter would abuse the privileges.

It is only relatively recently in history that the concept of positive management has emerged. Positive managers *encourage* their team members rather than threaten them. They control their negative emotions, recognize what is and isn't within their sphere of influence, and view problems as opportunities. It seems self-evident to me that positive management techniques work much better than negative ones. My experience has backed that up as well.

According to an August 2007 article in the *Gallup Management Journal*, Margaret Greenberg and Dana Arakawa, graduates of the Master of Applied Positive Psychology Program at the University of Pennsylvania, decided to run a study to try to determine whether managers who practiced positive leadership techniques—optimism in particular—fostered teams with better performance than managers who didn't apply these practices.[5]

Their research demonstrates that the answer is yes. *Engagement* is the payoff. Though they could not prove that a manager's optimism level directly affected the engagement level of his or her team, optimism does correlate with a stronger sense of engagement on the part of the *manager*. And that factor—the manager's level of engagement— has a strong, measurable effect on project performance. Employee engagement has a similar measurable effect. Engagement is strongly linked to productivity, profitability, employee retention, customer satisfaction, and workplace safety. Engagement, however, only occurs when employees feel a strong emotional bond with the company. And this, I would argue, only occurs through positive approaches.

Positive and effective managers tend to use a strengths-oriented philosophy as opposed to one that focuses on correcting weaknesses. They also keep a positive point of view when challenges arise (rather than lapsing into panic, threats, and reactivity) and provide frequent praise and encouragement to their team members.

In our society, many parents and teachers—and in turn, many *employers*—tend to fixate on an individual's weaknesses. They seem to carry an abstract standard in their heads as to the ideal qualities a child/student/employee should possess, and then try to "fix" individuals to make them fit the mold. If you've ever had a performance review at your job (or a report card from school), it's quite clear that most of the attention is typically focused on weaknesses, with little credit being afforded to one's unique strengths. Often, in fact, there are printed checklists of characteristics against which the individual is rated. And when an employee rates below a certain score in any area, it is considered a deficit.

Focusing on negativity is not a powerful way to leverage human resources and does nothing to inspire employees or bring out their signature strengths and talents. On the contrary, focusing on weaknesses only serves to undermine an individual's confidence. It also perpetuates a false notion that there is an ideal standard that we should all try to emulate. Thankfully, a new breed of management is slowly emerging. These new, positive managers have begun to realize that the way to get optimal results is to pay attention to *what the employee is good at* and how his or her strengths can be leveraged to benefit both the employee *and* the organization. Of course, that doesn't mean ignoring weaknesses—these, too, must be addressed—but it means putting far more emphasis on building upon strengths. Positive managers make themselves part of the solution rather than part of the problem. They build teams that use the best of what each team member can contribute. In this way, they achieve maximum creative output, rather than maximum *compliance*. Instead of, in effect, trying to form a musical band consisting of five mediocre guitarists, they recognize that a great band has a talented bass player, a gifted drummer, an exciting keyboardist, and so on.

This approach translates to entire companies. The truly visionary, market-leading companies don't spend the bulk of their time strategizing about how they can correct their flaws or worrying about what the competition is doing. They are too busy unleashing their signature products and services on the world. Could the iPod have been invented from a "weakness-correction" point of view? Would Velcro have been created if its originator was trying to improve the zipper? Would the automobile airbag have been developed if its inventors were trying to correct the bumper? I think you know the answers.

Recognition and Praise Are Crucial

Praise, encouragement, and strengths-based management lead to greater engagement, which leads to greater performance. One huge mistake managers often make is to wait until the end of a project to hand out kudos. By doing this, they miss a golden opportunity to provide encouragement on a step-by-step basis to those who are vitally important to the project's success. By failing to recognize project milestones and provide encouragement along the way, they rob employees of the fuel they need to carry on at peak performance long after the assignment is handed out.

Positive, effective managers, on the other hand, learn a trick that positive teachers and parents have known for years: "catch people doing well." That is, rather than wait for things to go wrong, pay conscious attention to what is going right. Notice the things your team members are doing that are unique, excellent, and praiseworthy, especially when these things flow from their unique strengths. Point out small successes at every opportunity: "Ed, you always do a great job on these reports. How did you learn to do graphics so well?" "Greta, you handled that customer with such patience. I don't think I could have done it!" "John, I'm really happy with the way you took initiative by making that follow-up call instead of waiting to be told." The great thing about catching people doing well is that it brings back positive energy toward *you*, too It feels much better to praise people than to criticize them! And the more of the former you do, the less of the latter is required.

In their book, *How Full Is Your Bucket?*, authors Tom Rath and Donald O. Clifton cite a 2003 Gallup survey that found 61 percent of employees in America received virtually no praise on the job. And yet, they also suggest that the biggest reason people quit their jobs is lack of appreciation! Hmm. It doesn't take Stephen Hawking to figure out that more praise and recognition would result in, at minimum, higher employee-retention rates. For this reason alone, all managers should make praise and recognition their daily bread.

The way in which managers coach employees, respond to their problems, and, above all, recognize their achievements—whether positively or negatively—has a profound effect on morale and engagement. Simply put, a positively engaged, positively motivated employee is a productive, responsible, and creative one. In today's rapidly changing and uncertain business environment, managers need to use optimism and praise more than ever to not only cope with challenges but to innovate and flourish in the face of them. Positivity equals productivity.

The Positive Brain

I hope by now you are convinced that, in business and life, positivity helps create success. A hopeful, positive brain has better resources for thought available to it than a stressed, frightened one.

But how else do we improve our positive-to-negative ratio? Another method is to take a page from the books of life coaches. They often use the principles of resistance and reward to increase positive habits and decrease negative ones. *Resistance*, we might say, is the hurdle we have to overcome to start a new action; *reward* is the "feel-good" benefit we reap from it.

Whenever we are contemplating taking a new action, there is a certain amount of resistance to overcome. Let's say you want to improve your diet while you're at work. There will naturally be a certain amount of resistance to this change. This resistance may stem, for example, from the fact that there happens to be a great burger place right next door and a pizza parlor across the street. The nearest place to get a salad or a smoothie is four blocks away—and the food is expensive. It's just easier and cheaper (and more fun) to eat poorly.

You can lower the resistance by bringing a healthy lunch to work with you, which is easier than going to get a burger. And because you're bringing food from home, you're saving money, too. Use this to *reward* yourself. If you stick to your new eating plan, at week's end, you can use the money you saved on burgers to buy yourself a special treat, such as a book or DVD.

You can also intentionally *create* resistance to stop an *addictive* habit, for example. Let's say you want to quit smoking. Give the cigarettes and lighter to your spouse or partner to hold, so when you want to smoke, you must ask for them. You don't want to seem weak to your loved one, so you are hesitant to ask. If you make it through a week without smoking, arrange a rewarding activity with your partner on the weekend.

Keep these ideas in mind if you want to run a positive business. Your managerial strategies should always work toward creating low resistance levels for positive work habits and high resistance levels for negative work habits. They should also offer frequent, immediate, and pleasant rewards for those who perform positive actions. In such a way you can help to "institutionalize" positivity in the workplace.

Allow for Peaceful Expression

Another way to avoid negativity in society and in all of its institutions is to make room for positive expressions of dissatisfaction. King constantly emphasized that peace could only be achieved by positive means and unconditional love.

Dr. King, following in the footsteps of Gandhi, was determined to show that unjust systems can be challenged and changed through nonviolent direct action. He saw this approach as highly positive and believed that it was, in fact, an effective way to *prevent* violence. How so? King repeatedly asserted that when you don't allow people a positive, peaceful means for expressing their dissatisfaction, they will eventually resort to violence. It is just human nature. In his "Letter from a Birmingham Jail," he pointed out that modern black Americans had accumulated generations' worth of intense anger and resentment. He urged leaders to allow them to release and express these emotions through peaceful, legal means. If this kind of "positive" expression was squashed, warned King, then the pressure would continue to build and violence would inevitably erupt.

History is filled with examples of people who have resorted to violence after being denied any peaceful means for working out conflict. The more recent ethnocentric conflicts in Rwanda and Sierra Leone show what happens when oppressed and repressed peoples' tensions are given no avenue for dissipation. When tensions are ignored and allowed to fester and grow, they eventually escalate into violence. The more repressive the regime, the more violence will be required to get its attention. King showed the world that conflict *can* be addressed effectively and realistically through nonviolent means. It is one of his greatest legacies.

This principle matters not only on the global political stage but in our homes and workplaces, too. If we don't provide peaceful, positive ways for workers and family members to express disagreement, and to express creative new ideas, tensions build until they reach a breaking point and destructive energy is unleashed. If we wish to encourage positive expressions of criticism, we must provide *the means* for this to happen. We can't slam the door on everyone who has a problem. We must offer a safe and positive forum in which differences can be aired openly and non-punitively, and we must provide meaningful mechanisms for making change when change is indicated. Otherwise, change will be forced upon us through chaotic, negative, and unpredictable means.

Feed Your Positive "Dog"

As we wrap up our discussion of the Currency of Positivity, I remind you that if you want to cultivate a positive attitude, you have to think healthy, nourishing thoughts. This is especially tricky to do nowadays in our media-driven world, which is so rife with negative messages. Fear sells, and so, in almost every news media outlet, we are fed a steady diet of fear fodder—violent crimes, accidents, cancer scares, terrorist plots, and dire predictions about the environment. Today's economy, too, can make it difficult to stay positive. At work and at home, we are constantly bombarded with talk of business closings, job cuts, benefit losses, downsizing, and home foreclosures. On top of that, there seems to be a resurgence of reported hate crimes and instances of discrimination on the basis of opinion, political affiliation, class, skin color, sexual orientation, and religion. There is a lot of anger out there and much of it is being misdirected—brother fighting brother and sister fighting sister, when we should all be focusing on the deeper source of our woes.

We all need to take deliberate steps to counteract the negativity. To do so, we can start with the simple stuff, which can actually be amazingly effective. Don't always read the newspaper, for instance, or heavy political books; see a funny movie or read a funny book at least once a week. Play with a child—your own or someone else's. Spend some time with friends, just laughing and having fun. Read an inspirational book for ten minutes every morning. Treat yourself to nice things: your favorite music, your favorite meal, a walk in the woods, or a warm bath. Look for a reason to find gratitude in every situation before you open your mouth to complain, berate, or express anger.

Mindfulness, meditation, prayer, yoga, and other means of quietly tapping into the spiritual "stream of positivity" can be immensely beneficial, on many levels. Everyone I've ever spoken to who tries one of these practices reports an increase in positive emotions and attitudes.

Another simple technique to increase positive emotions is to consciously aim for the magic 5:1 ratio mentioned earlier in the chapter. That is, always strive to have five positive thoughts or make five positive comments for every one negative thought/comment. Though it may sound simplistic, make a conscious daily practice of (1) reducing the frequency and intensity of your negative thoughts, and (2) increasing the frequency and intensity of your positive thoughts.

As with creating any healthy new habit, it will take perseverance, practice, and dedication. But it can be done. It may feel very artificial, at first, to monitor your mind and your mouth in this manner. However, the rewards you reap will affect every aspect of your life and business for the better. I have seen this in my own life and in the lives of others who have tried it.

If you are a manager or businessperson trying to increase positivity on your team, remember the advice discussed earlier: become strengths-focused instead of the reverse, offer lots of praise and encouragement to team members, and lower the resistance level to adopting positive habits.

In *Man's Search for Meaning*, Viktor Frankl, a famous Holocaust survivor, writes about how he chose to find happiness and purpose while in a Nazi concentration camp. "Between stimulus and response, there is a space. In that space lies our freedom and power to choose our response. In our response lies our growth and freedom."[6]

In order to counteract the barrage of negativity this world dishes out, I find it very helpful to surround myself with positive quotes from positive-energy people. I encourage you to do the same. Here are a few of my favorites:

"Persons are judged to be great because of the positive qualities they possess, not because of the absence of faults."

—JOHN F. KENNEDY

"Think like a queen. A queen is not afraid to fail. Failure is another stepping-stone to greatness."

"Do the one thing you think you cannot do. Fail at it. Try again. Do better the second time. The only people who never tumble are those who never mount the high wire. This is your moment. Own it."

—OPRAH WINFREY

"Formulate and stamp indelibly on your mind a mental picture of yourself as succeeding. Hold this picture tenaciously. Never permit it to fade. Your mind will seek to develop the picture."

"Become a possibilitarian. No matter how dark things seem to be or actually are, raise your sights and see the possibilities. Always see them; for they are always there."

—NORMAN VINCENT PEALE

"A pessimist sees the difficulty in every opportunity; an optimist sees the opportunity in every difficulty."

—WINSTON CHURCHILL

"There is little difference in people, but that little difference makes a big difference. The little difference is attitude. The big difference is whether it is positive or negative."

—W. CLEMENT STONE

"When you get into a tight place and everything goes against you, till it seems as though you could not hold on a minute longer, never give up then, for that is just the place and time that the tide will turn."

—HARRIET BEECHER STOWE

"If you don't stand for something you will fall for anything."

—MALCOLM X

"If you think about disaster, you will get it. Brood about death and you hasten your demise. Think positively and masterfully, with confidence and faith, and life becomes more secure, more fraught with action, richer in achievement and experience."

—SWAMI VIVEKANANDA

6

THE CURRENCY OF PERSONAL RESPONSIBILITY

One of the last public actions King took before he was assassinated on the balcony of the Lorraine Motel was to stand in solidarity with Memphis sanitation workers who had decided to rise up and take personal responsibility for the way they were being treated on the job.

After years of racial discrimination, mistreatment, humiliation, and dangerous working conditions, about thirteen hundred black sanitation professionals said, "Enough!" and walked off the job in protest during that famous strike. Most of them bore signs with the simple message, "I AM A MAN." This is what happens when people decide it is time to take their definitive purpose and destiny into their own hands by seizing responsibility for their actions. I am sure the frustration that drove these sanitation workers to action stemmed from thoughts very much like this: "I clean the streets with excellence. I report to work on time. I work overtime without complaint—yet I am paid less than my white counterparts and my humanity is questioned every day." These men got tired of waiting for someone else to fix the problem.

King was fond of quoting this famous passage from the Declaration of Independence: "that all men are created equal, that they are endowed by their Creator with certain unalienable rights, that among these are Life, Liberty and the pursuit of Happiness." He reminded us that we are all created in the image and likeness of God. Therefore, the quest for *economic* equality became synonymous with a quest for the recognition of basic *human* equality. It remains so to this day. For even though several new employment laws have been passed since King's death—and these have had a positive effect on economic opportunity for all—legislation cannot force the hearts and minds of mankind to open to one another, nor can it force businesses to practice true fairness. King was aware of this. He knew that economic equality had to be fought for from within ourselves and our communities, not just asked for from forces outside of ourselves, such as the government. It had to become a matter of personal responsibility.

During his historic "I've Been to the Mountaintop" speech from Mason Temple in Memphis, Tennessee, the night before he was shot, King called for the community of poor and disenfranchised blacks to harness their individual responsibility to leverage their collective clout. In doing so, he was also calling for *all* economically disempowered people to follow suit and claim their own power. King pointed out that although black people might be considerably poorer than whites as individuals, *together* they had more wealth than most nations. And together they could, and *should*, use their collective economic clout to exert pressure on companies, stores, and organizations that used unfair policies and practices. This economic pressure might include withdrawing their dollars from certain industries and institutions or making changes in their retail spending habits.

Nowadays many people might be fearful of committing "guerrilla" economic actions such as boycotts, "occupations" of merchants and retailers, and mass withdrawals of funds from banks and financial entities. I call such actions a matter of seizing personal responsibility. When a certain group of people is treated with institutional unfairness, those people are responsible for leveraging their economic power, in concert with others, to bring pressure to bear on the marketplace for the purpose of change. This does not need to be militant or confrontational. It can include simple but organized changes in shopping, investing, and lifestyle habits. For example, Molly Katchpole, a young woman who had only recently finished college and was holding down two low-paying jobs, became incensed when her bank,

Bank of America, announced its plans to institute a $5 monthly charge for debit-card users. She started a petition online, which quickly garnered three hundred thousand signatures as well as a good deal of press.

Father Eduardo Samaniego of the Most Holy Trinity Catholic Church in San Jose, California, in concert with PACT (People Acting in Community Together), took action against the same bank in a different way. Although Bank of America had been his parish's bank for twenty years, Samaniego withdrew $3 million from the institution and transferred the money to local credit unions. The result of this action? The second-largest financial institution in the country (Bank of America) rescinded its new fee and several other banks, such as Wells Fargo and JP Morgan Chase, canceled their plans to implement similar fees.

Katchpole and Samaniego were just everyday people exercising personal responsibility in the economic arena.

My Own Attempt to Exercise Responsibility

In 2010, I convened a focus group of entrepreneurs and influencers in Atlanta to help shape some of the small business legislation that was being drafted by the U.S. Senate Committee on Small Business and Entrepreneurship. Attorney Don Cravins, the committee's staff director and chief counsel, worked very closely with me on this. A hearing was held in Washington, D.C., with young entrepreneurs from the private sector and other small business owners and community leaders from around the nation. We made it our personal responsibility to get involved in the process of legislation and to ensure that our ideas about making more funds available for new small businesses were incorporated into the national policy.

Most of our ideas made it into the legislation that was passed. It was a great experience because we participants in the process actually felt like and operated as stakeholders. We were on the front end of *creating* law rather than on the back end of *accepting* laws that were passed while we were asleep or distracted. This bipartisan legislation became known as the Small Business Lending Facility. It was passed into law in 2010 and specifically designed to fund small business growth via community banks. The community banks were given very good incentives to draw down on these monies and lend to local businesses.

As I write this book, however, billions of the allocated dollars remain untapped because these banks have declined to shake loose the funds. Why? It's difficult to know the exact reason, but I have heard insiders speculate strongly that it is due to an orchestrated intention to see the Obama Administration fail. Whatever the reason, many small- and medium-sized businesses still haven't been able to access the critical lending necessary to expand and create jobs.

This disappointing real-world result showed me that, although participating in the policy process was important, at the end of the day, government can't *force* a bank to lend or a company to hire. Even when new laws are put in place, they can be difficult to enforce. And although new laws can and do create social and economic change, human beings can still resist them and defeat them in spirit. Thus the question, "What can I personally do to influence the outcome?" gained urgency.

I continued my journey and came up with another solution: a Business Development Company (BDC). Forming a BDC is a way in which individuals can come together and take personal responsibility for their economic futures. Typically, a BDC helps grow small companies in the initial stages of their development and is very similar to a venture capital fund, except that BDCs allow smaller, nonaccredited investors to invest in start-ups. In essence, they allow investments by the general public. This is a huge advantage. Having raised private capital for businesses before, I knew that private companies can usually raise capital only from accredited investors. Accredited investors, however, must have a net worth of at least $1 million and generate $250,000 in income per year.

The majority of people in America are considered to be nonaccredited investors. Through the concept of a BDC, however, we discovered a way to give all people an opportunity to do what banks and venture funds were failing to do: invest in exciting new start-ups. So I began talking with the people in my network and discovered that there was a loose group of professionals that were coming together for business networking and social events on a consistent basis. Now we are organizing a joint venture to expand our mall investment fund into a BDC that will enable us to receive investments or loans from more than 750,000 professionals.

Just imagine how many start-ups this investment company can make loans to; how many real estate ventures it can pursue; how many church properties it can acquire and refinance; how many contracts it can help fulfill. Can you say "jobs, jobs, jobs"?! As always, with a vision this large, it's going to require a tremendous amount of education, inspiration, and motivation. But the point is that we are doing something *real* to put our money where our mouths are. During this process, I have learned that although many people *talk* about their collective economic desires, few make the individual efforts to turn those desires into reality.

The Currency of Personal Responsibility is one of the most challenging currencies to act upon.

Personal Responsibility in the Job Market

I was recently speaking in Orlando, Florida, and was offered a tour of a community commercial retail property owned by The Hope Church under the leadership of Bishop Allen Wiggins. The owners' vision for that community is quite impressive and should serve as a model for revitalization and investment nationwide. Allen was able to reposition his church's land, form a community development corporation, acquire a dilapidated commercial property in a highly blighted area, renovate it, and lease it out. Using his model, land and structures can be repositioned to create jobs and stimulate growth in the worst and best of communities.

One of the retailers in this mini-mall operated a men's boutique that I took interest in and wanted to support. In his shop, I was drawn to a T-shirt imprinted with the purple and gold words, "I DON'T HAVE A JOB. I CREATE JOBS." I had to buy it.

This phrase resonated within me and excited my sense of personal responsibility to address the jobs crisis in America and beyond. I realized that in the economy of the twenty-first century, we must stop thinking of a job as something that is handed to us by someone else. We must start thinking of it as something we generate ourselves. We must reclaim that power.

> *In the economy of the twenty-first century, we must stop thinking of a job as something that is handed to us by someone else.*
> *We must start thinking of it as something we generate ourselves.*

If you have recently become unemployed, then it's time for you to create a job. If you have recently graduated from high school, college, or graduate school, then it's time for you to create a job. If you have ever thought of starting a business or becoming a private contractor, then it's time for you to create a job.

How do we create jobs? Well, entire books could be written about this topic. The main point I want to make here is that it's a mindset, first and foremost. We need to shift our psychology away from one of *finding* existing jobs toward one of shaping, defining, and creating new ones. There are many ways we can do that. We create jobs by offering our skills to people for a fee, as freelancers and contractors. We create jobs by writing a business plan, raising start-up capital, recruiting a skilled team of partners, and starting a small business. Yes, this requires risk and hardship, and many new businesses do fail. But even when they fail, they create jobs and teach new skills in the meantime. We create jobs by lending money, if we have it, to skilled individuals who are trying to go into business for themselves. Most start-ups, for example, launch with less than $25,000 in seed capital—imagine if we each invested $1,000 in a start-up every quarter by using crowdfunding platforms like Kickstarter,

Opportunity Hub, and GrowVC. We create jobs by selling specialty items online. We create jobs by asking CEOs and managers to envision new positions within their existing companies and showing them how this will benefit *them*.

The point is that we don't wait around for jobs to materialize. Long gone are the days when we could hope to land a job in a secure corporation and ride it till retirement and a gold watch. The twenty-first century belongs to the entrepreneurs and the entrepreneurial thinkers. It is the era of personal job creation.

Of course, creating jobs requires effort and sacrifice. It requires us to

- learn a trade or perfect a skill so that people will want to pay us for it;
- serve apprenticeships and give away our skills for free as we learn them;
- identify business needs in the marketplace and think up innovative solutions to meet them;
- market our skills and solutions in clever, attention-grabbing ways; and
- find creative crowdfund investments and make investments ourselves.

Creating jobs also requires investors to take risks with start-ups. And sometimes it may require business owners and existing employees to make sacrifices, such as taking less profit or pay for a season to make room for new people who will help the company thrive in the long run. Job creation really doesn't require special or advanced skills. A janitor, for example, might put together a simple proposal to clean his employer's offices on a contract basis and gradually build a cleaning business that way. A nanny might slowly develop a nanny-referral system, helping others get hired for a percentage of their ongoing pay. Eventually she may be able to move, full-time, into running her own agency.

The best way you will ever leverage your truest gifts is to make yourself indispensible via a job or business that you help create, directly or indirectly. You may not be ready to take this step now, but you can work toward it by developing the mindset that you, and you alone, are in charge of your career.

If Not Now, When?

Beginning now, nothing is more important to our collective well-being than to embrace the Currency of Personal Responsibility. For this currency holds the key to developing any of the other currencies of *Kingonomics*. Why? Without the commitment to become the masters of our fates and the captains of our souls, we will never personally embrace the currencies of Service, Connectivity, Reciprocity, Positivity, and Diversity. We will never try to execute the lessons of this book. If we don't get the fact that *we're* the ones who need to invest these currencies, we'll spend our lives complaining and waiting for someone else to step up to the plate.

Too frequently we attach our survival, sustainability, and growth to someone or something else. But we can't always look outside ourselves and our own resources for life's answers; we must look within. For there—sometimes buried very deeply—lies the motivation, intellect, and strength to take meaningful action. If we don't care enough to manifest our own ideas, who will?

An important thing to remember is that someone, at some point in the past, present, or future, is going to arrive at the same great idea you had. Have you ever seen a new product, service, or company, and said, "I thought of that! That was my idea!"? Well, you may have *thought* of the idea, but you lost the opportunity to benefit from it because you didn't take the action—didn't take the personal responsibility—to make the idea real. Every noteworthy business success stems from an individual making the decision to *act* on a good idea, not just tuck it away in the "someday" file.

Many times we allow people, hardships, circumstances, and "-isms" such as classism, racism, and sexism to prohibit us from recognizing that we have the personal power and responsibility to make our economic dreams come true. We tend to want presidents, senators, governors, and mayors to fix our lives and economic situations. But again, we can't continue to look *outside* of ourselves for what is clearly an *inside* job. Learning is an inside job. Building the self-confidence to navigate adversity is an inside job. Finding the compassion to serve and to help others succeed is an inside job. Innovating new ideas is an inside job. Being positive is an inside job. Believing in the future is an inside job. Managing our fear is definitely an inside job. Personal change is an intentional, internal process that no one can do for us.

Government is merely an *enabler* of change. It can't start businesses for us. It can't place us in satisfying jobs. Its main power lies in its ability to *remove* institutional barriers, not to proactively improve our lives. It can do its part to prevent unfair practices in the workplace, but it cannot make us happy and successful. Change will never happen if we don't live it firsthand. For instance, I voted for President Barack Obama, but I don't expect him to be my savior. Yes, he motivates me. Yes, I believe in most of his political agenda. But I will take personal responsibility for my own definitive purpose and destiny rather than wait for him or anyone else to "fix" it. I don't mean to attack government-sponsored social programs. There are millions of Americans that legitimately and rightfully utilize these services during economic transitional periods of their lives. But I do mean to "attack" the kind of personal thinking that *demands* President Obama, or any president for that matter, create all the jobs, but then never takes personal responsibility by (1) learning how government works and what a president's limitations are (especially if he or she isn't to become a dictator), (2) hiring within their own businesses, (3) marketing themselves creatively and aggressively to hiring managers, (4) starting a business themselves or in cooperation with others, and (5) becoming a private contractor/freelancer.

It's easy to sit around and talk about what America has to do to change for the better; it's much tougher to take responsibility for our day-to-day actions and results.

There are many, many things each and every one of us can do right now besides simply wait till the next election cycle to "vote and hope" once again. One of the most important things we can do is align our personal actions with the policies we want to see become law or remain law. Why vote for increased and legitimate taxes for the rich if we're going to fail to pay our own taxes? Why vote for alternative energy programs if we're going to continue to drive a huge gas-guzzler year after year? Why clamor for more small business loans to be made if we won't lend a family member a thousand dollars to launch a promising new Internet business? Why ask the government to enforce fair hiring and fair housing practices if we refuse to rent an apartment to a member of a racial or cultural group *we* don't approve of?

Even in matters of faith, we often ask God to fix our lives, when God has endowed us with a brain, an imagination, and the ability to innovate and create something from nothing. Rather than use our faith to beg for favors from the Almighty, we need to leverage our faith *in ourselves* as God's creations so as to innovate from within and create the reality we desire.

Personal Responsibility in Business

Renowned business guru Peter Drucker once said that the purpose of a business is to create and keep a customer. Milton Friedman, one of the most prominent economists of the twentieth century, said, "There is one and only one social responsibility of business: to use its resources and engage in activities designed to increase its profits so long as it stays within the rules of the game."[1]

For the past several decades, some business managers and entrepreneurs have hidden behind such business philosophies to avoid taking responsibility for bad behavior, such as producing shoddy products, polluting the environment, lying, or cheating clients and customers. Many have disavowed any responsibility to make the world a better place or even to be honest about their own behaviors. After all, if one's only responsibility as a businessperson is to make a profit and generate income for stockholders, then one needn't take personal responsibility for anything that doesn't affect the bottom line. Traditionally, the public has allowed business to get away with this, for the most part.

But things are changing. Today's consumers are beginning to demand more when choosing companies with whom to do business. Managers and executives are beginning to see that being transparent and personally responsible is the right way to behave and can benefit their firms in the long run.

As an example, the *New York Times* made an unprecedented move by publishing a front-page analysis of its own ethical crisis: the plagiarized and often fabricated reporting of one of its writers, Jayson Blair. This analysis, "Correcting the Record; Times Reporter Who Resigned Leaves Long Trail of Deception," was published on May 11, 2003:

> A staff reporter for the *New York Times* committed frequent acts of journalistic fraud while covering significant news events in recent months, an investigation by *Times* journalists has found. The widespread fabrication and plagiarism represent a profound betrayal of trust and a low point in the 152-year history of the newspaper . . .
>
> The investigation suggests several reasons Mr. Blair's deceits went undetected for so long: a failure of communication among senior editors; few complaints from the subjects of his articles; his savviness and his ingenious ways of covering his tracks.

Although taking responsibility for mistakes can be painful, doing so does more to bolster your reputation as a trustworthy business than any amount of "spinning" and dodging. The reality is that most people have more respect for an organization that readily admits its mistakes and comes up with a plan to avoid them in the future than for one that's never had so much as a black mark on its record. Whenever a failure occurs within a company, the opportunity arises to publicly spend the Currency of Personal Responsibility.

The fact is that even if everyone is extremely conscientious about their conduct, mistakes do happen. Some occur through carelessness or inexperience while others are just twists of fate. Messes can be physical, such as oil spills or asbestos in buildings, or can arise from simple human interactions ranging from innocent misunderstandings to outright bad behavior. Whatever the cause of the mess and whatever kind of mess it is, leaders still need to take responsibility and clean it up. Nobody has any respect for companies that play the "blame game."

But owning up to mistakes can be costly and, unfortunately, too many businesspeople fail to see the value that can be gained by combining a sincere apology with a genuine effort to correct problems. By taking the shortsighted approach of lying, denying, or blaming, they create bigger problems for themselves down the line. Toyota executives, for example, created a crisis of trust in 2009 by failing to acknowledge a dangerous "sticky pedal" defect with several of Toyota's vehicle lines. The crisis could have been averted had they viewed the problem early on as an opportunity to take personal responsibility and publicly prove their company was one that stood for safety and honesty. Instead, they ignored and denied the issue, which snowballed into a massive recall and an even more massive crisis of faith for a company that had always had a stellar reputation. The company is *still* working to rebuild consumer trust in the wake of this failure of personal responsibility.

Assuming responsibility involves four steps:

1. Acknowledge the problem.
2. Offer a sincere apology.
3. Repair the damage.
4. Take steps to avoid a repeat of the problem.

When a company follows these steps, it can limit the damage to its reputation by owning up to its mistakes and thereby keep the trust of customers. In the long run, this approach is better for both the company and its customers.

Domino's Pizza took this initiative in 2009 when, in a remarkable ad campaign, the company took full responsibility for the poor reviews its pizza was receiving from customers and began using better-quality ingredients and a new sauce recipe. The ad campaign generated very positive responses on Twitter and Facebook, and in March 2010, the company publicly stated that it had doubled its profits for the previous quarter. This indicates, not surprisingly, that consumers appreciate it when a company acknowledges its shortcomings, takes steps to correct them, and does so in a very public and transparent way (see Chapter Eleven).

Businesses and individuals that are respected thrive. And responsibility is what breeds respect. You have the power to turn your business around simply by presenting it as honestly as you can and by accepting personal responsibility for any mistakes or ethical missteps your company makes. In this social media–driven era, businesses that behave responsibly are receiving positive buzz online, while those that cheat, lie, deceive, or turn their backs on customers are being "outed" with record speed. Word now spreads faster than at any time previous in history. The wrong "tweet" from the wrong person can do instantaneous damage to your venture. Even if you don't believe business has a *moral obligation* to behave responsibly, it now has a financial obligation to do so.

Personal Responsibility to Fight Injustice

It's not just in the business arena that we need to be morally proactive. The Currency of Personal Responsibility also demands that we raise our voices loudly and clearly against *any* injustice we see in society and in our communities, *even when we might be personally benefiting from that injustice.* We need to remember that although we may be benefiting for the moment, we will be the victims of injustice next time around if we do not stand up. Injustice toward one person or group is injustice toward all.

One way to stand up is to speak out against falsehoods and half-truths that are perpetuated in the media and become accepted as facts. In America and around the world, for example, racist precepts have been recently masquerading as "good family values." But for whose "family" are these values good? Early in the 2012 presidential election cycle, Republican nominee hopefuls Michele Bachmann and Rick Santorum signed a pledge by the Family Leader, an organization in Iowa, that suggested black children who were born into slavery were, in some ways, better off than they are today, and that America's first black president was somehow responsible for this state of affairs: "Yet sadly a child born into slavery in 1860 was more likely to be raised by his mother and father in a two-parent household than was an African-American baby born after the election of the USA's first African-American President."

It is completely ludicrous to suggest that black children were in any way, shape, or form better off as slaves than they are today! Slave families were routinely broken up for sale at auctions. In many instances, rape, torture, and humiliation were practiced on *all* family members, and all were treated as property, with fewer rights than dogs have today. Yet somehow all of this abuse was supposedly mitigated by the fact that there were two-parent households? Chattel slavery was an utter outrage upon humanity, in every way.

It's a tragic state of affairs when major political candidates sign a pledge that openly suggests that life for young black children born into slavery was in any way better than for black children living during the administration of President Barack Obama.

As a father of six, I cannot sit by idly and let these kinds of statements go unchallenged. I must take personal responsibility to balance the scales, and I have done so. Via the Internet and public speeches, I have pointed out that it was illegal for slaves to learn to read, while most of my children are already reading; that it was illegal for slaves to own property, while my children are already planning to own their own business and purchase homes and investment property in the future; that it was illegal for slaves to go outside after dark or to leave their owners' properties without written permission. Today we have a black president. I take it as my personal duty to correct harmful lies when they are sold to the public. We all must.

We have a duty to not only challenge untruths but also to positively stand up for moral principles, even if it costs or inconveniences us to do so. We cannot allow the convenience of the majority to trump the individual rights of the minority. That was the mindset that allowed slavery to thrive. A modern example of this is the community that finds it much cheaper and more convenient to build public institutions that are not handicap-accessible, resulting in lower taxes for its citizens. But no matter how many benefits such a practice might bring to the majority, keeping disabled citizens out of public buildings would still be terribly unjust, and we would all have a personal duty to stand up and say so.

Personal responsibility demands that we shake our cowardly dispositions and stand up for principle—personally and economically—in any given situation. Those who stand to benefit economically from unfair policies must have the courage and virtue to forsake personal gain in order to do what is clearly right. Those who stand to *lose* from unfair policies must take personal responsibility by using their collective purchasing power to force change. Rights for African Americans have only been gained when courageous individuals in both camps have taken a stand.

Some Great Models of Personal Responsibility

Social evolution progresses by building on what works and discarding the miscues. Thus, we can look back and see what others did when faced with the same predicaments we face today. There is no shortage of references. Every injustice being perpetrated today, sometimes under the mask of "for the people, by the people," has been done before. So if our situations today are not fundamentally new, then what did great leaders of the past do to establish democracy, human rights, and the rule of law during bad times? They employed determination, hard work, sacrifice, and focus; all launched from the springboard of an unshakable sense of personal responsibility.

Like many of his countrymen, Mahatma Gandhi was opposed to British colonial rule in India. Unlike most of his fellow countrymen, however, Gandhi made it his personal responsibility to bring this form of governance to an end. He did so by becoming the modern face of nonviolent resistance. Although Gandhi could have asked his people to raise arms against the British, he chose, instead, to take the high road and follow the dictates of his conscience. He knew it would ultimately be pointless to win the political battle if his followers lost the war by resorting to actions that debased them, such as physical retaliation. He believed we all reap what we sow and he did not wish to see his followers create bad karma for themselves. He organized his people to practice brotherhood amongst ethnic and religious groups, to fight for women's liberation, to end the caste system, and to work for economic independence from the British. When the British imposed the "salt tax," Gandhi advocated civil disobedience and led his people to the ocean to extract salt. He openly called for the British to "quit India" and advocated the use of boycott, peaceful resistance, and labor strikes to achieve economic freedom for his people. Always practicing what he preached, Gandhi lived a simple life and went to prison several times for his nonviolent defiance against injustice. His famous statement, which perfectly summarizes what personal responsibility is all about, was, "You must *be* the change you wish to see in the world." As a result of this one man seizing personal responsibility for change, India was victorious. In fact, today it is the largest democracy in the world.

Dr. King was a student of Gandhi's philosophies. When faced with the scourge of segregation and unequal treatment, King, too, took it upon himself to make a difference. Like Gandhi, he believed in the power of peaceful resistance and the good that could be accomplished by using this form of protest. In 1955, he personally led the Montgomery Bus Boycott to end racial segregation on city buses. He urged black people not to ride the buses until their demands were met and, after much struggle and sacrifice, he and his nonviolent protestors won. Several years later, in 1963, more than 200,000 people gathered to witness King make his famous "I Have a Dream" speech in conjunction with the March on Washington, which he co-organized.

During Dr. King's journey for equality, he advocated the use of economic boycott, peaceful protest, and targeted strikes to achieve freedom for himself and his people. The Civil Rights Act of 1964 and Voting Rights Act of 1965 came about as a result of his focused and relentless determination. Taking personal responsibility means pouring our efforts into doing the right thing, even when victory may seem far away.

Much like Gandhi, Nelson Mandela also took responsibility for his beliefs and fought for them. Involved in the Youth League of the African National Congress (ANC) when he was a young man, he became deputy national president in 1952. Mandela was inspired by the teachings of Gandhi and the ANC and based his struggle to get rid of apartheid on the principle of nonviolence. He organized and led "peaceful protests" and was arrested several times.

The 1960 incident known as the Sharpeville Massacre, when peaceful protesters were gunned down by the regime, was a turning point in Mandela's thinking. He came to the realization that the nonviolent movement must sometimes be augmented by the use of force. Reluctantly, but believing it was his only choice, he took personal responsibility for leading Umkhonto we Sizwe ("Spear of the Nation"), the military wing of ANC; raising funds; and visiting several African countries to arrange military training and logistical support.

At his trial in 1964, the ever-defiant leader faced the all-white court and said:

> During my lifetime I have dedicated myself to this struggle of the African people. I have fought against white domination, and I have fought against black domination. I have cherished the ideal of a democratic and free society in which all persons live together in harmony and with equal opportunities. It is an ideal which I hope to live for and to achieve. But if needs be, it is an ideal for which I am prepared to die.[2]

Willingness to die for one's principles is, of course, the ultimate form of personal responsibility. As we all know, Mandela was found guilty of sabotage, along with other charges, and spent the next twenty-seven years in the apartheid regime's prison. His imprisonment gave strength to a new generation of activists, including the young and charismatic Steven Biko, who emerged to unite his people.

Biko took the struggle international and urged the West to boycott and divest from South Africa. He asked all of us around the globe to take personal responsibility for sending a message to the leaders of African apartheid. Like Gandhi and MLK, Biko understood that if we want to prevent the spread of injustice, we must be willing to take personal stewardship of our own minds. He wrote, "The most potent weapon in the hands of the oppressor is the mind of the oppressed."

He believed "the oppressed" had a personal responsibility to protect the space between their ears as a sovereign state.

The Soweto Uprisings were later organized and led by the Black Consciousness Movement (BCM) of which Biko was president. He was murdered shortly thereafter by the apartheid regime. He, too, was willing to give his life for his cause.

So what can these four courageous people teach us? They did not place total blame for their problems on other people, nor did they wait for their governments to fix their problems. Instead, they used the Currency of Personal Responsibility to motivate people to unite and stand up for what was right.

Seize Every Opportunity to Exercise Personal Responsibility

In 2006 I had the opportunity to participate in a series of meetings in Libreville, Gabon, with His Excellency Omar Bongo Ondimba, the now-deceased president of the Gabonese Republic. Bongo was commonly referred to as a dictator. Although my company was contracted by him to address his U.S. relations, trade, and investment opportunities, I used this platform to discuss how his influence could be a catalyst for peace and positive transformation throughout the world. As my team and I sat in President Bongo's equivalent of the Oval Office, I suggested he leverage his oil resources to engage in peaceful dialogue with rogue nations and states. Using MLK, Mahatma Gandhi, Nelson Mandela, and Steven Biko as examples of men who took responsibility for their personal destinies and the destinies of millions, I encouraged this billionaire oil leader to do the same. By seizing an opportunity to influence a world leader, I, too, was assuming personal responsibility for change (along with a good bit of risk).

Though some of my message may have been lost in the French translation, something was resonating in his eyes as we talked. Knowing that his re-election campaign was forthcoming, I asked him, with sincerity, not to take military action against the opposing party's leadership and to demonstrate diplomacy in dealing with his opponents. Of course, he won the disputed election months later, but the political casualties and civil unrest were far less severe than in earlier years. Whether I had any influence on this or not I'll never know, but I will take it as a win for peace.

The Gabon story continues. In early 2012, I learned that my very good friend Bishop Mike Jocktane, former chief of cabinet to the late President Bongo, was facing government persecution because of his decision to support a presidential candidate who opposed the present leadership. The lives of Jocktane's family were also threatened. I could have wrung my hands and let it happen, but instead I launched an interactive campaign across the social graph (i.e., Twitter, Facebook, Scribd). I also reached out to my business colleague, Mrs. Martha Tilahun, chairperson of the United Africa Group, a very successful business conglomerate on the African continent with close ties to the current Gabonese president, Ali Bongo Ondimba.

I asked Martha if I could copy her on a letter I wrote about Jocktane's troubles to the Gabonese president. Although she was compassionate about Bishop Jocktane's dire circumstances, she wanted to stay clear of any perception of affiliation with the opposing party. I followed up by speaking with Martha and candidly encouraged her to consider her personal responsibility to seek justice and freedom in Africa rather than sit back and allow the remnants of imperialistic governmental policies to continue forward. I encouraged her to seek significance in this process rather than success. For although she was already very successful—in reality, one of the most successful women on the entire continent—I believed this was an incredible opportunity for her to establish a new precedent that in order to do business with her, one must at least respect the basic free will of citizens.

Well, Martha finally agreed to my request; I copied her name on the letter. A few days later I received word that the president of Gabon personally went to the trumped-up trial of Bishop Mike Jocktane to guarantee his personal safety, the safety of his wife and children, and the sanctity of their church and ministry.

Once again, personal responsibility prevailed.

Make Personal Responsibility a Business Asset

As we wrap up this topic, I'd like to look at the Currency of Personal Responsibility from a slightly different angle.

In more than one of his speeches, Dr. King urged those of us who work in even the humblest of professions—such as sweeping streets—to do our jobs with the same dedication, pride, and loving attention that Michelangelo, Beethoven, and Shakespeare poured into their work. For when everyday people take personal responsibility for a job well done, heaven and earth sit up and take notice.

The point Dr. King was trying to make is that all of us should take personal responsibility for doing our jobs at the highest level possible. This is true whether we are artists, surgeons, entrepreneurs, customer service representatives, or janitors. We must lose the attitude of boredom and resentment that many of us bring to the workplace and instead make it our *personal calling* to serve with excellence. It is the right thing to do from a spiritual perspective and also makes sense from a business perspective.

A sense of entitlement pervades the attitudes of many young employees today. I've dealt with more than my share of customer service reps who roll their eyes whenever asked to go out of their way in the least and project an attitude of, "I am much too important a person to work at a job like this." But can we afford this attitude? Should we behave as if we're owed a good job by corporate America?

My belief is that employees of the present and future must think of themselves like motivated freelancers do and take personal responsibility for doing a great job and pleasing every customer. To survive in the economy of the twenty-first century, we must understand that each of us is a "brand" unto ourselves and make it our personal mission to embody exemplary brand values every day in the workplace.

Our parents grew up in a different world. Not only was the economy more robust, but business, as a rule, was much more stable. The great career model for Baby Boomers and members of "the Greatest Generation" was to get a steady job with a reputable corporation and steadily work your way up the ladder until retirement. The idea of securing "a job for life" was the prevalent goal amongst both employers and employees. Employees wanted job security and employers wanted long-term team members who would grow with the company. Though doing a good job was important, you didn't have to "fight for your job" day in and day out.

Today, few employees work at one job for more than three or four years. The workplace is much more fluid. Employees of the twenty-first century spend much more time *looking for new opportunities* than workers of past generations did. It really makes more sense today—whether you are a freelancer or salaried employee—to think of yourself as an independent contractor working a "gig" rather than a permanent position, because that is how companies now view their employees, too. There is no longer a sense of corporate responsibility for the long-term careers of workers. Employees are viewed as commodities that are brought aboard as needed and released when they no longer serve the company's immediate needs. There are very few "permanent" careers in "stable corporations" today. Every worker today must be much more conscious of building the right "personal brand" so that she or he can move easily into new job positions when needed.

In such a fluid employment atmosphere, your personal reputation becomes much more important than it ever was before. On a daily basis, you must actively and passively build your brand: consciously adopt a high set of values and then live those values every day, no matter what your present job is, because tomorrow your job may change. Continually work to make your stock rise, because you are always "auditioning" for that next position, whether moving laterally or upward. This simply will not happen, however, if you project an air of entitlement, laziness, surliness, or indifference. Take personal responsibility and present yourself—the distinctive "brand" that is you—in the best light possible.

THE CURRENCY OF SELF-IMAGE

At first glance, the Currency of Self-Image might seem like an odd concept to promote in this book. After all, the term *self-image* is often used by spiritual and self-help writers to describe the superficial concerns of the human ego. The advice often given is, "Don't be so concerned with your self-image!" But I use the term as it refers to two distinct but related concepts.

First, it refers to the image or idea we hold of ourselves inside, in our own minds: Do we know ourselves? Do we like who we are? Do we trust and respect ourselves? Are we proud of our own values and behaviors? Do we possess self-esteem?

Second, it refers to the image or idea of ourselves we project externally, to the rest of the world. Is this image an accurate reflection of who we are inside? Is it one that inspires trust and respect in others? Does our image allow us to lead by example?

What ties these two ideas together is *congruence*. That is, are our images *in full agreement* or *alignment* with each other? Is the external image fully consistent with the internal one? Is my outer behavior congruent with the values I hold—or *claim* to hold—inside? Congruence builds trust.

It's next to impossible to build trust and respect with others, especially in the business world, if you don't trust and respect yourself. Trusting and respecting yourself means you are confident in who you are and how you behave. It means you abide by moral principles in both your private and public lives. That is the way you build trust and respect in yourself. It takes a secure, self-respecting person to trust him- or herself, especially when money and capital are involved. Self-trust flows from knowing you will do the right thing, even when there are powerful incentives to do the opposite. When you confidently know this about yourself, others will know it about you, too.

> *Self-trust flows from knowing you will do the right thing, even when there are powerful incentives to do the opposite. When you confidently know this about yourself, others will know it about you, too.*

All of our relationships with others are based on the *primary relationship we have with ourselves.* People who truly love themselves naturally love others. People who trust themselves naturally trust others. People who believe in themselves naturally believe in others. Conversely, people who lack trust or belief in themselves have no basis on which to build trust and belief in others.

But how does trustworthiness get communicated to others? After all, many public figures master tricks of behavior and speech to *project* an outer image of trustworthiness, but this is not an accurate reflection of who they are inside. On the other hand, some very trustworthy people inadvertently project a flawed image that fails to reflect their highest inner qualities, simply because they lack basic presentation skills, social skills, or media training.

Long-term behavior, of course, is the truest measure of trustworthiness. Trustworthy people keep their promises . . . even if it takes a lifetime to fulfill them. If a trustworthy investor tells you that she is going to invest, she lives up to her word and does so. The same applies to keeping appointments, attending meetings, repaying debts, and delivering products and services in a timely, professional manner and completed to the very best of one's ability. Genuinely trustworthy people and companies perform with integrity even when others are not watching. Eventually this kind of congruent behavior gets recognized by customers and associates.

In a very real sense, as I mentioned in the previous chapter, each of us is a "brand" unto ourselves. Just as a company breeds trust or distrust in its brand by the way it delivers on the values it espouses, so do *we* build trust in our individual brands by behaving with congruence. Your brand must not only begin with a firm inner sense of self-knowledge and self-esteem, but project an outer image that is fully aligned with your personality, values, and skills. You then *build* your brand's trustworthiness by consistently delivering on your promises in both your personal and business lives.

Lead by Example

Dr. Martin Luther King, Jr. probably didn't use the word *brand* to describe his own self-image, but he clearly understood the importance of *embodying* the values he preached. He knew that it does absolutely no good to talk to your followers about excellence, courage, and compassion, for example, if you are not willing and able to exemplify those traits yourself. King was committed to personal development and was constantly re-evaluating how to best live his life and how to best evolve as an effective leader, teacher, and human being. He knew that it was vitally important not only to *be* whatever change we want to see in the world, but also to *be* whatever values we want to encourage in others.

Not long before he died, Dr. King urged our society to develop leaders who "embody virtues" that we can all look up to and emulate. He stressed how important it is that the leaders themselves possess the moral principles they seek to inspire in others. He did not say, "We will have to develop leaders who *talk about* great virtues." He chose the word *embody*, which demonstrates that he felt strongly about the idea of congruence—of not only practicing what we preach but *living* the virtues we wish to instill in others.

It is by embodying values and virtues that we can all truly become leaders in our own lives, whether or not we hold a public position. Leaders lead by example, plain and simple. Every parent learns, sooner or later, that it is the behaviors they *model*, not those they preach, that are copied by their children. "Do as I say, not as I do" just doesn't work. If you tell your children to adopt healthy habits and avoid addictive substances, but you smoke and drink in front of them every day, it is your behavior that becomes the true teacher. If you act compassionately toward neighbors and always speak honestly, your child will learn these traits whether or not you specifically "teach" them. We are all leaders to the extent that we act congruently, allowing our outer behavior to fully reflect the values we hold inside.

Though Dr. King inspired millions with his words, those words would have meant very little had he not backed them up by consistent, courageous behavior. One of King's greatest legacies was that there was no apparent dissonance between his own self-image and his public image. In his book *Martin Luther King, Jr., on Leadership: Inspiration and Wisdom for Challenging Times*, Donald T. Phillips recounts the following story:

> One night, while back in Atlanta, Martin left the house without telling anyone where he was going. He had been concerned about a pending strike against a local factory's discriminatory practices because many of the company's employees were members of his congregation at Ebenezer Baptist. Martin's mother, who had been extremely worried about her son's recent depression, had been keeping a close eye on him. When he left without warning, she feared the worst and called an old friend of Martin's, Howard Baugh, who was the highest ranking African-American police officer in Atlanta. Also alarmed at Martin's unusual behavior, Baugh jumped in his car and began cruising the streets in search of his old childhood friend. Remembering the ongoing strike, on a hunch he drove by the factory around midnight. It was there that he found Martin standing outside the entrance. He was waiting for the shift to change so that he could encourage and give hope to the workers.[1]

And that, my friends, is a stellar example of outer behavior reflecting inner values and qualities. During a dark time in his own life, Dr. King looked inside himself and, despite being depressed and physically ill, was able to act on and embrace his highest self—a leader who stood for equality and justice. He lived his values even when—*especially* when—it would have been easier to rest on his laurels. And he did it without fanfare and without calling in the film crews. He knew that only when we embody what we truly stand for are we able to set the sort of example the world so desperately needs for inspiration.

The Two Aspects of Self-Image

"Looking back, you realize that a very special person passed briefly through your life—and it was you. It is not too late to find that person again."

—ROBERT BRAULT[2]

Again, self-image, as I use the term, refers to congruency with (1) the image of ourselves we hold internally, which, needless to say, must be a strong and trustworthy one if we are to believe in ourselves and build a foundation for relating positively to others, and (2) the image we project to society. We need to be sure that the persona we present to the world reflects our highest "version" of ourselves, the version we truly believe in and work hard to manifest. For the purposes of this discussion, we can refer to the two types of self-image as Outer Self-Image and Inner Self-Image.

Throughout the past few decades, both types of self-image have taken on an increasingly important role in society, politics, and the business world. Why? Well, we live in a very transparent, media-rich world today. Cell phone cameras, security videos, and recording equipment of all kinds are becoming omnipresent, making it increasingly important to be "on" at all times. At the same time, it is becoming increasingly difficult to live a "double life," in which you preach one thing publicly, but behave in an entirely different way in private. Simply put, if you misbehave, there's a much greater chance than ever before that you will get caught and exposed. But even if this were not the case, congruence is critically important.

Let's look at both the outer and inner self a little more carefully.

Outer Self-Image

Outer self-image has much to do with behavior. Congruent, trustworthy behavior will do much to compensate for any physical quirks or shortcomings you may possess. Still, it would be foolish to pretend that appearance is unimportant. Such qualities as your manner of dress and your personal hygiene are crucial in business, no question about it. For example, neither consumers nor employers like to see retail staff in clothes that have not been cleaned and ironed, or with messy hair and scuffed, dirty shoes. Personal hygiene and good grooming are essential to self-image in business. If you do not present a clean and hygienic self-image, it is unlikely that potential employers will be interested in hiring you. Even if you *are* hired, you are less likely to bring in business because customers will not take you seriously. Inevitably, unless you correct the problem, you will get fired.

Presentation is even more important if you are an entrepreneur. I recall a gentleman who ran a sandwich shop in my neighborhood when I was a child. He was habitually unshaven and always wore a very stained, dirty apron. I don't know if his hygiene was actually poor or not, but because he projected such an unhygienic image, I was always reluctant to buy a sandwich in his shop.

There are no hard and fast rules about physical appearance. What is brand-appropriate at one type of business may not be at another. For example, in the computer game business, it is customary to dress extremely casually. Game-company presidents are known to show up at staff meetings in cutoff jeans and a Batman T-shirt. Wearing a three-piece suit to work at such a company would cause coworkers to question your sanity. Similarly, showing up at a corporate finance office in shorts and a T-shirt would result in a consultation with the company counselor. Starbucks baristas dress and present themselves differently than insurance salesmen. You must understand the company brand and present your own image within these parameters. (But poor hygiene and lack of self-awareness are never desirable in any industry.)

You must be true to yourself while realistically taking into account how others will perceive you. Strong choices in physical appearance can evoke strong reactions. Black leather clothes, tattoos, and body piercings, for example, make a certain kind of statement to the general public whether you like it or not. So does a plaid polyester business suit from 1978. It is important to note that the judgments of others may differ from your own perception of your self-image.

There are many *behaviors* that deter customers and coworkers, too. You may feel there is nothing wrong with chewing gum, drinking a Slurpee, reading a book, or keeping a cell-phone conversation going while talking to customers, but many customers might find it off-putting, as I do. Therefore, look closely at your projected self-image to ensure that your dress and presentation befits your role in the company. Outer appearance, rightly or wrongly, communicates something about your inner qualities. If you dress smartly and appear clean and organized, others will assume you possess similar inner traits, unless you do something to prove otherwise. The opposite is also true. If you present yourself in a slovenly, disheveled way, it will take time and effort to prove to others that you are actually meticulous and dependable. Attractive, reasonably stylish hair and clothing will evoke a positive reaction from those you wish to serve, whether your employers or consumers.

Body language is another area of self-image to consider. One aspect of this is our facial expressions. We often don't realize the message we are sending with our faces. Sometimes that message is at odds with our intention. I know one very sweet-natured gentleman, for example, who always appears to be angry or upset. When colleagues inevitably ask him what's wrong, he seems genuinely surprised and flashes them a warm smile. My guess, though, is that for every person who asks him what's wrong, there are ten others who will simply judge him as angry and avoid him.

Some people come across as bored or discourteous, even though this is not their intention. This may be a simple result of failing to make eye contact or folding their arms in a way that suggests irritation. Even the way we sit communicates a message. If we sit facing forward with our shoulders squared and our head held high, we put ourselves in a welcoming position. If we sit hunched over, arms crossed and shoulders facing away from the other person, we portray a closed-off attitude, which tells other people that what they have to say is unimportant to us and we have no desire to begin an exchange with them. Open postures and facial expressions, in general, project open attitudes, while closed postures and gestures suggest, "Don't bother me."

Many other aspects of physical self-image are also important— tone of voice, physical distance, etc.—but we needn't cover them all here. (There are lots of great books dedicated to this topic alone.) The main point is that you need to objectively consider the self-image you are portraying to others and moderate it to suit the business environment in which you work. This usually means being polite, physically open, and attentive, and making another person feel as if his or her needs are important to you.

Make efforts to align your outer self-image with the inner one. If the two are in discord, then adjust one. Either you must change your outer behavior to more accurately reflect the kind of person you are striving to become, or you must work internally to become a better person, so as to "live up to" the image you're portraying.

In addition to our actual physical appearance and gestures, there are some other important factors that play a part in creating the outer image we project to the world. These factors include the following:

- **Vocabulary and word choice.** Like it or not, we are judged by the words we speak. For example, if you are in a position that requires some social sophistication and your vocabulary is limited, you may be perceived as intellectually limited, and this can affect the trust others place in your ability to do a complex job. Similarly, if you use words that are inappropriate to the social, trade, or business situation, others will judge you in ways that can harm you. You don't have to be a poet or orator, but your ability to communicate well has an effect on the types of customers and partners you can attract. If verbal communication is not your strength, find someone who can speak effectively in your place.

- **Written communication.** You cannot expect to be taken seriously within a professional community if your e-mails, proposals, and business letters are full of grammatical errors and misspelled words. If you have any doubts about your writing abilities, run all of your writing—yes, even your e-mails and tweets—past a trusted editor or, at minimum, through a word processor's spelling and grammar check before sharing them with the world.

- **Business collateral.** All of the physical aspects of your business, from the sign in front of your store to your business cards to the car you drive when doing business, say something about your brand. (And remember, you *have* a brand even if you don't own a business.) Your physical trappings need not be opulent but should be professional. Your workspace should be clean, well-organized, and thoughtfully arranged. The way you "package" every aspect of your product, service, or paid work is an opportunity to demonstrate how you feel about your brand and how you wish others to feel as well.

- **Internet presence.** To be taken seriously as a professional in a way that is consistent with the personal brand you're promoting, make sure you don't have an embarrassing or inappropriate online persona. It is very easy for business associates to google you. If your Facebook page projects you as a party person or your blog is dedicated to hobbies that others may find objectionable, it could damage your image. Even something as simple as a thoughtless e-mail prefix or Twitter ID can send a message that is misaligned with your brand values (FoxxxyGrrl@ or @BeerLover, for example). Every online photo of you, or post *by* you or *about* you, can come back to haunt you. Treat your presence on the Internet and social graph as an important part of your brand.

- **Social and public behavior.** *You* may draw a line between your professional and personal life, but the rest of the world does not. How you behave on city streets, in restaurants and grocery stores, and even in your own backyard can reflect powerfully on the brand you are creating for yourself and your business. If you are rude and inconsiderate to waiters or appear slovenly at the grocery store, others will take note of that. Once we create a negative impression, it cannot be "un-created."

Inner Self-Image

Although there is much overlap between the outer self-image and the inner self-image, the latter is based upon our own perceptions of who and what we are. It entails concepts such as self-belief, self-confidence, and self-esteem. If you do not feel good about yourself, no one else is likely to feel good about you, either, and this will have a major dampening effect on your career and your business. Think about it. If you do not believe you deserve your own respect, then naturally you will not believe you deserve respect from others. Consequently, you will dress and act in ways that invite disrespect. Many criminals, for example, are profoundly lacking in self-respect, and so they behave in ways that force the world to confirm their damaged self-image.

One of the most important elements of inner self-image is positive self-belief. That is, *you* must believe you possess positive and admirable traits, such as moral goodness, compassion, dependability, talent, and intelligence. Although we must recognize our own shortcomings, it's more important to believe powerfully in our strengths, for it is through our strengths that we make our key contributions to the world. And if we cannot recognize and acknowledge these strengths, we cannot leverage and maximize them in the world.

For some people, it does not matter how successful they are or how often they receive praise from others; they still don't really believe it. Look at certain well-known athletes who, despite being highly talented in their particular sports, never have the confidence to be winners and are forever relegated to runner-up status. This does not stem from a lack of talent but from a lack of self-belief. Such athletes have an inexplicable tendency to "choke" at critical moments, as if unconsciously confirming their own poor self-images. Other athletes, like Tom Brady, Hakeem Olajuwon, David Ortiz, or Mariano Rivera, become known as "clutch" players because of their uncanny ability to deliver a big play at crucial moments. These players have such a strong sense of self-belief that they refuse to accept loss as a possibility and, when the money is on the table, perform at a level even higher than their own apparent talents.

The problem with lack of self-belief in a business environment is that if *we* do not believe in ourselves and project this positive belief outwardly, others will not believe in us, either. Why would they? Why *should* they? Consequently, we may be passed over when it comes to promotion and career advancement. Big projects may be handed over to other employees, or consumers may choose our competitor's products—not because we're not good enough, but because we do not project sufficient belief in ourselves and our offerings. When we worry that we are not good enough, others absorb that concern. We cannot expect someone to hire us or purchase our offerings if we lack confidence in our own abilities, products, and services.

Self-worth is a related concept that is equally important. It is crucial to believe not only in our capabilities and strengths, but also in our *inherent worth* as human beings. Sadly, many of us picked up the message early in life that we were not as good as others or were flawed in some fundamental way that made us undeserving of life's highest blessings. African Americans, for example, have had to struggle with this phenomenon. And it was not a subtle thing. African Americans were told, flat out, that they were not as good as their white neighbors and colleagues. Only several decades ago, blacks were still forced to drink from separate water fountains and sit at the back of the bus. So a collective sense of self-worth is something black Americans are still working to develop. Other communities, such as Native Americans, Irish Americans, Jews, and gays, have faced—and still face—parallel struggles at various times in America's history.

If we as individuals feel we are unworthy of good things, we will consciously or unconsciously push away success, reject the aid of those who can help us, and subtly confirm the belief that we are worthless. This is called self-sabotage. Psychologists say that most of us like to stay within a certain "comfort zone" regarding the way the world treats us. When we step out of this comfort zone—even in ways that can improve our lives—we become uncomfortable. We then subconsciously engage in behaviors that shrink our success back to the level where we have traditionally felt comfortable. It is almost as if we have a self-worth thermostat in our brains. We set it to a certain temperature and when life's circumstances take us above or below that temperature, we do whatever it takes to get back to the original setting.

How many overnight movie stars, sports stars, and music stars, for example, throw their newfound success away through partying, drugs, and reckless spending? Or consider lottery winners. I have heard that more than half of major lottery winners lose most of their winnings within about a five-year period. In many of these cases, families and friendships are destroyed along the way. Why is this? I will suggest one of the main reasons is that these people didn't feel worthy of their good luck. Their success was more than their sense of self-worth could support, so they did whatever it took to get back to their comfort zone.

In the self-help movement it is often said that whenever we fail to achieve our goals in life, it is due to one of two things: we did not feel *competent* or we did not feel *worthy*. Both of these beliefs are key components of our inner self-image.

Without a strong, confident, and worthy self-image, we will mostly follow others and seldom be innovators and pioneers. We will doubt ourselves so much that even when we do have a great idea, it will either remain unspoken or be defeated by self-sabotaging behavior. Have you ever thought of an exciting new product only to convince yourself it couldn't possibly be viable? Have you then sighed with regret a year or two later when someone else made a million dollars with the same idea? We have all come across people in business who constantly berate or second-guess themselves. After we try to lift their spirits a few times without success, we give up and take our business to someone who projects an attitude of self-worth. Others do the same with us. So if *we* want to be pioneers and winners, it is essential that we carefully invest in the Currency of Self-Image. It is critical that we instill within ourselves a positive sense of self-belief that convinces us not only that we *can* excel but that we *deserve* to excel.

To Thine Own Self Be True

As we discuss the importance of projecting a positive image, we need to understand one thing: an obsessive concern with how we look *to others* is not what is meant at all. Many people in business misguid-edly go to extraordinary lengths to become what they think their consumers, suppliers, and employees want them to be. Such efforts are doomed to failure. No one wants to build long-term relationships with individuals or organizations that are false or confused. Most clients would rather work with someone who is secure with him- or herself, even if it means accepting some personal quirks they may not be crazy about. Being secure with one's self is not found through pleasing people and trying to live up to external images.

A strong self-image is built from the inside out, not the outside in. External projections mean nothing if they are not backed up by inner truth.

Awareness Is the Key

As I hope I've shown you, self-image has both an inner and an outer aspect that affect our business and personal lives immensely. We do, however, have the power to change the adverse aspects of our self-image into positives. Awareness is the key. We have an opportunity for growth the moment we become aware that we are projecting an outer image that is inconsistent with who we believe ourselves to be within. At such moments, one of two things is true: (1) we don't know ourselves as well as we thought we did and our outer behavior has revealed an inner flaw we need to work on, or (2) we need to work on our outer game to more accurately reflect the highest aspects of our inner selves that we want the world to see.

It is very helpful—albeit sometimes painful—to seek feedback from others in this regard, because they can often see us objectively and notice qualities and behaviors in us that we are unable to see in ourselves. It's very important to seek feedback from people we can depend on to give us honest opinions; friends, family members, and employees may not always be the best providers of feedback because they may not want to risk offending us, or otherwise have something to lose by being honest.

If you have a very high-profile job position, it's not necessarily a bad idea to work with an image consultant if you can afford one. Though this might sound like a superficial "Hollywood" tactic, an objective consultant can help you become aware of things you're doing that may be harming your brand. A consultant can take inventory of your speech, mannerisms, body language, clothing, hairstyle, etc., and objectively tell you a great deal about the image you are presenting. Donald Trump, for example, may be able to get away with the world's worst comb-over, but you may not, especially if your brand is all about honesty and self-acceptance. A bad comb-over, after all, might be perceived as nonacceptance of your own baldness or trying to hide something. A skilled consultant can work with you to align your outer image more congruently with your inner self and the message you want to send. Should you discover that your *inner* self needs more work than your outer self, consider consulting a psychological counselor or spiritual advisor.

For lasting success in our careers, it is critical that we create—both within ourselves and without—a respected and effective self-image that positively draws others toward us rather than pushes them away.

Self-Esteem and Extraordinary Success

High self-esteem—that is, a positive inner self-image—not only improves our effectiveness when dealing with others, but also gives us the confidence and determination to reach our goals. High self-esteem is a character trait possessed by most CEOs and world leaders, as well as by countless successful pros in the worlds of entertainment, sports, and the arts. Let's summarize three public figures whose unshakable belief in themselves helped elevate them to the levels of status and success they enjoy today.

Bill Gates is certainly one of the wealthiest and most influential men in the world. When you read his words and watch him in interviews, it is clear that he is fueled by a robust sense of self-esteem and self-confidence. Born in 1955 to successful, well-educated parents, he was raised with education as a high value. He attended prep school and entered Harvard in 1973. But he couldn't contain his curiosity about computer programming or his hunger to start his own business. Finally realizing he didn't need a college degree to validate himself in the world, he left formal education behind. He walked out of Harvard and began the technological and entrepreneurial work that would lead to Microsoft.

Gates is a visionary and an unapologetic workaholic, but as we all know, he has also had to face an endless tide of detractors and lawsuits. Due to his extremely high self-confidence, however, Gates has always stayed true to who he really is—an inventor and a computer nerd. Everyone can respect that. And if they don't, Bill Gates doesn't really care.

Warren Buffett is one of the most successful investors and business owners of the modern era. Known as the "Oracle of Omaha," he routinely ranks in the top three on the *Forbes* Billionaires list. Buffett started making money at the age of six, going door-to-door selling items such as soft drinks, magazines, and gum. Later, he bought a used pinball machine and placed it in a local barbershop; before long, he had his own barbershop pinball "franchise." When he was only eleven, he bought his first shares of stock. Of course he is now known as president of Berkshire Hathaway and his philanthropic endeavors are the stuff of legends (more than $30 billion donated at last count).

What *really* distinguishes Buffett from most other businessmen and high-profile personalities, however, is his remarkable self-esteem and self-confidence. He cares not one bit about what others think of him and always follows his own instincts. He's not afraid to admit his mistakes and is never swayed by the social pressures that often drive other wealthy people. As revealed in the film *The World's Greatest Moneymaker: Warren Buffett*, for example, he still lives in the same modest three-bedroom home in Omaha he has owned for fifty years. There is no wall or security fence around it. He does not socialize with movie stars and other billionaires. He still drives his own car. He has no entourage around him. He flies on commercial airlines. When he comes home from work in the evening, he makes himself a bowl of popcorn and watches TV or plays bridge. Buffett is a man eminently at home in his own skin, his own mind, and his own sensible pajamas.

Oprah Winfrey is another splendid example of how a high sense of self-worth can lift one to unimaginable heights. She routinely tops the lists of the wealthiest and most influential women in the world, and was designated the richest black American of the twentieth century, yet the challenges she has surmounted have been nothing short of astonishing. Striking out in the world of media and entertainment as a young woman, she faced the perfect storm of obstacles: she was black, she was female, and she was "overweight" by runway standards. But that was just the tip of the iceberg.

Winfrey had to rise above an even tougher set of *internal* challenges. She was born into the poverty of rural Mississippi (where she was ridiculed by peers for wearing dresses made from potato sacks), then later raised in the tough inner-city environs of Milwaukee. She was sexually molested by a family member growing up and became pregnant (by her molester) at age fourteen. She suffered parental neglect, the death of her baby, and the perils of running away from home as a young teen. She had no models for success and no visible opportunities as a child. These hurdles would have crushed the spirits of the vast majority of us, but she had an enduring sense of self-belief that somehow pushed her to follow the advice of MLK and strive for excellence in all areas of her life.

By the time she was in high school, Winfrey had forged herself into an honors student. Before long, she won a speaking contest and earned a full scholarship to Tennessee State University. She also won the Miss Black Tennessee pageant. Because of her accomplishments, she was hired by WVOL, a local black radio station, as a news reader. The rest is amazing history.

Now think about some of the challenges *you* face. How might an Oprah-sized dose of self-confidence enable you to rise above them? Oprah would be the first to tell you that you are just as capable as she is. All you need to do is believe it.

Here are several of my favorite Oprah quotes about self-esteem, self-worth, and self-belief:

Self-esteem comes from being able to define the world in your own terms and refusing to abide by the judgments of others.[3]

Only make decisions that support your self-image, self-esteem, and self-worth.[4]

In every aspect of our lives, we are always asking ourselves, "How am I of value? What is my worth?" Yet I believe that worthiness is our birthright.[5]

It is confidence in our bodies, minds, and spirits that allows us to keep looking for new adventures, new directions to grow in, and new lessons to learn—which is what life is all about.[6]

Every time you state what you want or believe, you're the first to hear it. It's a message to both you and others about what you think is possible. Don't put a ceiling on yourself.[7]

Let your light shine. Shine within you so that it can shine on someone else. Let your light shine.[8]

Every time you suppress some part of yourself or allow others to play you small, you are in essence ignoring the owner's manual your creator gave you and destroying your design.[9]

THE CURRENCY OF DIVERSITY

Have you ever dreamed of a diverse, color-equal (notice I didn't say "color blind") society built on mutual respect, where people would be judged by their character and not the melanin in their skin? As we all know, Dr. Martin Luther King, Jr. articulated this premise very poignantly in one of his most famous speeches, "I Have a Dream," in which he described the world he hoped his four children would grow up in. He then led a historic movement that helped bring that imagined world closer to reality. Again, he didn't get us all the way to the Promised Land, but he certainly got us closer than any other American in history.

Dr. King was a drum major for the principle of inclusion and focused his laser-like vision on the goal of unity through diversity. We continue to honor this great man because of the commitment he made not only to black Americans but to every human being who walks this Earth. The dream of true equality is closer for me, for you, and for our children and their children because of King's revolutionary spirit and lifelong vision for a diverse and mutually respectful world.

Why is diversity such a challenge for us? Why do we have such a difficult time learning to accept those who look and sound different from us, despite the fact that both history and science show us that human populations are strengthened, not weakened, by increased variety? Our very system of genetic reproduction mixes the

chromosomes of two different parents and carries forward varied genetic traits from many generations of ancestors on both sides. It is
meticulously designed to encourage diversity and prevent repetition.
It is not designed to promote homogeneity. In fact, it is commonly
known in human biology that illness and birth defects tend to develop in populations where the gene pool is too homogeneous.

Nature itself knows that diversity is the key to a healthy, thriving, and
ever-evolving human population. Why can't we follow nature's lead?

Diversity Is Good for Business

Whether or not biological examples resonate with you, diversity is
clearly good for free enterprise. King was a huge advocate of stepping
outside of our racial and cultural comfort zones when doing business.
But the sorry fact is that in business we often fall into the habit of
turning to the same kinds of people for advice and ideas; people with
whom we are comfortable. And with whom are we most comfortable?
Why, those who look, talk, and act just like us, of course!

Kingonomics declares that we must diversify our decision-making
process by deliberately including those who aren't of the same ethnicity, religion, gender, or social background as we are. Success in
the new global marketplace lies with those who are willing to follow
King's advice and look to new faces and places for opportunity.

As mentioned earlier in the book, we don't need to be best friends
with everyone on the planet, but we do need to develop enough curiosity about our fellow man to encourage exploration into the vast
array of new opportunities that today's interconnected world offers.
When we learn to *welcome* and *appreciate* diversity instead of just tol-
erating it, new ideas will rapidly take flight and old, unworkable ideas
will rapidly evaporate.

King encouraged us to work toward a world in which all working
people are truly one, without regard to race, religion, or cultural background, and in which character is no longer equated with skin color.
Interestingly, though, the way we will get to that place is by openly
acknowledging, respecting, and honoring the ways in which we are

different. As long as we continue to avoid and judge one another out of fear and ignorance, we cannot come together at all. We must first celebrate and grow comfortable with our differences before we can begin to look past them with a spiritual sense of unity.

Diversity in the Workplace

The United States is a melting pot of cultural "oddballs," with each new wave of immigrants contributing vitally to our cultural, religious, and ethnic heritage. Interacting with people from different nationalities and religious backgrounds is almost unavoidable in America, and yet we seem to go out of our way to avoid it.

Diversity is our nation's heritage, plain and simple. Unless we are of Native American blood, all of us descend from immigrants (and, of course, even the native people immigrated here at some point). Since the days before we were even a nation, immigration has brought waves of people from every part of the planet to our shores. Although many people today seem to regard immigration as a problem to be fixed, our rich diversity gives our nation a distinct business advantage, if we would only seize it and leverage it. With the current trend toward globalization, companies are reaching out to all corners of the world to expand their sales and marketing. And yet we in the United States hold a microcosm of the world in our very hands. Why not reach out to diverse people *right in our own neighborhoods* and assemble internal teams that reflect the colorful global marketplace we are trying to penetrate? Why not use diversity as a business tool?

The importance of diversity in today's workplace cannot be overemphasized. If we are not motivated by the call of brotherhood or the love of humanity, we should at least be motivated by economic self-interest. Diversity helps us to not only develop products and services that have greater cross-cultural appeal, but also to market and sell them on the world stage. We must challenge the habit of homogeneity in the workplace and overcome long-held stereotypes and misconceptions if we truly wish to sell our wares to diverse cultural and ethnic sectors worldwide.

> *We must challenge the habit of homogeneity in the workplace and overcome long-held stereotypes and misconceptions if we truly wish to sell our wares to diverse cultural and ethnic sectors worldwide.*

With the steady devaluation of the U.S. dollar and the steady increase in the relative value of many foreign currencies, what businessperson today can afford to snub the international market? Of course, you might say, "I have a local business; global rules don't apply to me." But even if your business is a bakery or a car wash or a gas station that can't be marketed overseas, don't you wish to make it appealing to as many *domestic* customers as possible? Let's say Hispanic residents comprise 35 percent of the neighborhood around your convenience store. Maybe you should consider selling hot rice and beans alongside your pot of chicken soup and hiring a Latino teenager to work the evening shift. If your photography studio is in a town where much of the population is Vietnamese, you might want to hire a receptionist who is bicultural and bilingual. Perhaps he or she can help you develop a line of picture frames that is more appealing to an Asian aesthetic.

We have certainly made progress in the workplace since the days of Dr. King, though we are miles from reaching a perfect balance. Today's business environment may be a more colorful and diverse place than it used to be—thanks largely to equal opportunity laws, fairer hiring practices, and a slowly changing public mindset—but many companies still struggle with issues of diversity and acceptance when it comes to the hiring, promotion, and treatment of employees.

Though some of this reluctance to diversify can be pinned on management, part of the problem is that segregation doesn't only occur from the top down. There is also inherent resistance among the various groups themselves. People of similar background, culture, and race naturally gravitate toward one another and attract new people who fit the same mold. While this can feel comfortable to all, it can actually be detrimental in the long run.

Sometimes institutions, in their well-meaning attempts to support cultural diversity, can trigger such self-perpetuating segregation. For example, a college might offer courses in African-American studies, provide funding for culturally based clubs and organizations, and host social events featuring relevant music, dance, and dress. But who attends these venues? Mostly African-American students. So, without interest from students of majority and other minority ethnicities on campus, nothing changes. It is not realized that African-American studies are just another part of American history, and not "foreign" studies. Therefore, out of sheer mutual interest, as with the rest of the student body, these black students continue to spend more and more time together and naturally form bonds with one another, especially when they are not included (or comfortable when included) in other settings. So, the designated "black students' table" in the cafeteria—or Latino, Asian, African, or Jewish table—continues to be a place of acceptance and familiarity, just as it did in the mid-1960s. No one intends for this to occur, but, ironically, that's what can sometimes happen; the same if it's the football players and fraternity or sorority members deciding to dine and fellowship together. I'm not saying it's a bad idea to host culturally based clubs and events or spend time with people of your own race, ethnicity, and culture. It's necessary. I'm just saying that we have to watch for the subtle ways that segregation can rear its head in our midst, even when we're aiming for exactly the opposite effect. Self-imposed segregation is just as nondiverse as institutionally enforced segregation.

In today's increasingly global marketplace, the ability to effectively communicate and interact with people (often clients and customers) of different cultures and backgrounds is a critical business skill. When we diversify the workplace, these skills are learned naturally. People learn to relate to other cultural groups as a result of everyday office interactions and teamwork. Sensitivities are learned, comfort is developed, and humor even begins to emerge as the awkwardness of intermingling is overcome.

Naturally, when groups of diverse people learn to work together, workplace discrimination and intergroup tensions begin to lessen. Once you get to know a single individual of a certain group—whether it is identified by culture, gender, physical mobility, age, or sexual orientation—you are far less likely to show prejudice toward other members of that same group. Open sharing of ideas, traditions, rituals, and cultural points of view helps all employees to develop understanding of one another and abandon biases and stereotypes. Once fears and resistances are overcome, team members begin to see how diversity is an asset well worth fighting for.

Another powerful benefit of diversity is that it encourages individual creativity and innovation. In an atmosphere where everyone feels accepted and valued, team members feel *safe* and *motivated* to make their unique contributions. Instead of feeling they will be subtly (or overtly) mocked for speaking up, team members feel as if their input is actually *desired*. As a result, innovative and creative ideas are more freely contributed and each individual feels encouraged to achieve his or her full potential. The importance of this dynamic cannot be overstated.

Customer Diversity Begins with Internal Diversity

Our world's population is becoming more interconnected by the day, thanks to new modes of real-time communication, superfast Internet connections, the preponderance of networked devices, and the ever-growing availability of Wi-Fi networks. People the world over have much greater access not only to *one another* but also to competitive products and services worldwide. The entire global community has suddenly become everyone's marketplace at the click of a virtual button. Customers can satisfy their unique tastes and needs as never before.

Whether a gay single parent in California; a Pakistani software engineer caring for a large, extended family; an African-American bachelor doing volunteer work in Ethiopia; or a seventy-five-year-old disabled veteran trying to adjust to living alone after the death of his caretaking wife, people have unique tastes, needs, and product requirements. And thanks to the Internet, we can now expect to have them met by innovative and competitive businesses. We are free to spend our dollars globally with whatever business best demonstrates that it understands us, our life situations, and our special needs. Today, consumers put a lot of emphasis on whether or not a company "gets" them personally. It's no longer a world where *businesses* decide, in a top-down fashion, what products and services they're going to offer and then consumers are forced to adapt. Sellers no longer run the show in this globalized and specialized world. *Customers* now dictate the scope and pace of business, and their buying decisions are based, to a large extent, on whether a company's products and services are fine-tuned to their demands, tastes, lifestyles, cultures, and desires. If one company doesn't get your tastes and needs—and this is often evident after a few seconds on its website—you can easily find another one that does. And the number of global competitors is growing exponentially. In an interconnected world, if you're not offering a service or product that speaks to consumers, then someone else is.

How can we possibly expect to understand and appreciate our diversity of customers if we insist upon maintaining a homogeneous workplace? In any enterprise with global reach, management should strive to ensure that the internal talent reflects the customer base with which the company does business.

Diversify the Workplace

Admittedly, diversifying is a challenge. Everything seems simpler when the whole office team is made up of the same basic social and cultural group. And it is always easier to *keep* things the same and stick with familiar patterns, including those used to attract, recruit, select, and hire staff.

But here's the key point: easier doesn't mean *better*. Change is well worth the effort it takes. But how do we accomplish change in a positive manner that works for everyone?

Well, for one thing, instead of turning a blind eye to differences—which is what happens when we pretend to be "color blind"—we must acknowledge, appreciate, explore, and *celebrate* cultural differences. For example, instead of requiring every individual to adapt 100 percent to the existing corporate or office culture, we might try adapting our culture to new staff members to some extent; that is, find some ways to welcome them and make them comfortable and productive. This means being flexible and open-minded.

Let's say, for instance, you hire a devout Muslim employee whose faith requires him to break for prayer a few times over the course of the day. Instead of insisting he take his breaks at the same times and in the same manner as other staffers, why not encourage and support him in his uniqueness? Let him take breaks on a flexible schedule, maybe even offer him a quiet spare room to use for praying. If you show him this respect, he will almost surely return it to you threefold. And if he feels his important spiritual needs are being met (rather than ignored or challenged), he is far likelier to be happy and productive on the job. Perhaps some of the other staffers will learn a thing or two about his faith as well, and lose some of their prejudices.

We should encourage *communication* about differences rather than make such communication taboo. This means doing things such as devoting staff meetings to the topic of cultural differences, making it the focus of individual supervision, and writing about the topic in company memos and newsletters. Actively look for signs of tension or discomfort among team members and *address* them rather than deny or ignore them. Always consider whether workplace unease might have its roots in issues related to race, gender, religion, or culture. Although we don't want to look for racial tensions where none exist, we should keep an open mind to the possibility of it, and we should have the courage and clarity to deal with it openly. Often we remain silent about racial or cultural issues in an attempt to "be respectful," when the truly respectful thing to do would be to address these issues openly. Discomfort grows in the dark shadows of secrecy and denial; it evaporates in the bright light of openness and sincerity.

Anytime a major change, such as diversifying the workforce, needs to happen within a company, you must create a sense of "buy-in" with your team members. If they don't accept the *need* for change or see the reason for it, they will fight it and resist it. Even worse, they may behave with passive aggression, sabotaging new initiatives before they have a chance to be implemented. Work to convince your employees that diversity is good for your company and good for them as individuals. Explain how it can positively affect the bottom line. Show how diversity can improve your organization's performance in terms of sales and market penetration. If you can successfully show your staff members how they will *personally profit* as a result of diversifying, they will likely become allies of change rather than obstacles in your path to it. Moreover, include all employees in the designing of your diversity initiatives, which is a great way to create buy-in, generate creative ideas, and foster the very atmosphere of inclusion you are trying to create. Mostly, make sustained efforts to *reinforce* your diversity philosophy in as many ways as possible—it can't just be a one-off thing where you issue a memo or rewrite part of the company handbook and hope that change occurs.

For diversity to be accepted in the workplace, there must be long-term, integrated plans in place that are supported by other company policies and constantly reinforced in a variety of ways. Here are several things you can do to implement and reinforce this change:

- Ensure diversity on the board of directors, throughout all levels of the company, and in outside vendor relationships.
- Hold workshops about the benefits of diversity and offer advanced training to key employees.
- Devote a few hours every month to cultural-awareness activities, such as lectures, films, or artistic events.
- Develop mentoring programs in which members of different cultural or ethnic groups with differing skill levels are paired together to form learning relationships.
- Create a diverse "diversity committee" comprised of staff members at varying levels of the organization and give them some concrete and important responsibilities.
- Offer a weekly or monthly platform (as part of a staff meeting, for instance) in which a featured employee can share issues, concerns, or interesting facts about his or her culture or group identity.

- Create an online forum on the company website for discussing diversity issues.
- Reward and celebrate those employees who take compassionate, courageous, and innovative steps toward inclusion.

Remember, just as nature has proven that a diverse gene pool makes our species stronger, business owners and managers must show their team members how a diverse workforce is a strength, not a weakness. When everyone on the team begins to see the benefits of working with a wide variety of teammates and appealing to a broad range of customers, resistance to diversity begins to melt away.

Problems with Implementation

Employers, employees, and hiring managers must face and solve the challenges of implementing diversity. Stereotypical thinking affects almost all of us, on both a conscious and an unconscious level, so it is up to everyone to work together to change stale ideas and habits. Communication is the key. But there must be a clear intention to *truly* make diversity work; instead there is often a subtle intention to prove that it's a failed idea.

A common problem with implementing diversity is that even when new laws or initiatives are put in place, people resist them in subtle and unconscious ways. Employers may still decide not to hire an individual based on race, but can always claim other criteria for their decisions—just as landlords can always claim other reasons for not renting to someone whose race or culture makes them uncomfortable. And it's difficult in most cases to *prove* discrimination. One gentleman I know, for example, has had repeated problems getting hired in a youth-dominated industry due to his age. When he submits his creative work online, potential employers are unfailingly excited and impressed. The phone interviews always go beautifully. But when they meet him in person and see his white hair, there is an inevitable cooling-off period and the position goes to someone else. He can't *prove* discrimination, but he has accumulated enough experiential evidence to strongly suggest it.

This is why hiring quotas have been established in some industries. Although by no means an ideal or completely fair solution, quotas are one way of counteracting subtle discrimination on a large-scale basis. But if we would only welcome diversity for its obvious benefits, this type of measure would no longer be needed.

Employers, managers, and coworkers often act with discrimination toward those of certain racial and ethnic groups because they consciously or unconsciously believe the stereotypes. The problem is, these beliefs become self-confirming due to a little trick we play with our minds. That is, we pay attention only to evidence that *supports* our beliefs and minimize or ignore evidence that *contradicts* them. If a manager truly believes that Mexicans are lazy, for example, he may constantly look for evidence of laziness among his Mexican employees yet ignore evidence of energetic engagement within the same group. If he sees an Anglo employee taking frequent bathroom breaks, he may not attribute any significance to it. But if he sees a Mexican employee doing the same, he may say, "See, Mexicans are always trying to avoid work!" We witness this type of thing in the political arena all the time. Radio talk-show hosts trot out anecdotal evidence to "prove" that members of the opposing party or belief system are morally corrupt yet ignore the bad behavior of members of the group they support.

There's an infinite variety of ways that employers and managers can sabotage attempts at diversity. I was told a story recently that illustrates one particularly insidious strategy used in a company that had a large percentage of Latino employees but virtually no Latino management. There was a subtle, unstated perception among the Caucasian managers that Latino workers were not good "management material," and resistance among many Caucasian *workers* to report to a Latino boss. But pressure was mounting within the organization for management to diversify, so the executives promoted a Latino woman who was known to have character and competency issues. Why did they promote this individual? No one can really know another person's motives, but it seems pretty obvious that the management team deliberately chose her because they *knew* she would fail and possibly even disgrace herself. In this way, they could "prove" their unspoken theory about Latino (and female) managers.

There are many other subtle ways managers and coworkers can punish and discourage people who try to rock the boat of the status quo. Opportunities can be withdrawn, promotions can be withheld, excessively difficult demands can be made, and faults can be exaggerated, while faults of those in different groups are ignored. It is critically important that we be alert to any ways, subtle or obvious, in which we allow a hostile atmosphere to defeat our attempts to create a more vibrant, diverse, and mutually respectful workforce.

Acceptance Versus Tolerance

In today's Age of Collaboration, diversity must be backed up by true acceptance, not mere tolerance. Tolerance isn't good enough. For one can *tolerate* a diversity plan without authentically accepting it. Many people grudgingly go along with diversity but privately consider it part of a suspect overall agenda of political correctness. They do not embrace the concept deep within themselves. Diversity in hiring needs to flow from a whole-hearted acceptance that says, "I genuinely *want* you on the team because I value you and the contribution you will make," rather than, "I am doing this because I have to." The day we all *personally* embrace the message of inclusion is the day we will no longer need to pass laws to make sure it is enforced.

America's unwillingness to take full responsibility for past and present injustices toward many of its citizens—chattel slavery, Black Codes, unfair housing practices, financial redlining, voter suppression, and unfair lending practices, among others—continues to be a roadblock in the way of diversity. From religion to politics to industry, leaders have consistently failed to leverage their positions to insist upon equity, parity, and corrective actions. Selfishness and cowardice have instead ruled the day. Leaders have not seized their opportunities to make a difference.

In his book *Leadership Is an Art,* Max De Pree wrote the following:

Recognizing diversity gives us the chance to provide meaning, fulfillment and purpose, which are not to be relegated solely to private life any more than such things as love, beauty and joy. The art of leadership lies in polishing and liberating and enabling those gifts. In addition to all of the ratios and goals and parameters and bottom lines, it is fundamental that leaders endorse a concept of persons. This begins with an understanding of the diversity of people's gifts and talents and skills.[1]

Many leaders, of all races and backgrounds, passively tolerate diversity, but the time has come for them to courageously *embrace* it, in spite of what their peers, neighbors, and family members might say. It is time for us all to stop paying lip service to this idea and to make a personal stand for it via our own actions, decisions, and commitments. If there is any group that we are personally reticent to embrace, we need to challenge ourselves to rise above our biases and take the kind of inclusive actions we'd be proud to tell our children about. It's time to recognize, once and for all, that the "brotherhood of man" comes in all genders, body types, skin colors, sexual orientations, cultures, and religions, so that the memories of past injustices can finally fade away. Only then can we start *using* our differences boldly and creatively.

> *It's time to recognize, once and for all, that the "brotherhood of man" comes in all genders, body types, skin colors, sexual orientations, cultures, and religions, so that the memories of past injustices can finally fade away. Only then can we start using our differences boldly and creatively.*

Diversity when Networking

In order for diversity to really take root in all sectors of the economy, it must extend beyond the walls of the workplace. We must include diverse members in our *informal* business networks as well. And members of minority groups must make special efforts to network with other like-minded minorities. There is power in networked numbers.

A June 2011 *Washington Post* "ideas@innovations" blog post, titled "We Need a Black Mark Zuckerberg," describes a group of eight owners of minority start-up companies who are renting a house in Mountain View, California. Together they have launched an organization called NewMEAccelerator. Although the level of diversity in Silicon Valley is quite high, the article points out that there is still an alarming lack of representation among blacks and Hispanics in the business leadership community. To help correct this imbalance, this pioneering group—led by Angela Benton, CEO of Black Web Media, and her entrepreneur friends Wayne Sutton and Toby Morning— hosts dinners at their homes and invites the Valley's top business leaders to visit and speak with them about a variety of topics focused on what it takes to build a successful start-up.

As we all know by now, a major key to success is to learn from others and to network, and that is exactly the process NewMEAccelerator is trying to facilitate. It aims to offer its members some of the same advantages that are being provided by other networking accelerators such as Y Combinator, Founder Institute, and Tech Stars. These advantages include access to investment capital, mentorship from successful businesspeople, and introductions to top clients, potential employees, and key players. Although minorities are not specifically excluded from the business accelerators mentioned above, Benton and her partners realize that in a world where minority business starters have historically had an unfair *dis*advantage, they need to make up a lot of ground. So NewMEAccelerator focuses its attention exclusively on providing minority start-ups with the same networking opportunities that have long been enjoyed by non-minorities.

"This is important," states the blog post, "because innovation flourishes when there is diversity, and we desperately need more innovation and startups to heal our economy. We can both improve the quality of U.S. innovation and uplift disadvantaged communities by mentoring minorities."[2]

I suggest you take a moment to look at the makeup of any and all social and professional networks to which you belong. Are they mixed populations or are your networks made up mainly of people who are in the same cultural, racial, and economic groups as you are? Diversity begins at home. What steps can you take today to diversify your own networks? Remember that the ultimate beneficiary of this action will be you.

Pass On the Knowledge

Recently, while at an art exhibit with my wife and children, I noticed an image of a paper pie plate with the following words carefully printed on it in a multitude of colors:

> *He drew a circle that shut me out—*
> *Heretic, rebel, a thing to flout.*
> *But love and I had the wit to win:*
> *We drew a circle that took him In!*[3]
>
> —EDWIN MARKHAM

What this poignant little verse means to me is that we who have been placed "outside the circle" must be vast enough in spirit to practice inclusion ourselves, particularly inclusion of the very people who have shut us out in the past. As is so often the case with social injustices, those who have been victims themselves inherit a special responsibility to erase the evils of the past. For it is only when the excluded practice forgiveness toward the excluders that the "healing circle" becomes complete.

Many people who hear advice like this become fired up with righteous anger. "I'm the one who has been the victim of discrimination," they say. "Why should *I* have to be the one to change it?!" This is a very understandable position to take and I sympathize with it. But the truth is, only those of us who have been wounded by exclusion—from jobs, from social positions, from neighborhoods, from financial opportunity—know the depth of pain and suffering that this kind of treatment can cause, and only we can understand all the subtle levels of exclusion that exist. It falls on us to educate others and to lead by example, because if we who have been placed outside the circle are willing to draw a circle large enough to accept everyone within it, including the hate-filled groups that have been our tormentors, then what excuse does anyone else have not to join in the cause?

We cannot afford to carry forth the hatred and bitterness we might be "entitled" to, because we cannot afford to pass that kind of poison on to another generation. We cannot afford to teach our children to extend to others anything less than the level of acceptance we want *them* to receive. If we are bitter and fearful and filled with vengeance, we will pass it on to them, plain and simple. Children are naturally accepting; they need to be taught otherwise. If we act fearful or resistant toward any particular "type" of person, our children will learn to react in the same way.

Children, like sponges, absorb all they see and hear from their adult role models. And it is our *behavior* that really instructs them, not the nice-sounding lessons we try to impart at bedtime. Therefore, it is our responsibility—whether we come from a heritage of exclud*er* or exclud*ed*, or from some hybrid of the two, or from neither—to ensure that what our children are taught, in both word and deed, is to love and respect one another. By learning to *give* love and respect to all, they simultaneously learn to *expect* the same for themselves. There is no gift that will serve children better as they forge the course of their personal destinies. On the other hand, if they are taught to withhold acceptance of certain people, they will learn that having the same thing withheld from them may be acceptable under certain conditions.

What we are taught to give is what we are taught to receive.

I hope I've managed to persuade you, even a little, that diversity is not just the right thing to do—it's a vital currency for business success in our interconnected world. Tribal thinking served its purpose in a globe divided by technology, geography, culture, and language. But diversity is the principle that is needed to drive today's world. In fact, it is already doing so. The question is, will you resist it or leverage its power?

9

THE CURRENCY OF CHARACTER AND DIGNITY

The so-called "I Have a Dream" speech (originally titled "Normalcy, No More") contains some of the most immortal words ever spoken by Dr. Martin Luther King, Jr. As noted in the last chapter, King famously dreamed of a day when the content of one's character would be judged as more important than the color of one's skin. And although these words are usually (and rightfully) used to illustrate his hopes for a diverse world of equality for all, they contain another, equally important concept. That is, that *character* is paramount amongst human traits. In his immortal words, King was not making the point that it is a good idea to judge one another, but, rather, that character outweighs any superficial traits we might exhibit as human beings.

Perhaps no other individual, renowned or otherwise, more powerfully personified strength of character during his lifetime than did Dr. King. He was constantly willing to stand up for what he believed to be right and to take inconvenient positions in the name of his beliefs. He was also, as we've seen in previous chapters, willing to "do the right thing" even when the cameras were not rolling or when there was tremendous personal risk involved. He even had to overcome the ridicule of his own culture and community, which had become accustomed to the status quo of inequality and didn't really perceive any hope of true change. King could have quit and simply rested on the laurels of his early accomplishments. He was married with a young family. He was educated with an earned doctoral degree and had a promising future ahead of him as a leader in ministry. Yet he put it all on the line to do what he believed was right for those without a voice. There is perhaps no greater measure of character than that.

The concept of dignity is closely related to character and one that King also modeled in a most exemplary way. We'll talk about dignity later in the chapter. Let's begin by looking at character.

What do we mean by character? Character begins with having a firm sense of ethics, principles, and an understanding of "right and wrong," but it goes much further than that. It also entails being willing to *act* on that sense of ethics, even when there might be a high personal cost for doing so. Needless to say, it is the latter part of the formula that is the most challenging. Though most of us have a pretty good idea about what we believe to be right and wrong, we are not always enthusiastic about *acting* on that knowledge. It is this second aspect of character that we will focus on primarily.

Character in Business

Character is an extremely important business currency because, as we all know, actions speak louder than words. It is by our actions that we are judged by customers, partners, suppliers, and employees. This is why business ethics are so important. Having a solid sense of business ethics, and being willing to act on it, is the main way in which we bring character into the arena of commercial enterprise. In other words, business ethics can be thought of as the manifestation of character in the business world.

Make no mistake about it—the ethical impression you leave on others communicates volumes about your character. And it is your character that will ultimately determine whether someone wants to do business with you over the long term. It also determines the *kind* of people you will attract. Businesspeople of good character attract customers and partners of good character. Businesspeople of low character attract the opposite. (Note how criminals bond with other criminals.)

Initially, people may judge you based on your clothing and appearance, but their lasting impression of you will be based on your actions. Character-driven action is what builds lasting business relationships. Lack of character, or even the *perception* of lack of character, is what sinks businesses.

> *Lack of character, or even the* perception *of lack of character, is what sinks businesses.*

A crisis of character perception is not just reserved for liars, cheaters, and bad guys; it's a problem nearly anyone can face. Just because you're "basically" an honest person doesn't mean you can't wake up tomorrow and find yourself facing a full-fledged ethical dilemma. Perhaps you were just in the wrong place at the wrong time or you neglected something you should have been paying more attention to. Perhaps you allowed panic to trigger a thoughtless decision or you did something truly regrettable and wish you could start over. No matter what the slipup was, it can make a lasting impression—and one that may take a good deal of time and effort to overcome.

In a courtroom, jurors are instructed to issue a verdict based on facts, not assumptions of character. But we don't live in a court of law, we live in the real word. People *do* judge you for acting badly; it's as simple as that. And you are always being watched. Even if you say something or do something in strict confidence, those words and actions may come back to haunt you. Although damage control may set the record straight to some extent, a wounded reputation is difficult to heal.

In the long run, acting with character saves you time, energy, and mental torment. Your conscience is always your surest and simplest guide when making decisions. It may not make your decision *easier*, but it will make it less complicated and convoluted. When you act with character and honesty, you never have to worry about a troubled conscience, second-guess yourself, or remember which story you told to whom. Doing the right thing frees our minds for more creative and productive pursuits.

Humility is a parallel trait that is vitally important to cultivate. Nobody is perfect. Knowing that you're capable of messing up—even when you have the best of intentions—is crucial. Arrogance is the enemy of character growth.

In those instances when you do make an error of character or ethics, it's important to accept responsibility in an open, transparent manner and make a sincere, visible effort to change your behavior and make reparations. Let everyone know that you (1) are aware of the error, (2) fully understand why your actions, or your team's actions, were wrong, (3) accept responsibility for the error, (4) plan to make things right with anyone who was harmed, and (5) are taking serious steps to avoid repeating the mistake in the future.

Safeguard Your Professional Reputation

Although it is important to do the right thing for its own sake, it is also important to consider how others perceive you and the way you conduct business. A *perception* of an ethical lapse can occur even when your character is sound. Remember that you are being judged *all the time*, whether you know it or not, especially if you are in a position of leadership. The surest way to avoid negative impressions is to consistently act with character and ethics. All of your actions must be exemplary. If you keep this in mind every day, then others will define you on the basis of your known, reliable character, not on those rare instances when you may let your ethical guard down.

When you truly care about doing the right thing and allow others to see this, then colleagues will be much more forgiving and understanding if a mistake is made. That's because they will assume the mistake was made with the best intentions. Sometimes when trying to serve a higher good we are forced to take actions—such as firing a well-liked employee or making a painful budget cut—that might appear "wrong" on the surface. When others are made aware of the higher principle upon which we were acting, however, they can better understand why we made such a choice. They may not always agree with us, but they will respect our character nonetheless.

Let me re-emphasize this point: avoid even the *appearance* of ethical lapses. Even if you *know* you are acting with integrity, do not place yourself in a position where this can be legitimately questioned. For example, do not serve on the board of an agency that regulates an industry in which you earn income nor allow family members to do so. Even though you may be perfectly capable of acting with integrity in such a situation, you can potentially create an impression of ethical fuzziness. Similarly, your ethics may be called into question if you give a promotion to a personal friend, even if that promotion is wholly justified, or if, as a college professor, you give an "A" to a student others know you have dated. That's why it's best not to even put yourself in such a position. Don't hire personal friends to work under you. Don't have relationships with your students.

Appearances are not *more* important than actual integrity, but in the world of business they are *equally* important. Just as attorneys are bound by their professional codes of conduct and canons of ethics to "avoid even the appearance of impropriety," so, too, should you strive for this goal at all times. Treasure and safeguard your ethical reputation like the priceless commodity it is. Don't allow others to doubt your character; don't give them that opportunity. If you find yourself in a potential ethical challenge or in a situation where your character *may* be questioned, clearly explain your ethical stance to those who may be directly or indirectly affected. The more carefully you explain your ethical rationale up front, the less room you give to others to draw the wrong conclusions.

Each morning, as you dress and prepare yourself to look your best for work, don't forget to run through your character checklist as well. Remind yourself that your reputation is your most valuable commodity. Just as it is important to dress and groom yourself in a way that it is consistent with your brand values (see Chapter Seven), it is also important to groom your mind to behave with character on a daily basis.

Character Does Not Take a Day Off

The currency of character has implications well beyond the business realm. It is equally essential in the development of a satisfying and well-balanced personal life. Just as our business partners, customers, and employees notice our behavior, so, too, do our children, neighbors, spouses, and friends. When we strive to be *models* of good character for those who are closest to us, we invest a priceless currency that pays dividends for the rest of our lives and beyond. We also play a real and vital role in making the world a better place. In fact, behaving with character may ultimately be the *most important thing we do in our lives*, whether we are CEOs or street-sweepers. When we act upon principle—particularly in small matters—we tell our children and friends that values *matter* and are more important than convenience. We inspire others to behave with character as well. Their behavior, in turn, sends further ripple effects out into the world, and these ripples can even affect future generations. One courageous, character-driven act can sometimes be enough to change the lives of our grandchildren, great-grandchildren, and even *their* great-grandchildren. (Think about Rosa Parks or the "unknown rebel" at Tiananmen Square in Beijing, China.) In fact, I believe every act of true character echoes throughout human consciousness for all eternity. Every day we are given the opportunity to commit such acts. Think about that the next time you are tempted to take an ethical shortcut!

Remember, when it comes to your behavior, someone is always watching—and that person is you! Once *you* develop deep faith in your own character, it will rarely, if ever, be doubted by the world at large.

"Character"-izing Our Current State of Affairs

Character is not just a personal issue. It is a societal one as well. For example, as America continues its collective hypocrisy with respect to the black community, systematic discrimination continues to keep many blacks, other minorities, and women from gaining access to the capital and financing they qualify for. This is a failure of character on a grand social scale. For instance, the Center for Responsible Lending, in its report "Lost Ground, 2011: Disparities in Mortgage Lending and Foreclosures," states, "the majority of people affected by foreclosures have been white families. However, borrowers of color are more than twice as likely to lose their home as white households. These higher rates reflect the fact that African Americans and Latinos were consistently more likely to receive high-risk loan products, even after accounting for income and credit status." Yes, there is federal legislation that prohibits this type of discriminatory lending practice. But if businesspeople in the marketplace lack the character to adhere to both the letter and the spirit of the law, then we will continue to replicate the same injustices that have been visited on the black community since Abraham Lincoln emancipated the slaves in the South.

Over the last few years, I have been making contact with the policy makers at various government agencies regarding such unfair discrimination. Although we finally seem to be having some productive conversations, it has been an uphill battle to engage and include underserved communities in these administrative initiatives. As mentioned in Chapter Six, I recently organized a focus group with the U.S. Senate Committee on Small Business and Entrepreneurship, the arm of government that helped shape the legislation that established the Small Business Lending Fund. This legislation allocated $30 billion to community banks for loans to small businesses. Yet, even though the law has earmarked the funds within the U.S. Treasury Department, during my last conversation with the Senate Committee's chief of staff and a colleague at the Treasury Department, I learned that the community banks were reluctant to draw down the monies and lend to businesses in their communities, particularly in underserved communities. Why? Well, it seems you can't legislate character. You can't *force* loan officers at community banks and decision makers at venture capital firms to lend money to, or invest in, people they insist upon seeing as bad risks (i.e., people of color), even though this is an unjustified opinion based on inaccurate perceptions about how the borrowers' respective communities execute their business plans and ventures. (Note that lenders and investors don't make similarly sweeping presumptions and judgments against our white brethren when they come seeking capital, even when their business "communities" show a history of business failure, bankruptcy, white-collar crime, and in some cases, grand-scale fraud and theft.) History has demonstrated that people of color always have to "work harder and make less; spend more and get less; innovate more and own less."

Though we now have some great new lending policies, I feel that poor character is shaping the way those policies are carried out on Main Street. I have concluded that although governments can provide a road map for fairness, true fairness will only occur when individuals decide to act on the basis of *character* rather than external obligations, mandates, and quotas. Again, each time any of us acts with character, we send ripple effects out into the world that multiply that goodness over and over. Each time we fail to act with character, we reinforce the built-in prejudices and unfair practices that have become our society's "dirty little secrets."

"Character"-izing Government and Business

In today's governmental arena, character is seriously underemphasized. Political figures seem to judge one another mainly on the basis of how well they manipulate policy for themselves or their own parties' agendas, rather than on the basis of character. And because the vast majority of politicians come from the privileged sectors of society, the result is that the rich get richer at the expense of everyone else. As lawmakers, they also end up with the law on their side, even though the law may be wrong.

Much of the business world operates in a similarly character-free way. Any individual who makes money for a company tends to be highly regarded, whether his behavior is ethically admirable or not. A good businessperson is one who *wins*. Period. It matters not if his victory comes at the expense of others, or at the expense of the economy or the environment.

But I believe business can, and must, be a force for change. When we, as businesspeople, begin to act with courage, integrity, and character, consumers will recognize this and they *will* reward us with their business. This is already happening in many places. Consumers have shown that they are willing, for example, to spend more for fair-trade coffee and for "green" products and services because they believe the companies that offer these choices are doing the right thing. Though character-based actions may cause us to miss an occasional short-term opportunity, they will help us gain long-term trust and loyalty. Customers who trust us will ultimately give us their business and refer their friends and relatives to us. (In the next chapter, "The Currency of Openness and Transparency," we will see some examples of businesses that are succeeding by doing just this.)

Business experts and ethicists disagree on what ethics should mean in business and whether the term should be used in business at all. Some believe business to be an amoral institution in which traditional notions of ethics don't apply. Others, such as Richard Branson, founder of Virgin Atlantic, feel that if you're not in business to do good, you shouldn't be in business at all. My loyalties lie with the Branson camp. For if it is true that business's only moral obligation is to turn a profit and/or to make money for stockholders, then that opens the door for businesspeople to behave as unscrupulously as they please. Not getting caught becomes the primary measure of "morality." And none of us want to live in a world like that.

I am reminded of a famous case in which a company called Allied Crude Vegetable Oil Refining Corp. secured large business loans from Bank of America, American Express, and other major lenders by putting up its salad oil inventory as collateral. It brought its ships into the docks and invited the inspectors to take a look. Indeed, the ships appeared to be carrying thousands of gallons of salad oil. In truth, however, the ships' holds were filled mainly with water, with a thin layer of oil on top so that the cargo appeared to be 100 percent salad oil. The stunt, uncovered in 1963, ended up costing the financial institutions a sum of money that would be more than a billion dollars today.

If businesses have no moral obligations except to make money, then Allied Crude Vegetable Oil did nothing "wrong." Its only mistake was getting caught.

But I believe consumers have grown sick and tired of unscrupulous business practices. Look to the Occupy Wall Street movement of 2011 as evidence of this. A spirit of rebellion against unprincipled greed is growing. And consumers now have powerful new weapons—such as social media—with which to exert influence. Today's social graph-savvy consumers are becoming much more conscious of character considerations when choosing companies with whom to do business. And they are making their opinions known to others.

I believe that the more companies act with ethics and character, the more we will come to *expect* such behavior from our business leaders. I also believe that, in matters of ethics, commerce leads and politics follow. As we slowly come to see that character is good for the bottom line, more and more business leaders will behave with integrity. This trend will inevitably change our expectations for government leaders as well.

So *how* do we bring more character into the workplace? One simple way is to employ individuals who demonstrate strong character qualities. Instead of looking solely for experience, education, and training as the main criteria of a candidate's worthiness, companies must learn to give character equally high priority when making hiring decisions.

A friend of mine recently told me about an experience she had at a fast food restaurant. As she entered the restaurant she had to walk around an employee who was lounging outside the door smoking a cigarette. He didn't make room for her to get by. When she got inside, the counterperson did not greet her, did not even look at her, and acted irritated that she had interrupted her flirtation session. I am sure these employees were not fulfilling the wishes of the storeowner or manager. I am sure the owner would have sincerely preferred those employees to show honor and respect for customers. The problem was, the owner probably didn't pay enough attention to *character* when he was hiring and training these employees. Sometimes you have to dig beyond paper qualifications and put people in uncomfortable situations to discover how they will really represent your company.

If you're a hirer, I suggest building a character assessment into your job-interviewing process. One way to do this might be to present some hypothetical situations to potential hires. Ask them how they would behave in tricky ethical scenarios. Then ask probing follow-up questions. Based on the way interviewees respond to challenging questions and the kinds of principles they rely on for their answers, you can get a sense of whether or not they take character seriously. You might also want to build a few real-world character tests into an employee's probationary period. Without "entrapping" that person or putting safety or laws at risk, deliberately set up a situation where a character-based response is called for. That might involve using a "secret shopper" to interact with the employee, or perhaps leaving a small amount of cash unaccounted for. See how your employee behaves. Remember, it is always possible to teach a person of good character new job skills. It is almost impossible, however, to teach character to someone who doesn't possess it. And it is character, in the long run, that will serve your company or cause, large or small.

Character Takes the Lead

Lincoln once said, "Reputation is the shadow. Character is the tree. Our character is not just what we try to display for others to see, it is who we are even when no one is watching. Good character is doing the right thing because it is right to do what is right."

Dr. King echoed similar sentiments when he pointed out that people are not measured by how they behave when everything is going swimmingly, but rather by how they behave when conflict and controversy arise.

I believe both of these great men would have said that character is *the* most important quality of any great leader. Character is primary; everything else is secondary. If you think I am wrong, then just look at our current economic challenges. Many of the recent national mortgage scams and Wall Street investment schemes are glaring examples of what happens when leaders serve their own needs over the needs and rights of those they are supposed to be leading. This is nothing new. If you look at bad economic trends throughout history, you will see that they are often preceded by a period in which business and government leaders were behaving with rampant lack of character.

Again, it is actually simpler (though not always *easier*) to act *with* character than without it. After all, we usually know, in our hearts and our guts, the "right thing to do" in most cases. When we rely on that unerring gut sense as our guide, we don't need to take opinion polls, run focus groups, or build consensus. We don't need to make "pros and cons" lists. We don't need to look over our shoulders or worry about the potential fallout from an unpopular decision. We simply do what we know to be right and then deal with the consequences. Most of the time, we *know* what the right thing is without having to give it too much thought. In cases where we don't, we ask for the counsel of trusted team members—not to tell us what to do, but to help us see the situation from all sides so that we are aware of all the issues and variables in play. And *then* we do the right thing.

Character-based decision-making is a much simpler way to live and lead. The added bonus is that we get to sleep well at night, resting with the peace of mind that comes from following our conscience instead of our quarterly financial goals.

> *Character-based decision-making is a much simpler way to live and lead. The added bonus is that we get to sleep well at night, resting with the peace of mind that comes from following our conscience instead of our quarterly financial goals.*

Character Heard 'Round the World

One of my most respected historical figures of strong character is Miep Gies, a woman who risked her own life to supply sustenance to Anne Frank and her family and friends during the years they spent in hiding from the Nazis.

In 1933, Miep began working as a secretary to Anne's father, Otto, at his trading company. Miep met Otto's wife, Edith, and their daughters and developed a deep friendship with them. In the spring of 1942, Otto asked Miep for help in hiding his family from the Nazis and she readily agreed, even though she had nothing to gain personally, and much to lose. Along with her husband, Jan, she took it upon herself to ensure that Otto, his family, and another family, the Van Pels, were supplied daily with food, water, and other essentials. Meanwhile she continued to help keep the business going.

Eventually, the families in hiding were discovered and arrested. Miep, not being Jewish, was allowed to remain free. She found the pages of Anne Frank's diary on the floor and hid them in a drawer in her desk. Shortly afterward, the Germans combed the Franks' hiding place, but Anne's diary was kept safe. In the summer of 1945, Otto Frank (the only survivor of the group) learned that his daughters had died in the concentration camps, and that's when Miep gave him Anne's precious diary. That diary, of course, was eventually published for the whole world to read.

King believed that eventually there comes a time for all of us when we must do what is right, not because safety concerns or public opinion demand it, but because our *conscience* does. Miep did what she did because her conscience told her it was right. She put concern for her own personal safety aside and took a huge risk to help those in need, making her a person who stands tall upon the "character" pillar of history.

Dignity

Personally, in order to ensure that I act with character, I use the Currency of Reciprocity as my moral compass for navigating life and business. By that I mean the Golden Rule, "Do unto others as you would have them do unto you." It is a highly reliable guide, one that has stood the test of time.

The problem with the Golden Rule is that after years of mistreatment, many people are not even kind to themselves. Why? Self-hatred. Low self-esteem. Feelings of inadequacy. These traits become instilled through centuries of mental, verbal, emotional, and physical abuse; centuries of being told "you are worthless," "you are an animal," or "I am better than you by nature." This pattern in our nation's history actually began in Europe before America was born. For example, the early settlers were from the lower European social and economic classes—many of them indentured servants—who had endured years upon years of abuse from a top-down system of classism and social castes. "When one is systematically hated, torn down, and disrespected by others, that hatred cannot help but filter down to oneself. The proclivity to *tolerate* mistreatment then becomes a manifestation of this low self-worth. It also leads to a tendency to mistreat others. This helps explain—but not excuse—why some of these same settlers would then turn around and practice chattel slavery and other forms of institutional abuse. Like the abused child who becomes an abusive parent, more often than not, the person inflicting the mistreatment is actually a self-loathing, insecure individual, one who can only find respect for himself or herself at the expense of others. The point I'm making is that it is very difficult to act with character when you have no historical precedent for self-respect and self-worth. Self-loathing begets self-loathing.

This is where dignity comes into play. Dignity is a concept Dr. King championed throughout his life and career. It means, essentially, the belief in one's own inherent worth and the inherent worth of *every human being* on this planet. When I say *inherent* worth I'm referring to the sacred, essential value we naturally possess, beyond the *relative* value we provide to employers, family members, and others. King believed, as I do, that it is vitally important that every human being not only carry him- or herself with dignity, but also treat every human being on Earth, from the president of the United States to a homeless person, with the same degree of dignity. Dignity is the basic worth we all inherit, just by being born human in the "image and likeness" of our Creator. We are all capable of behaving in ways that honor that dignity or in ways that negate it.

Though this is not meant to be a spiritual book, we cannot really talk about King's concept of dignity without straying into the "spiritual realm" a bit. King was a man of deep, Christ-like faith who firmly believed that all human beings, due to our fundamental relationship with the Creator, are divinely endowed with dignity at birth. King spent much of his time and energy trying to awaken this sense of dignity in both the oppressed and their oppressors. He thought that every human being had an obligation to behave with dignity and that, to paraphrase one of his famous remarks, if we wished to be a first-class society, we must not tolerate the idea of second-class citizens.

King saw man's inherent value as flowing from the fact that we are all united in God. He believed we are not ultimately separate beings, but are one in spirit. And the oneness we share with each other is the same oneness we share with God. We are all, in fact, living avatars of God, His embodiment here on Earth. As such, we must treat every human being, starting with ourselves, as a facet of the Creator Himself. In his speech "Paul's Letter to American Christians," King quoted the Bible, Acts 17:26, which says, "God that made the world and all things therein hath made of one blood all nations of men for to dwell on all the face of the earth." This was a fundamental precept of King's beliefs. When King himself didn't have a clear road map of his own future, he relied on his sense of dignity to guide him toward his definitive purpose, which was ultimately to become as much like our Creator as possible.

If we truly believe, as King did, that all humans possess divine worth, then behaving with mutual dignity should be second nature to us. Segregation and discrimination should be regarded as laughably absurd. Rather, we should always strive to meet one another in the spirit of *namaste*—an Eastern greeting that means, essentially, "The God in me bows to the God in you." Dignity should become the gold standard for all human relationships and all business relationships. For if we all truly share the same basic, inherent worth, and are united as one divine being, then whatever we do to anyone, we quite literally do to ourselves. Or, as Christ said in Mathew 25:40, "Whatever you do to the least of my brethren, you do unto me."

A sense of spiritual dignity is often the only power strong enough to overcome the deep self-hatred and malaise that results from centuries of psychological, political, and economic abuse. Opening oneself to the power and presence of one's own divine nature can erase any amount of self-loathing that may have accumulated in our psyches from earthly sources. In one instant, an infusion of spiritual dignity can erase decades of poor mental habits.

Treating ourselves and others with love is what awakens this shared sense of sacred dignity. King made this point over and over. Each time we act with love and connectedness, we look past the superficial differences that appear to separate us and honor the deep spiritual bond that connects us. In fact, it is impossible to be a truly spiritual person and to also treat your fellow man with anything less than absolute dignity and respect. In King's "Paul's Letter to American Christians" speech, he pointed out that segregation is an inherently unChristian act because it fails to honor our mutual unity in Christ. Instead it relegates some people to the status of "things," while others rise to the status of human beings. To behave with dignity is to fully respect your own humanity and the humanity of everyone with whom you interact.

> *To behave with dignity is to fully respect your own humanity and the humanity of everyone with whom you interact.*

Character and Dignity

Character and dignity are inextricably intertwined. For when we believe in our own fundamental dignity and that of all people, we are impelled to act with character. How can we do less? On the other hand, when we lack a belief in the inherent dignity of humanity, we find ourselves adrift in a world of moral relativism. Cheating, lying, deceiving, and putting our interests ahead of those of others become perfectly acceptable. We are able to convince ourselves that others are inferior to us and deserve whatever ill treatment it conveniences us to dole out.

Just as dignity leads to character, behaving with character can also lead to dignity. How so? Well, sometimes the only way to find your way *back* to dignity and self-respect is to act with character, even when you're not completely "on board with the program." Each time you find a new way to act with character, especially when no one is looking, you reclaim a little more of your dignity. It starts with the little things and builds up to the big ones. The day eventually dawns when you have built up such a strong sense of dignity and self-respect that you demand to be treated with respect by others. And it is *then* that you develop the true capacity to live by the Golden Rule. When you come to deeply believe that you deserve to be treated with respect, dignity, and fairness, you can then extend those same considerations to others.

This is the foundation of acting with character. And character, in turn, is the foundation of a society worth living in.

CHAPTER 10

THE CURRENCY OF DREAMING

Of all the venerable nouns we can hang on Dr. Martin Luther King, Jr.—leader, prophet, organizer, rebel, writer, spiritual figure—perhaps the one that "sticks" the most is *dreamer*. Dr. King was nothing if he was not a dreamer. It is no accident that he is probably best remembered for the "I Have a Dream" speech we have been referring to in the last couple of chapters.

King was a dreamer, but he was not a fantasist. Nor was he an empty talker. He was a realist, a "solutionist." He only invested his dreaming energy in goals that he deeply believed to be possible and was willing to work on himself. Then he used his dreams as fuel for himself and others to continue striving toward those goals, even when hope seemed slim.

King's grandest and most inspiring dream was for the freedom of all people—not just black people. He understood, fundamentally, that humanity is one, and that when some of us remain suppressed, we all remain suppressed. This is why institutions like slavery can never work as long-term solutions. Those who "own" slaves are, in their own way, as enslaved as their human chattel. They are forever bound to blindness, corruption, and willful ignorance. They are forever captives of evil and merchants of blood money. Their souls cannot rise to their greatest heights because they are forever shackled to unholy beliefs and barbaric practices.

Similarly, none of us can truly be free while some of us are being kept from the table of economic opportunity. Such freedom is an illusion. That is why I believe King's biggest dream involved the economic liberation of all people. He knew it would not be enough to liberate only black people. Rather, all people must be economically liberated (ultimately including those who might *appear* to be holding all the cards at the moment). In other words, the economic *system* itself must be free.

King's dream was prophetic. In Memphis, the night before he died, he declared that he had "been to the mountaintop" and "seen the promised land." I believe he was able to see into our collective future and envision what we could be as a society. King embodied the dream of Moses, who was invited to the biblical mountaintop to communicate with the Creator, receive His laws, and stand in His presence. Moses didn't see God literally, but he was able to view the future of humanity—God's greatest creation. Similarly, King spent much time with his Creator, in prayer and meditation, and sometimes felt in direct communion with Him. This communion allowed King to see and to dream beyond his own death. We can live in the Promised Land he glimpsed, but we *must* keep the dream alive, each in our own way.

King's dream was disruptive, as all good dreams must be. It caused much of the world to feel very uncomfortable. Change is inconvenient. It pulls us out of our comfort zones. King understood that any dream worth having was worth sacrificing—even dying—for. Because of his dream, King faced threats from all communities, even his own. His religious denomination ostracized him. Only a minor percent of the black community of his time supported him; the others had been conditioned to believe that the status quo of segregation and discrimination was somehow "for the best," while many were afraid for their jobs and their lives.

King paid the ultimate price for his dream—his earthly existence. Yet, because he was willing to pay the price, his dream lives on today. I see it on the faces of my own children and in *their* hopes and dreams. I feel it in my own heart in profound ways. It has been *the* major driver in my quest to innovate and tackle the challenges that face society today and beyond. King's dream resonates deeply with my definitive purpose. King manifested his purpose by influencing policy and legislation at the federal, state, county, and city levels of government. I choose to complement that dream by influencing entrepreneurship, business, and economics at a local, state, national, and global level. But his dream and mine are, in essence, one and the same.

Interestingly, as I wrote this book, I was thirty-nine years old, the same age King was when he met an assassin's bullet and transitioned from mortality to eternity. It is humbling to carry his torch forward, even in my small way. I believe practicing *Kingonomics* will help bring to fruition the economic aspects of his dream, and that this may well be the final straw to break the proverbial camel's back of racism, bigotry, and hatred. King's life on Earth was tragically and prematurely ended. Yet, as his co-dreamers, we can remain hopeful and optimistic—even in the face of the resurgence of hate in its new guises today—that his dream of opportunity for all people can still be realized.

Dreaming the Right Kinds of Dreams

The ability to dream is what makes human beings truly unique. Other animals can experience pleasure and pain; some appear capable of abstract problem solving; some may even share some human-like emotions; but they don't dream as Homo sapiens do. I believe this capacity was embedded in our DNA by the Creator of the universe. The human soul, the source of dreams, is what differentiates us from other animal species.

The human soul encompasses our intellect, emotion, and will (or choice). Our *intellect* gives birth to thoughts, which not only provide us with the ideas and information necessary for living our lives, but also sow the seeds of our dreams. What elevates dreams above ordinary thoughts, though, is the *emotion* we invest in them; emotions such as hope, desire, and excitement. And, because of the emotional investment we place in our dreams, they have the added power to summon our *will*. A powerful dream can drive a human being to extraordinary acts of courage, endurance, and discipline. A powerful dream, born of the soul—and harnessing intellect, emotion, and will—can draw others into its spell and unite entire nations of people. The problem with dreams today is that our dreaming mechanism has been hijacked by the media. It has been robbed of its soul, heart, and spirit. Today, many of us dream largely about *things we wish to acquire* rather than about *changing the lives of others*. In sharp contrast, Dr. King dreamed of changing the world to make it better for all of us. That was what he truly cared about and felt was important.

Such an idea almost seems quaint today. Look around at our culture. Flip through any magazine or glance at any billboard and you'll see extreme consumerism at work, often against the backdrop of poverty and depravity. Citizens of today's "first world" are encouraged to dream about automobiles, sexual conquests, fancy homes, gadgets, vacations, and money. As a result, we have homes filled with more *stuff* than at any point in history. Did you know that one of the fastest growing industries in America, for some years now, has been the self-storage industry? That's right—an ever-growing number of first-world citizens can't fit everything they own in their homes anymore! They need to rent extra storage space just to hold their belongings (even as others in the world are struggling mightily).

But have we become happier and more fulfilled as a result of this material focus? I would argue that we have not. I challenge anyone to argue otherwise.

What if we dreamed, instead, about the *right* things? What if we followed the inspiration of Dr. King and began dreaming about things like collaboration, innovation, and exploring new ways we can work together as human beings? What if we dreamed about ideas that would make the world a fairer and saner place for our grandchildren?

Human dreams have the capacity to mobilize entire civilizations. But to what end? Perhaps we need to reevaluate our dreams. Perhaps we need to reroute them from Madison Avenue to Martin Luther King, Jr. Boulevard. Perhaps we need to realize that dreams have power, but only if they are powerful, ennobling dreams. Perhaps it's time to begin harnessing our dreams in service of something bigger and more meaningful than our selfish, personal needs.

The way we do that, I believe, is to flip the switch from *getting* dreams to *giving* dreams. We stop dwelling on what's in it for us and start dwelling on how we can contribute to the world with maximum impact. We must dream new dreams that build community and cooperation toward common goals. We must dream new dreams that bring more people to the table of opportunity. We must dream new dreams about innovative products and services that can enrich human hearts and souls and make better use of our shared resources. And we don't have any time to waste. The world's economy is reeling and resources are running thin, even as the population has broken the 7 billion mark. Superficial, material dreams are not the answer to humankind's dilemmas. The time to nurture spiritually liberating, humanity-connecting dreams is now.

But first, of course, you must *unlock* your dreams.

Unlock the Dream Box

Many of us keep our dreams tucked away. It's as if we have a safe-deposit box somewhere that holds the vision of what we would really love to accomplish in our lives. We create the dream, we put it away in the box, and then we accept a disappointing life and career, doing something lesser. Every now and then we sneak a peek inside the box just to make sure the dream is still there. Then we lock it away again and go back to "punching the clock," literally or figuratively.

Well, I call upon you to crack open the locked box! Take out your cherished dreams and throw away the key. I'm not talking about the dreams of things you'd like to own (though that kind of dream has its place, too), but of things you'd like to *accomplish*. There are few things more painful than looking back on one's life with little more to show for it than a handful of unrequited desires.

Unlocking your dreams is not just important for you, it's important for the world. You were brought here to this "mortal coil" for a reason: to contribute your gifts at the highest level. Would the airline industry exist today if the Wright brothers hadn't had the dream that man could fly? Would the music industry exist if Edison hadn't dreamed of the phonograph? Or how about Dr. Jonas Salk? He dreamed of a cure for a disease that was maiming and killing thousands of children before his very eyes, and through his optimistic dream, the vaccine for polio was discovered. Was it easy? Risk free? Of course not. Transforming abstract dreams into concrete realities rarely is. But braving those risks is what separates the perennial fantasists, who die with hopes and little else, from the "action dreamers" who make a difference.

If you have any kind of dream at all—for a new business, a new form of creative expression, an invention, a book, a unique product or service—what are you waiting for? To be "discovered?" To be "rescued?" To be sponsored? To be invested in? Those things may well happen, but first *you* must commit to unwrapping your dream and turning it loose in the light of day for all to see. You must become your dream's number one champion. You must take the first steps.

I have found, as have countless creative pioneers, that the moment we begin to act on an important dream, we set wheels in motion that we never could have predicted at the outset. People show up to help us, doors open, and opportunities arise when we least expect them, often in quite mysterious and confounding ways. I believe the Divine approves of dreaming and supports us, as long as we are willing to take action. I also believe that the more our dreams serve humanity as a whole, the more "help" we get.

So begin! Take one step, today, in service of your highest, most noble dream. *Then* the next step will reveal itself. And then the next, and the next . . .

A Dreamer Who Changed the World

When talking about the power of dreams, it is almost impossible to ignore the story of Nelson Mandela. Though you may already be familiar with the general outline of his life's accomplishments, I feel compelled to sum them up briefly here as an illustration of how a single individual's dream can bear fruit on the world stage.

Mandela, as you may know, had a lifelong dream to abolish apartheid in his native land of South Africa. Little did he know how severely that dream would be tested.

Mandela, whose given name was Rolihlahla (which means, oddly enough, "troublemaker"), was born in 1918 in a small village on the eastern Cape of South Africa, the son of a tribal chief of the Tembu tribe. He could have followed in his father's well-respected footsteps, but he chose not to. Already dreaming of better opportunities, he became the first person in his family to attend school (where he received the name Nelson from one of his teachers). He eventually attended Clarkebury Boarding Institute, where he excelled as a student, and then went on to attend the University of Fort Hare. He showed his rebel spirit early and was asked to leave the university following his involvement in a boycott against school policies. Eventually he became a lawyer, then further displayed his disruptive spirit by starting the first black law firm in South Africa. He was already *acting* on his dream of opportunity for all.

In 1944, when he was about twenty-six, Nelson Mandela joined the African National Congress (ANC). The ANC was an organization made up of chieftains, leaders, and church officials from various African nations dedicated to fighting for greater rights for the African people. In 1948, when Mandela was about thirty, the National Party assumed power in South Africa, instituting its official policy of apartheid in a nation that had already endured decades of "unofficial" segregation. The ANC and Mandela stood in firm opposition to this policy. Mandela, inspired by the work of Gandhi (like MLK), advocated only nonviolent forms of resistance, but after the shooting of some unarmed protesters in Sharpeville, South Africa, in 1960 and the banning of the ANC and other antiapartheid organizations, he reluctantly changed his approach.

In 1961, Mandela became the leader of the newly formed militant faction of the ANC known as Umkhonto we Sizwe. He left South Africa to obtain military training and, upon his return in 1962, was captured and given a five-year jail sentence. Two years later he was convicted of treason and sentenced to life in prison. Rather than accept his fate quietly, he continued his education in jail and repeatedly refused to back down on his antiapartheid views (when doing so would have set him free), becoming one of the most influential black leaders in South Africa while still in prison. Holding on to his dream to end apartheid, he came to be seen as a martyr, a political prisoner, and a worldwide antisegregation symbol. In 1990, South African President F.W. de Klerk finally lifted the ban on the ANC and released Mandela from prison. Mandela then used his fame and stature to help dismantle apartheid. A new multiracial democracy was finally formed in South Africa and Mandela and de Klerk shared the Nobel Prize in 1993. The following year Mandela was elected the country's first black president.

But he wasn't finished dreaming. Moviegoers may remember the film *Invictus*, which dramatized Mandela's efforts to unite a nation torn apart by decades of segregation by rallying it behind the nation's pro rugby team. Many doubted that this attempt would be successful, but, again, the power of Mandela's dream silenced the naysayers.

Mandela's autobiography, *Long Walk to Freedom*, was published in 1994. Since his "retirement" he has remained an active and influential figure on the world stage, speaking out often regarding important issues. In one of his greatest moments, Mandela was invited on stage for a commencement speech by one of the very judges who sentenced him to prison. And what did Mandela do? Offered the man an embrace.

In 2005, Mandela again captured world attention when, after his son died of AIDS, he pleaded with the people of South Africa and the world to lift the taboo on this terrible disease and to talk about it openly and plainly.

If you ever doubt the power of a dream or need inspiration to hold on to your dream when times get rough, look no farther than the life of Nelson Mandela, one of the greatest living dreamers in the world.

Dreams Fuel Our Lives

It is easy to think of dreaming as a romantic or poetic notion—something we do when the pace of life slows down a bit and we have time to indulge the imagination. But dreaming has far greater importance than this. It is not just the icing on the cake of a satisfying life; it is the *foundation* of one. In fact, a powerful dream—or vision—is the very engine that powers us to live extraordinary lives.

Performance psychologist and author Jim Loehr has done some fascinating work and writing in this area. In his book *The Power of Full Engagement*, and in some of his other books, he makes the case that humans operate on four types of energy and that all four types must be operating at a high level if we wish to be happy and fulfilled. This is a state he calls Full Engagement.[1] A fully engaged person is operating on all cylinders and living at the highest level of human contribution and fulfillment.

The most important point he makes is that a powerful dream—or "story" as he calls it—is what feeds these four levels of energy. It takes a vital dream to *make* us fully engaged. Why? Well, a compelling story about the big picture of our lives is what gives us a sense of purpose higher than ourselves, higher than mere survival. And it is this sense of purpose that drives us to harness and maximize all four kinds of energy.[2]

On the other hand, if we're just trying to "survive" or "get by," we will fail to maximize our energy and settle into a low-level, disengaged existence. Many, many people, in fact, live in just this way, dragging themselves to an unsatisfying job and collapsing on the sofa at the end of the day. No dream, no energy.

Big, compelling dreams are the antidote to this; they are the fuel that makes us fully human, rather than mere animals living in survival mode. Let's look at how this works. Again, it's all about maximizing the four kinds of energy as presented by Loehr.

The first type of energy is physical.[3] This is the basic bodily energy that gives us strength, endurance, healing, and the fuel to do our daily activities. The need for a good level of physical energy is obvious for athletes, dancers, laborers, and others whose bodies are critical to the way they make a living. But even those who *think* for a living or work at desks and computers need a high level of physical energy. As Loehr points out, the brain weighs only 2 percent of our body mass, but requires nearly 25 percent of our body's oxygen.[4] Thinking is hard work. There's a reason professional chess players exercise rigorously; they need a high level of physical energy to play at their best and maintain concentration and stamina.

But, of course, it's very easy to neglect our physical energy. It's easy to eat fattening food and avoid exercise. Having a passionate dream not only gives us instant energy—notice how lethargy evaporates the moment we start doing something we're passionate about—but also provides our *motivation* to take better care of ourselves. It helps us give up bad habits that are not serving our purpose. When more than just our small selves are at stake, we *want* to live longer and stronger. We take our health more seriously.

Emotional energy is next.[5] Emotional energy controls our enjoyment of things and determines whether we have a fundamentally negative or positive approach to life. It has been proven in numerous studies that positive emotions lead to greater health, longevity, effectiveness, and life satisfaction. But many of us spend our lives mired in negativity. We spend much time in the fight, flight, or freeze modes that make life a fearful, stressful experience. A powerful dream or vision provides hope and meaning, which increases dopamine levels in the brain and triggers solution-oriented thinking. A sense of higher purpose toughens us against negative emotions. It allows us to summon courage and optimism when setbacks occur. It allows us to transform stress into a *challenge*, rather than a hindrance. Without a dream to motivate us, we tend to succumb to stress. But a powerful dream lets us harness our emotional energy toward a higher goal.

The next form of energy Loehr presents is mental energy.[6] This is the energy we need to concentrate, focus, solve problems, and organize data. Good mental energy is crucial in managing our lives and doing our jobs. Nothing hampers accomplishment more than an inability to focus and concentrate. Where does dreaming factor into this? It gives us a grand, overall "desired outcome" for our lives and careers. This allows our brains to "shepherd" our thoughts in productive directions, rather than let them wander about randomly, reactively, and haphazardly. And, as Loehr points out, each time we think thoughts along an organized pathway, we solidify that pathway and make it easier for thoughts to travel that same path the next time.[7] *Meaning* becomes the force that organizes our thoughts, and dreams are what give meaning to our lives.

Finally, there is the level of spiritual energy.[8] Whether you are a person of faith, as I am, or not, spiritual energy provides the "why" of life. Why am I doing what I am doing? What is my purpose? If our only goal is survival and getting our selfish needs met, we operate at a very low level of spiritual energy. And so our motivation level tends to be very low. When we adopt a sense of purpose that is bigger than our self-interest, however, we ignite our spiritual energy at a very high level. High spiritual energy supercharges our other three energy levels and infuses a sense of purpose into everything we do. But without a powerful dream, we are unlikely to *have* high spiritual energy. A dream is what gives our lives a sense of purpose beyond earning a paycheck.

I hope you can see, then, that a dream is not something we entertain only when all of our other needs are met and we have a bit of spare time. Rather, a dream is the very wellspring from which all of our energy flows. When vision (dreaming) permeates every living cell in your body, it provides you with the energy to press beyond your pain, press beyond your setbacks, and press beyond your present reality. It is not something we can afford to put off till later, but, rather, a matter of immediate urgency.

Do you have a big dream for your life? If so, start working on it today. If not, what are you waiting for? No one else can craft the dream for your life!

A Dream (Vision) Gives Purpose to Business

In 1982, Disney World finished work on Epcot, formerly the Epcot Center theme park. At the opening ceremonies, company executives invited Walt Disney's widow to the microphone. As the emcee introduced her, he remarked, "Mrs. Disney, I just wish Walt could have seen this!"

Mrs. Disney smiled and said, "He did."

Imagining a "theme park of the future" on 3,000 acres of swampland in central Florida was only one of the many dreams of Walt Disney, which also included Mickey Mouse, *Fantasia*, Disney Productions, the Carolwood Pacific railroad, Disneyland, and Disney World.

When Disney was a child, he was already filling his schoolwork pages with doodles of talking rats and ducks with hats. Disney is now a business empire, unparalleled in the entertainment industry. Vision came first, success later.

There's a good reason most business plans start with a "Vision" section. Without a vision, or dream, there is no point in even starting a business. And a business vision must include more than simply "making a profit." Making a profit is a given, a necessity for any business to thrive. But making a profit does not constitute a vision, nor does "success." Rather, a vision is your dream for what you want your business to accomplish *beyond* making money. According to *Kingonomics*, this should always be a positive goal, a way of adding unique value to the world and to society. For only positive visions fuel us with the heroic energy needed to overcome obstacles and do "impossible" things.

Personally speaking, vision is the compass that helps me navigate the process of building businesses from the ground up. An inspiring, specific vision provides me with a road map to see beyond today's reality and to imagine future opportunities. It ignites my four levels of energy and gives me the "heart intelligence" I need to connect with the right people at the right time. For instance, I have a very large network—8,000 contacts. Some are potential advisors. Some are potential investors. Some are potential employees, contractors, vendors, partners, early adopters, or clients. All of them are talented. Yet, every contact is not relevant to every business idea that I launch or grow. My vision for a project or company is what allows me to intuitively reach out to just the right people for any particular venture. It's not just talents and capabilities I'm looking for, but shared values and passions. Without a vision, I would have no intuitive guidance.

Dreams are an essential requirement for growing a business. And dreams should always be bigger than what we can currently see in front of us. *Executing* the dream may require concrete planning, but the dreaming stage itself should always look beyond our current capacity or reality. Having a big vision is why King was able to disrupt the status quo of his day. Dreams inspire innovation, and innovation (as we'll discuss in Chapter Twelve) is the heart of business. Without a dream, though, innovation can be exhausting. Without vision to fuel all of the energy levels of all of the team members, a business doesn't stand a fighting chance in the long run. Again, dreams are not poetic niceties; they are the highly pragmatic engine on which a business runs.

Finding and Developing Your Authentic Dream

As you try to identify your main dreams for your life and your business, it is crucial that you choose only those dreams that are authentically your own. That can be difficult in today's media-saturated world. Everywhere you look or listen, it seems, someone is trying to sell you *their* version of a dream (so they can sell you products!).

Real dreams emanate from the soul. They are not gaudy and loud. They announce themselves quietly, but insistently. In order to cultivate your own authentic dreams—not those of your parents, your neighbors, your teachers, your bosses, your friends, your spouse, or the media—you must do some soul-searching. That means spending some time in silence, asking fundamental questions such as:

- Who am I?
- What is the meaning of life as I understand it?
- What is my purpose in life?
- What do I deeply believe in?
- What are my core values?
- What do I want my legacy to be?

I believe genuine soul-searching means tapping into nothing less than God's omniscience.

Soul-searching can be painful and difficult. Our real dreams do not appear at the push of a button or the click of a mouse. They cannot be bought; they must be *revealed*. That often happens slowly and painfully. During the vision-crafting phase, it is not what we see or hear that is painful. It's what we *don't* see or hear. Seldom are our dreams announced by bands of angels blowing trumpets. Rather, our dreams whisper to us from the subtle creases between our thoughts.

Soul-searching can be lonely and confusing. It requires that we turn off all the noise—opinions and suggestions from friends, family, and the media. And yet, if we do this with the humble intention of seeking guidance, we *will* receive what we seek. Our dream will reveal itself. "Ask and ye shall receive."

I soul-search daily. I find it an indispensable tool for maintaining and honing my business visions. I often soul-search in retrospect as well. For instance, I did a lot of soul-searching when I was ousted from the day-to-day operations of my growing start-up new-media company in 2002. During this process, I learned that I had to better manage my ego in order to see and live the true purpose that lay before me.

Dreams do not typically arrive full-blown (although that can happen). Usually, they go through a delicate, embryonic phase. I am careful about the people with whom I share my dream in those early days. For me, my wife is my confidant for all phases of my vision; all is transparent with her. If my vision is a "go" with her, I usually then select three people with whom to share it in more detail. I then develop the vision further and pursue twelve "early adopters" to bring into the fold before I take it to the masses. This is parallel to how Jesus operated on the earth. He had his brother John; then he had Peter, James, and John; then he had the Twelve Disciples; then the Seventy; and then the masses. I highly recommend growing and refining your dream with a core team that is connected to the fullness of your vision.

With humility, I can say that I have finally developed a clear vision for my career. I believe I am called to bring dignity, knowledge, access, and opportunity to people, worldwide, as they seek to fulfill *their* purposes on earth and beyond. In this current season of my life, I believe I can best accomplish this through economics and entrepreneurship. And the best *way* I can do it is to disrupt industries, sectors, and spaces by introducing innovation, knowledge, and opportunity in empowering new ways.

Before you launch *your* business or career, it is critical that you do some soul-searching to discover your true dreams, desires, and values. Only when you know what your true dreams are can you conceive of a business or career that is fully aligned with those dreams. And there's no other kind of business worth pursuing.

Passion Is the Second Key

Along with soul-searching, another vital way to uncover your authentic dreams is to honor your passions. Passion is what drives people to work on ideas and serve causes without thought of being compensated with money. Passion is what causes people to become so absorbed in their activity that they enter the state of "flow" and lose track of time. Usually, our biggest dreams unfold via the things we are most passionate about. Passion is God's way of ensuring that we fully utilize the gifts He has given us.

In my case, a passion for music unleashed a tremendous amount of creativity and improvisational skill in me. It remains the basis for my ability to innovate and develop new opportunities in diverse sectors and spaces. Learning to play the piano, keyboard, and Hammond B3 organ was a passion-driven challenge. It required hours upon hours of practice, as well as learning hundreds of chords in different keys. It taught me how to fuse discipline with love, theory with practice. As I came to realize that I could earn income with my music, it also opened the doors of entrepreneurship. Without following my passion for music, I would never have discovered my larger purpose in life and business.

Your dream *must* be rooted, in some way, in your passions, or else it will feel like drudgery and duty. Your head will be in it, but your heart will not.

Last but Not Least

Here are a few other important points to remember about the Currency of Dreaming:

Dreams Must Mesh with One Another.

As you're developing dreams for your life, business/career, and relationships, make sure your dreams are compatible with one another. I have met many people who complain that their fondest dreams are not becoming manifest. Often this is for the simple reason that their dreams for one aspect of their lives are incompatible with those for another. Their career dreams, for example, may be at odds with their relationship or lifestyle dreams. It's difficult to be a working jazz musician and also live in a rural state with few big cities. It's tough to be a hang-with-the-kids-after-school type of dad when you're serving as the head of surgery at a busy urban hospital. It is all but impossible to develop a deep spiritual life while running a Ponzi-scheme type of business that cheats people. This may seem obvious, but your dreams for all areas of your life must be able to coexist in reality.

Dreams Must Be Bold but Doable.

Though it is very important to dream boldly and to look beyond the confines of your present reality, it is also critical to keep a sense of balance and moderation. Anything, including a dream or vision, that is taken to extremes will often result in error. If your dream is so ambitious that you won't be happy without becoming the president of the United States, a movie star, or the richest person in America, then it probably needs tempering. We have rational minds for a reason—not to hold us back, but to make sure we're not straying into the realm of self-delusion. You may indeed become president, but leave such results to God. Meanwhile, just do everything you can to use your gifts at the highest level possible.

Action Is Essential.

No matter how inspiring your dream, it will wither on the vine if you keep it stuffed away in your lockbox or settle for talking instead of acting. The only thing worse than acting without vision is dreaming without taking action. *Hoping* one's dreams come true, without taking real steps, is a naive and childish enterprise. Hope and action together, though, can be an unstoppable combo.

Finally, before reading further, I ask you to pause for a few minutes and ask yourself these questions, fearlessly and honestly:

- What are your biggest dreams for your life and career?
- Are you taking action on those dreams?
- How do your dreams intersect with the new age our world is entering?
- How do you want to define your life? What are your absolute core values?
- How do you want your loved ones, and the world, to remember you when your earthly life is over? If you died today, is that how you *would* be remembered?

Carrying King's Dream Forward

As practitioners of *Kingonomics*, it's crucial to develop unique, original dreams for our lives and businesses, but I believe these dreams should also be in sync with King's dreams. Abiding by the currencies of *Kingonomics* will help to ensure that they are. Moving forward, we must not only celebrate King's birthday each January, but also honor his life and learn from it. In fact, each of us, in our own way, must *live* the life King lived, not just satisfy ourselves with visiting his monument on the National Mall in Washington, D.C. King was a model for dreaming paired with action.

Dreaming means vision. You can't live a dream that you can't see. "Where there is no vision, the people perish," says the Bible. Society as a whole needs fresh visionaries in order to find its direction, dignity, knowledge, and opportunity for the future. But vision is also needed at the micro level by the people who depend on us every day—our spouses, children, family, friends, neighbors, and employees. Without a vision, we cannot really lead anyone. But *with* a vision, we can provide meaningful, inspiring leadership at every level of our lives.

CHAPTER 11

THE CURRENCY OF OPENNESS AND TRANSPARENCY

K ing was a great believer that noble ends do not justify shady means. He urged us to use "pure" means in the pursuit of pure goals. When our actions are pure, we are not afraid to be transparent to all. Transparency, in turn, helps *ensure* that our actions are pure.

We live in an age of distrust of corporate America. Certainly, recent corporate behavior has done little to lessen that distrust. From Bernie Madoff to the Enron and Tyco scandals to the deliberate selling of "junk" financial instruments to the hapless public, it seems that lack of character in corporate America is running amok. Many blame the government's lax regulations, or shareholder neglect, or the failure of financial analysts to pick up the problems. But the common denominator of all these scandals and abuses is that bad character is being allowed to operate in secret.

The antidote to this, of course, is an increase in openness and transparency. Earlier I made the point that business ethics is the manifestation of character in the workplace. If that is true, then openness and transparency are the *mechanisms* by which character is revealed. By running our organizations in an open, transparent way, we unlock the shutters of secrecy and invite the world to take an inside look at our values, our character, and our decision-making processes. A policy of openness and transparency says, "We have nothing to hide," and this, more than anything else, gives consumers confidence in a company's character. Organizations and individuals of good character are more than willing to share their inner workings with anyone interested in seeing them.

Many corporations are accustomed to the safety of operating behind closed doors. They are afraid that increased transparency will lead to increased scrutiny, which may invite criticism and negative publicity, which, in turn, might result in loss of share value, government investigation, or even exposure to lawsuits.

Some of this fear is perfectly natural. We all feel vulnerable when we make ourselves or our businesses transparent. After all, what if we're unknowingly doing something stupid or illegal? What if we've made a costly mistake we aren't aware of? What if our profits are lower than our estimates? What if our competitors find out something they can use against us? What if consumers decide to openly criticize our products and services or our corporate decisions?

But the real, long-term question is, what will happen to the public's trust in our company if we are *not* open and transparent? In the Information Age in which we live, there is a growing sense that openness equals trustworthiness, while closed doors equal trouble.

As a very simple example, consider what often happens when a power outage or other utility failure occurs. Typically the utility or cable company will place a message on its customer service number that says something like, "We are experiencing technical problems in your area and are working to correct the problem as quickly as possible." This kind of message feels generic and unhelpful to the consumer. It does nothing to set the callers' minds at ease that the problem has been diagnosed and is being corrected, nor does it provide any sense as to how long the solution can be expected to take.

In a refreshing move toward greater transparency, AT&T recently turned to Twitter to keep its customers abreast of a fiber optic cable cut that was affecting thousands of its customers. According to the April 2009 CNET article "AT&T Uses Twitter During Service Outage":

"AT&T began 'tweeting' updates about the massive service outage in California around 7 a.m. PDT, with the first message saying: 'CA customers: We are aware of a cable cut situation impacting services in Santa Clara and San Jose areas.'"

The article goes on to say: "From then on the company has sent about eight more 'tweets' or messages informing customers that technicians have been on the scene and service would be restored as quickly as possible. The company apologized for the outage and also informed its followers that the outage was likely caused by vandals who had cut the fiber cables.

"The company's most recent 'tweet' actually notified its Twitter followers that AT&T is offering a reward for anyone [with information about the individual(s)] responsible for vandalizing the company's infrastructure.

'AT&T offering $100,000 reward for info leading to arrest/conviction of those responsible for CA vandalism. Call 408-947-STOP.'

". . . Janine Popick, CEO of VerticalResponse, whose company has been affected by the outage, said the only way she has stayed on top of the situation has been through Twitter. 'All of my real time updates have been coming from the AT&T Twitter feed,' she said."[1]

AT&T continued to update its customers in real time about the nature and extent of the cable cut until it was repaired. And although many users were not able to access Twitter due to the very fiber optic problem that was being discussed, some 2,400 customers "tuned in" regularly and were, no doubt, pleased with the company's transparency, if not with the problem itself.

Some other common examples of transparency in today's business world include real-time, online tracking of shipped packages through FedEx; personal communications with company executives who post their names and photos on their websites; and "About the Company" web pages that describe a company's structure, business philosophy, and leadership team in detail.

Openness and transparency lead to trust, and trust is the glue that holds a customer base, as well as a society, together. I'm not saying that a company should divulge its trade secrets and proprietary technologies. Not at all. That's not what transparency means. I'm talking about providing customers, employees, and the financial community with enough ongoing information about the company's inner workings so that every potential stakeholder can have reasonable insight into the company's values and decision-making processes.

Openness and Transparency: The Solution Is Clear

Every business has setbacks and challenges. Managers make tough decisions and companies make mistakes—sometimes big ones! Being open about your business's mistakes is an opportunity, not a setback. Rarely will openness and transparency be criticized by the market or investors. People in these groups probably already know about your mess-ups anyway. (After all, it is tricky to keep a secret in today's Web-connected world. Policies of secrecy and conspiracy are getting harder and harder to maintain.) To borrow one of Dr. King's commonly used expressions, "the truth shall set you free." When you are open about your mistakes, you are able to clear the air about them. You are also able to show your human side. Owning your mistakes gives you an opportunity to share your values and concerns with your public and to solicit valuable suggestions for going forward.

Revealing one's shortcomings has historically been seen as a sign of weakness, both in commerce and social intercourse. That's because most people live behind a mask, presenting a day-to-day persona that is often far removed from the authentic self. In an ideal world, it would be acceptable to project vulnerability and openness. In our society, however, this is still not the norm (though we are finally moving in that direction). Guarding oneself from the potentially adverse opinions of others is standard operating procedure in virtually all walks of life. This kind of insincerity, however, impedes progress, rather than encourages it. Look, for instance, at how it affects our personal lives. Although it's true that hiding behind a social persona does help us feel less vulnerable, we pay an enormous price for this when it comes to our personal development. That's because growth only occurs when we rise to difficult challenges. But how can others authentically challenge us when they don't know our true feelings, thoughts, and values? Insincerity allows us to hide in safety, but not to grow. Transparency is a necessary condition of growth.

This is true in business as well. Although it may be considered "normal" for a company to "put on its best face" and keep its behind-the-scenes activities private, too much of this kind of behavior can ultimately stifle innovation and success. In an atmosphere of secrecy, consumer trust withers and companies lose the extraordinary opportunities for growth that openness offers. When a company openly shares its plans and goals, as well as its ethical dilemmas, it opens the door to valuable feedback from customers and partners. This can sometimes be painful at first, but many of the best ideas about any business come from the consumers of that business. After all, it is the consumers who use the products. They are the experts on what works and what doesn't. They can often spot the drawbacks in a new strategy that the designers of that strategy cannot see.

Many companies recognize the value of consumer testing and focus groups but are still reluctant to share their upcoming products and ideas with the general public for fear of losing a competitive edge. But perhaps a lesson can be gained from software companies, particularly those that develop ambitious online products such as multiplayer games. It is now common practice in this industry to openly share in-development projects with large beta testing groups. The latter often consists of *thousands* of individuals who agree to use the software product for a period of weeks or months and voluntarily provide unvarnished feedback to the developers in open forums. In this way, the future consumers of the product become, in effect, part of the development team by helping to solve problems, proposing new features, and giving "thumbs down" to ideas that sounded great in the conference room but don't work very well in reality. This is a very high form of transparency indeed. Most computer game companies today wouldn't dream of releasing a new online game that had not undergone extensive beta testing and revising.

It is especially fascinating to see how a company's *character* and values are revealed within a beta testing system. For example, whenever one of these software companies makes a product decision that is solely driven by profit rather than customer friendliness, the executives responsible for such a decision are mercilessly taken to task in online forums. Corporate decisions are often reversed because of this.

There is no place to hide when you throw open your company's shutters and let the sun shine in. And this is ultimately a good thing, for both consumers and stakeholders.

Honesty

Of course, if openness and transparency are to have any real value, they must be accompanied by honesty. In fact, transparency *implies* honesty, for to be transparent while lying is not to be transparent at all. But honesty is a very difficult business challenge, especially for managers and executives who have come of age in the era of "spin" and "deny, deny, deny."

Honesty is often said to be "the best policy," but it can be easier in theory than in practice. Why? Because *dis*honesty often seems more rewarding, at least in the short term.

For one thing, a huge part of building a successful business—from going after business loans, to attracting investors, to hiring the best personnel, to selling products and services—involves presenting one's business in the most flattering and positive light possible. And in a company's attempts to make itself look good, there is always a temptation to shade the truth or to lie outright. There is a fine line between hype and hyperbole. Fiction easily becomes mixed with fact. It is also tempting to minimize or omit facts that work against the business's image. The telling of half-truths, which can be more insidious than outright lies, may seem alluring.

In addition, there's the fact that dishonesty can often generate short-term profits, while honesty can lose business. Take the simple example of an auto repair shop. Let's say I take my car to the shop because of an apparent engine problem. The auto technician looks at it and determines that the cause of the problem is a simple loose wire that will take only minutes to fix. He is now faced with a dilemma. Perhaps his business is slow and he really needs a few high-paying customers this week. He can be honest and do the simple, inexpensive repair for a few dollars *or* he can lie by telling me that the problem is a much more serious one. He knows, after all, that I am ignorant about automotive matters and am totally reliant on his expertise and honesty. By charging me $400 for a bogus engine repair, he makes some fast money and I am none the wiser. By being honest, on the other hand, he loses badly needed business in the short term.

But—and this is the crucial part—by being honest he likely creates a customer for life. Telling me the truth not only makes me hugely appreciative, it also gives me confidence that I have found a technician I can trust. I am now likely to bring all of my future business to him.

Every act of business honesty is an investment in the long-term future of your company. Every act of deceit, by contrast, is a nail in your company's coffin. Though you may occasionally be able to turn a dollar by being dishonest, eventually word gets out and your reputation suffers. As a matter of *policy*, honesty truly does work the best, especially in today's transparent, Web-connected world.

> *Every act of business honesty is an investment*
> *in the long-term future of your company. Every*
> *act of deceit, by contrast, is a nail in your*
> *company's coffin.*

Transparency as a Financial Asset

Transparency is the ideal vehicle for showing your company's honesty and exemplary character. But even when you take character out of the formula, transparency has some obvious business value. Part of this is purely financial.

The term *transparent* as used in the business world often refers to a company's financial statements. If a company is "transparent" to the financial community, that means its financial statements appear to be clear and understandable to potential investors and analysts. On the other hand, if a company has "opaque" financial statements, potential investors may find it difficult to understand and, therefore, trust the company. The fact is that the simpler and more transparent a company's structure, the easier it is for everyone to understand its business.

To look at a simple example of this, take two corporations of basically the same market cap size, earnings, and growth projections. One produces a very simple line of products for one specific market, while the other has many subsidiaries producing many products for many markets around the world. In simple dollar terms, the companies are virtually identical. Which one will be better received by the financial world? The smart money would be on the simple, single-market company. Why? Because its financial statements will be far easier to understand for the analysts who make buy/sell recommendations to the investing public. A higher value will thus be given to its shares, and its bond offerings (if issued) will most likely get a higher rating from the rating agencies. This is simply because the company's inner workings are more obvious to the marketplace.

Of course, some companies are, by nature, more complex in their business structures and markets than others. For instance, a multinational corporation like General Electric will naturally have a much more abstruse financial picture than will, say, a domestic dough maker that sells its product only to pizza parlors. There are simply more moving parts with the giant multinational. A certain amount of "opaqueness" can't be helped in these instances.

Some companies, however, are unnecessarily complex in their financial reporting and business literature. They employ obscure technical jargon and expect the reader to interpret complicated numerical data. This naturally invites outsiders to conclude that the company has something to hide. That may not be true, but, again, perception is everything. Just remember, if you run a business, the simpler it is for others to understand, the more confidence they will have when it comes to investments, loans, partnerships, and referrals. Unnecessary complexity does not make you look more professional; it just makes you harder to understand and trust.

Google It

One of the most illustrative examples of how openness and transparency can lead to explosive growth and profitability can be found by looking at Google. Google was established in 1998 and has now grown to become one of the top fifty global corporations. So how did

Google create such explosive growth over such a short period? How do they continue to run their company in a manner that keeps them at the top of their game? There are many answers to this, but one big reason Google has succeeded is because of the open, transparent corporate culture it adopted right from the start.

To foster a culture of openness, the company clearly states its direction and philosophy to everyone who works there, and everyone is expected to know what matters to the company. New ideas under consideration are published openly on the company's intranet, and employee comments are actively solicited by management. That's because management understands that its people and their talents are the foundation of the company. This atmosphere of openness creates an environment where individual talents are nurtured and allowed to grow. Google employees understand the company's business strategies and can clearly see how their efforts directly affect the company as a whole.

Says former Google CEO Eric Schmidt, "[Team members] are going to do what they are going to do, and you're there to assist them. They don't need me, they are going to do it anyway. They are going to do it for their whole lives. Maybe they could use a little help from me. At Google, we give the impression of not managing the company because we don't really. It sort of has its own borg-like quality if you will. It just kind of moves forward."[2] Schmidt is describing an organization that strongly departs from traditional corporate culture in which only a few select individuals at the top of the organization are "in the know."

Google's open strategy allows decisions to be "owned" where they need to be owned. What that means is that the people making the decisions are ultimately held accountable for them, for good or for bad. When you arm people with a clear sense of purpose and accountability, they see that it is in their best interest to do their tasks with excellence. In this way, openness and transparency become a self-governing force. People in such a corporate culture become self-actualized and highly responsible. This inevitably releases vast amounts of creative power. It also creates an atmosphere where the best and brightest want to work, because they know their contribution will make a difference.

Transparency Is Good for Business

Even as recently as ten years ago, the idea of transparency as we now think of it would have been beyond the comprehension of most company executives. The standard business model was always the old "closed doors" approach. But, as the Internet has become more integral to our daily lives, many companies are now seeing the light. They know that anyone with a computer and a web connection can be a potential ally or a deadly enemy. All people have to do is tap into the blogosphere, social media outlets like Facebook and Twitter, or sites like Angie's List and Yelp to read and post instant public reviews of companies. And even one properly positioned anonymous post can have an enormous effect on a company's business.

So if you are a manager, how do you handle this pesky thing called transparency? I would suggest that instead of trying to hide your dirty laundry, you air it out. The bottom line is that customers want to know *who they are dealing with*, not just what your products or services are. They want to get a sense of what your company believes in. They want to know your company's "personality." They don't mind so much if you're facing challenges at the moment, as long as you are open and honest about them. In short, they value authenticity more than slick PR. Here are a few examples of how the new "openness" is remaking corporate culture and behavior.

- In an article titled "The See-Through CEO" (Wired.com), Clive Thompson presents the following scenario. Glenn Kelman became CEO of Redfin Real Estate several years ago. At that time, Redfin was unique in its approach to real estate brokerage in that it charged only one-third of the usual broker's fee of 6 percent on a sale. Needless to say this did not sit well with the other real estate brokerages; it significantly undercut their commission structure. However, homebuyers and sellers fell in love with Redfin because they were saving 4 percent on sales transactions. The other brokerages retaliated by refusing to allow Redfin's customers to bid on the multiple-listing homes where they had exclusive broker rights. This cut into Redfin's inventory of available homes. Out of sheer desperation, Kelman started a blog in which he laid out his company's philosophy and what he thought the industry was doing wrong. His competitors began attacking him on his own company blog and he began responding to their comments. This back-and-forth between Kelman and his competitors went on for some time and caught the attention of his customers. They rallied around him. As the criticism went on, Redfin's business grew and grew. Kelman attributes Redfin's success to the complete transparency displayed on the company blog.[3]

- In an unusual move, GM recently entered the blogosphere and wrote about the repayments it made on its bailout loans from the government. This was a wise move because most Americans were not in favor of bailing GM out in the first place. GM went on to expand its web presence from there. It now has a company blog that announces things like key personnel changes, new products coming to market, and other company news. This type of communication gives its employees, customers, and investors timely access to important information and shows that even a stodgy old behemoth like General Motors can get with the times and become at least somewhat transparent.

- Zappos has been a major player in the transparency game. This was most apparent in 2009 when Amazon acquired the company. In a reversal of the way many companies behave during a takeover, Zappos' CEO posted a letter on the company blog, going into great detail about the sale and the company's anticipated reorganization. Although many employees had been upset about the rumors swirling around the merger, when the CEO laid out the bald facts the employees felt more at ease. At least someone was telling them the truth! This is a much better approach than standard management protocol, which is often to say nothing until the pink slips start going out. As a result of this initiative, Zappos' employees have remained loyal and have even created a blog called "Inside Zappos" where any employee can ask management questions, make recommendations, and even post personal stories and self-made videos about life inside the company.

• An unusual example of corporate transparency occurred on the blog of Paul Levy, the former CEO and president of Boston's Beth Israel Deaconess Medical Center (BIDMC). His "Running a Hospital" blog became nationally known after he asked BIDMC hospital personnel to voluntarily take a pay cut until things improved financially at the hospital. He made this unusual request so that he would not have to fire several employees, most of whom were at the low-paid end of the spectrum. The response he got astounded everyone. Many of the staff quickly donated part of their pay to help their fellow workers. The media picked up on this and it became a national news story. On hearing the story, several other hospitals began sending BIDMC their overflow patients. This led to a 10 percent increase in patient volume, which put the hospital in the black once again. Transparency was the key to increasing not only esprit de corps among the company's staff, but also tangible revenues as well.[4]

• Toro is a well-known manufacturer of power lawn equipment. Numerous customer injuries occur every year, due sometimes to product misuse and sometimes to simple accidents. This has led to several lawsuits over the years. Back in the 1980s, this situation was putting the company at substantial financial risk. As part of a new CEO's efforts, Toro sent representatives to the injured customers' homes to see what the company could do to help. Toro's response team became so effective that it has experienced only one personal injury lawsuit since the new policy was put in place. Openly acknowledging the injuries and expressing concern for injured customers not only cuts down lawsuits but engenders enormous goodwill as well. Toro's approach is totally the opposite of what many companies do when faced with lawsuits, which is to deny, clamp down, and out-lawyer the plaintiffs. Openness and compassion have served Toro very well.

Transparency, of course, has to be genuine and consumer-oriented in order to gain trust.

- President Barack Obama promised on the campaign trail in 2008 to run a highly transparent administration if elected. Once in office, he directed his staff to fulfill his promise of transparency, which they did by revamping the White House website to make it much more user-friendly, timely, and informative. The number-one goal of this site is to publish information that is truthful and correct, because the readership is none other than the citizens of the United States! Most people think the president has done an admirable job in this regard.

Dr. King was prescient in his vision of how the world would become smaller due to the advances in technology. He concluded that this would, by necessity, require all people and organizations to be more open with one another if true progress was to be made. Again, the Currency of Openness and Transparency goes hand in hand with the Currency of Character and Dignity, because only in an open and transparent system is our character on display for all to see. And character, of course, is "King."

THE CURRENCY OF CREATIVITY AND INNOVATION

D r. King was keenly aware of the rapid pace of global change. He spoke with a fierce sense of urgency about the need to "stay awake" and to remain vigilant and mentally nimble in the new era that is now upon us. Though it was still the 1960s, King could see that we were entering a time of rapid social and economic change, and that the pace of change would only accelerate in the decades to come. King knew that we would need to shed our old ways of thinking if we wished to take advantage of global change, rather than be trampled by it. And he knew we would need to respond to change quickly and creatively, or else we might miss our opportunity.

Dr. King was a prophet and an innovator. He was able to envision a whole new world beyond the mindsets, practices, and policies of his day. He was also able to leverage new ideas and apply bold new approaches to old problems. He encouraged his followers to be innovators like him. He knew that for our society to remain competitive in the modern era, and for the economy to improve for all of us, constant innovation would be required. One of his biggest fears was that we would "fall asleep" and fail to rise to the challenge.

Today the world is facing problems on a scale, and of a nature, that it has never faced before. Therefore, it is critical for the passengers on this great spinning globe to meet those challenges with ideas, practices, and mindsets that have never been implemented before. "Tried and true" solutions have become tired and untrue. They will not serve us any longer. We are in desperate need of creativity and innovation, in all dimensions of life.

The trouble with innovation—and Dr. King implied this in his speeches and writings—is that it isn't easily embraced or implemented. New ideas often appear frightening or strange. Innovation can be downright disruptive, and no one likes disruption. Most of us strive to cling to the status quo, even when the status quo is bringing us only frustration and staleness. And yet, in this new millennium, it is innovation that will bring our nation and our businesses the competitive edge they need.

Innovative visionaries have always led to breakthroughs that have paved the way for the major advances in civilization. Geniuses like Jesus Christ, Imhotep, Benjamin Banneker, Thomas Edison, Dr. Charles Drew, the Wright brothers, Gandhi, and Steve Jobs all looked at the world in a fundamentally different way and, in doing so, changed it.

Where will the innovators of today and tomorrow come from?

It is tempting to always look toward the world of technology. Technology is certainly a great *enabler* of innovation. We now have a vast array of tools and platforms that allow for seamless collaboration amongst innovators, partners, investors, early adopters, and users. And yet technology is also one of our greatest challenges. Because of the rapid speed with which technology is evolving and the global market it has awakened, many of us are finding it harder than ever to make *meaningful* change and easier than ever to get lost among the noise. We are tempted to innovate simply for the sake of technological coolness, with no greater purpose in mind.

King cautioned us not to let the pace of scientific advancement outstrip our moral growth. He warned against the dangers of using technology and innovation to become materially rich while failing to become spiritually rich. He feared that even as we pulled the world together technologically, we would continue to distance ourselves from one another on a human level. King encouraged us to embrace change and to boldly develop new technologies and solutions, but to do so in a way that brings us closer together rather than farther apart.

Creativity in Business

Today, increasing competition from around the world, due to the globalization of the economy, is leading to accelerated product and service development cycles. More and more players are entering every viable business arena. And they're all looking for the edge that will set them apart. As a result, employers and corporations are desperate for creativity and innovation.

It appears that the pace of creative innovation will continue to accelerate. Studies show that half of the profits of most major global companies have come from products launched in just the last ten years. Most analysts believe that this turbocharged pace of innovation will continue for the foreseeable future.

The purpose of any commercial enterprise is twofold: (1) to grow revenue, and (2) to deliver exciting, value-adding products and services to customers. Both are necessary, and innovation is the driving force behind these achievements. No business can stand still today. We all must learn to *surf* the waves of change, rather than erect sea walls against them. Though stability and steady progress may have been the hallmarks of a successful business in the post-WWII era, stability and steadiness now sound the death knell for business. Nimbleness, innovation, and the ability to anticipate and adjust to change are the new measures of success.

As Darwin observed, only the fit survive in nature. In today's business world, fit means not only *keeping up* with the marketplace but becoming a market leader. To do this, a company must continuously look ahead, never resting on its laurels. Whatever value a company had yesterday, or even today, will wither tomorrow if it does not dynamically adjust its product line and strategic vision to the changing market. This puts businesses in a strange, but ultimately exhilarating, position—their greatest potential value lies in something that is *presently unknown.* Adaptability, not certainty, has become the new business mantra.

Today, being a market leader means innovating creatively at every stage of a product's development, from strategic vision, to initial ideation, to design, to testing, to manufacturing, to marketing, sales, and distribution. At each stage, we must ask such questions as:

- What can we be doing better?
- How is the market changing?
- Is this the approach that today's consumers *really* want?
- How can new technology help us reach new markets and better serve existing ones?
- What value can we add that others have not thought to add?
- Are we relying on any old assumptions?
- How will this change serve humanity and make a positive contribution to the world?

Innovation has become so crucial that many businesses, both new and old, now include it in their mission statements. And yet, while most managers and CEOs *talk* about innovation in theory, many do not fully embrace it in practice. There are many reasons for this, but most of them boil down to this: human resistance to change. Innovation requires risk. And risk stirs up fear. Fear stagnates creativity and innovation.

Most corporate cultures and personnel structures are built on principles of selfishness and self-advancement, rather than a true spirit of cooperation, collaboration, and teamwork. Many managers still operate in a *positional* way; they believe that asserting their position to their subordinates is what reinforces their leadership status. They often miss the fact that leaders lead by example and not simply by organizational authority. When leaders learn to set ego aside and serve as models for a more collaborative creative process, their team members begin to operate less fearfully. Innovation is given room to flourish.

In my experience, most creativity and innovation begins with the founders of the company. There is something in the entrepreneurial spirit of founders that is inherently creative and innovative. Business starters seem to be the type of people who are willing to take risks by creating something new from their ideas. Employees, on the other hand, must often be taught or "given permission" to be creative. That's because—as a very general statement—people who seek employment within existing structures are often hoping to follow existing processes, policies, and procedures. Though most people do have a deep-down desire to be creative and innovative, sometimes this must be "pulled" out of them. Good managers must seize the challenge of "turning on" their employees' creative powers. Business owners must do everything in their power to infuse their own innovative drive throughout their companies.

Innovation in the U.S. Versus Around the Globe

It's interesting, and sad, to note that the United States is no longer revered as the most innovative nation on the planet. Why is this? I believe one reason Dr. King would have offered—and admittedly I am filtering this through my own perspective—is America's inability to address its longstanding issue with race, diversity, and mutual inclusion. This issue is like a cancer that is metastasizing throughout every organ (organization) within our nation. We must eradicate it or it will eventually consume us. It's a simple truth: when people hate, they can't innovate. Hate fosters an "us against them" mentality, which stifles creativity. Love, on the other hand, fosters inclusion, cooperation, and encouragement, the very soil in which innovation flourishes.

Another reason the United States is losing its edge in innovation is its education system. In the article "The 30 Most Innovation-Friendly Countries," *Bloomberg Businessweek* reported on a study done by the Boston Consulting Group that set out to determine which countries in the world had the best conditions for developing and attracting innovation. Though the U.S. still ranked in the top ten, several other nations now supplanted it at the top of the list, including Singapore, South Korea, Switzerland, Iceland, Ireland, Hong Kong, and Finland. When analyzing the contributing factors for this, one of the main reasons cited was a well-educated workforce.[1]

Education has become a serious problem in the United States. It is a well-known fact that many nations are now outpacing us educationally, and we are also making it extremely difficult for young people to *afford* a quality education. Many college and grad school students today must take on staggering amounts of student loan debt, which they then find nearly impossible to repay when entering the job market, especially at an entry-level position. Hence, they are forced to make career decisions out of fear, not talent and inspiration. Common sense tells us that this situation is not conducive to a healthy, creative workforce.

We must learn to regard the education of our workforce as not just an individual problem, but a societal one as well.

Nokia, the Jewel of Finland

It is interesting to note that Finland, which *Bloomberg* placed ahead of the U.S. in terms of innovation-friendliness, is now ranked number one educationally, in both math and science, around the globe.[2] It also "happens" to be the home of one of the most successful and innovative companies ever to have appeared on the world stage: Nokia.

From the early handset telephones it built in the 1990s to the smartphones of today, Nokia has kept its edge despite extremely fierce competition in this highly innovative and technology-driven market.

Today the company has more than 132,000 employees in 120 countries and boasts annual sales of over $50 billion. In 2010 it controlled nearly 35 percent of the mobile device world market. Every step of the way, Nokia has been an innovator in this new industry, and the results have been astounding. Today, a substantial percentage of the world's citizens carry smartphones and have come to rely on them as essential business and social tools. Even fifteen years ago this would have seemed strange. A mobile phone was not something that "everyday" people needed or could afford. Smartphones barely existed and were used only by a select few businesspeople. Nokia, more than any other company, was responsible for turning this around. As Steve Jobs did with the iPod, Nokia showed the world that it needed something it didn't even know it wanted.

A major secret to Nokia's success is that it never relied on someone else's technologies or designs. Instead it went directly to its consumers to learn their likes and dislikes, desires and attitudes. Thus, Nokia has always been able to stay one step ahead of its competitors. Its sensitivity to its customer base has made it a leader in what is probably the most competitive and technologically innovative product market in the world.

Innovation the P&G Way

Though many of the hottest innovators in the world are relatively new companies, it *is* possible for an old dog to learn new tricks. Procter & Gamble is the largest consumer goods company in the world at the time of writing. It offers a diverse product line that includes everything from pet supplies, to shampoos and razors, to pharmaceuticals and household supplies. Interestingly, P&G has also recently become an innovation leader through its unique approach to "open innovation."

Before 2000, P&G was the typical big company adhering to a "closed" innovation approach. That is, it relied almost exclusively on its internal team to provide all the impetus for innovation. But company managers became convinced that there was a whole world of researchers, scientists, and innovative teams out there that could be tapped.

This led to what is perhaps P&G's greatest innovation: its "Connect and Develop" (C&D) model. This is a program by which the company actively seeks collaboration with external scientists, product developers, researchers, labs, and the like. The company hosts a C&D website whereby start-ups, inventors, and others looking for a partner or a buyer can contact its full-time C&D staff to discuss new inventions and ideas, as well as possible partnerships and supply relationships. Within six years of establishing the C&D program, Procter & Gamble found that its research and development productivity had more than doubled, while associated expenses had dropped.[3]

Clearly, P&G is relying on the Currency of Connectivity as well as the Currency of Openness and Transparency to help spur its growth in innovation. Some other companies that come to mind as innovation leaders today are:

1. Apple, Inc. (consumer technology)—Leads the world in introducing new technology to consumers and making new ideas cool, comfortable, and indispensible.

2. ShaunKing and Hopemob (nonprofit causes)—Pushes the envelope beyond traditional nonprofit fundraising strategies by raising money and support via platforms such as Kickstarter, Twitter, and Facebook.

3. LifeChurch.TV (faith and spirituality)—Innovatively uses new technology such as streaming media, satellite locations, and mobile apps to take its message outside the four walls of the church.

4. BreakingVoices (the social graph)—Disrupts media moguls by giving users an innovative new way, via social and mobile media platforms, to "discover, bookmark, post and share breaking news."

5. Twitpay (social commerce)—Offers a creative new platform for raising capital for nonprofit causes and selling products and services within the Twittersphere.

My Own Humble Stabs at Innovation

In my life, I have had the good fortune of meeting many innovative visionaries who have inspired, challenged, and encouraged me. I like to think that I have been a bit of an innovator myself. A few of my own forays into innovation that have taught me the most are:

1. In 2000, I cofounded Multicast Media Technologies. We innovated the delivery of inspirational content on behalf

of churches, ministries, and social causes via a platform we developed called Streamingfaith.com. This new platform could deliver content live, on demand, or on a continuous-play basis—similar to an MSO (DIRECTV, Dish) or network (MSNBC, CNN, BET). We didn't innovate streaming itself; we innovated the delivery of streaming to niche markets, and the management platform for delivering the content. We called it DMMS (digital media management system). Multicast Media Technologies was sold to Kit Digital, a NASDAQ company, in 2010.

2. In 2006, I established Intellect Inspire, which has become a publisher of inspirational content on Audible. com, an Amazon company. Today, Intellect Inspire is partnering with Audible on the ThinkUp project— designed to aggregate, produce, and publish one hundred thousand inspirational works and audio books for digital consumption. Again, we didn't innovate the technology, but we are innovating a new space for the use of the technology. That's an innovative trend I have adopted. I seek out brilliant new ideas in the world of commerce and technology and bring them back to unusual niche markets such as underserved populations, the inspirational community, the African-American community, and Africa itself.

3. In 2008, I became a founding partner in an innovative social network that connects entrepreneurs and investors from around the world. These entrepreneurs share expert knowledge, seek investor capital, form new relationships, collaborate, and save costs on key services that can help grow their businesses.

4. Currently I'm innovating an "economic dignity" investment crowd fund and learning company. Its objective is to educate and encourage individuals, companies, and

organizations in underserved communities to pool their monies together to collectively invest in innovative projects around the world that will ultimately impact the future of those very communities. This application of cutting-edge investment structures and traditional development techniques to an investment vehicle that is funded by members of the underserved community is, I believe, highly innovative. It is *Kingonomics* in practice.

It's *all Kingonomics*, actually. What my attempts at innovation have taught me, more than anything, is how interdependent the currencies of *Kingonomics* are, and how they feed one another to catalyze creativity. The currencies of Connectivity and Diversity, for example, enhance creativity by tapping into the power of new perspectives, experiences, and expertise. The Currency of Service is vital because trying to serve the needs of others is what helps us conceive many of the most innovative solutions. The Currency of Dreaming is all about developing the vision and imagination needed to be a true innovator, and the Currency of Positivity is all about keeping hope and confidence alive while you take the scary risks that innovation sometimes requires. And of course, the Currency of Personal Responsibility is what impels us to take action, rather than stow our innovative ideas in the closet and wait for someone else to bring them to life.

Encouraging and Stimulating Innovation Within an Organization

Today more than ever before in history, the main concern for any company's management should be how to encourage creativity and innovation. Fresh-mindedness must occur *throughout the organization*, not just in the research and development department. This does not happen automatically. Management must establish policies, attitudes, and practices that support the innovation process. The following are some ideas and principles that I have found especially helpful in that regard.

1. Take an honest, unbiased "innovation inventory." One of the most important, albeit difficult, things management can do is take an honest, top-to-bottom look at what the company needs to do in order to become more innovative. It often makes sense to bring a skilled consultant and advisor to help with this. After all, management may not see things objectively. Change may require eliminating cherished parts of the company. It may mean laying off workmates and friends. It may mean admitting to mistakes in management and running the risk of looking foolish. Still, it is absolutely crucial that managers find a way to step back and take an objective look at where their company stands in terms of innovation. Is the company a market leader? If not, why not? What can be done, objectively, to move it in a more innovative direction? What new strategies might help?

2. Create a risk-taking culture. Creating a risk-taking culture starts with senior management. Company leaders must learn to adopt a point of view that embraces risk and sees it as a vital tool. This is no easy or casual task. Once top management is on board, they must pass this new view on down the line to their managers, and, from there, to the other employees.

Next, management must establish clear guidelines as to the company's expectations for creativity. If you expect innovation, then you must create a structure by which innovative behavior is rewarded. This is the opposite of the way most companies actually work. Typically, *blame* is assigned whenever risk-taking fails. But instead of pointing out risk takers' failure, managers should praise their initiative and view any failure as a welcome opportunity for all to learn a valuable lesson.

3. Expose your team members to creative people and their work. When you just *talk* about creativity and innovation, most team members don't really "get" it. Actual exposure to creative people, ideas, and environments, however, can really birth creativity. College campuses, business incubators, business lounges, and business accelerators are good places to look for models. If possible, it can also be very helpful to expose your team to the inner workings of businesses that may be very different from yours. Sometimes unrelated businesses may be making just the kinds of innovations that will spark one of your team members to invent the "next big thing." (Businesses in different industries are also more likely to share their secrets with you because they won't view you as competition.) Try to arrange "field trips" to innovative companies and/or invite speakers to come in and share their creativity secrets. Creativity workshops can help, too.

4. As leaders, engage in dialog and debate. Healthy dialog and debate amongst the experts or leaders in an industry can create a stimulating, challenging atmosphere in which creativity can flow freely. Smart leaders recognize that, even though there may be competition between companies, the industry as a whole grows richer and stronger when open dialog occurs amongst leaders. Fun intercompany challenges can also inspire team members to bring out their "A" game.

5. Establish quiet, creative space. The business world is noisy, but creativity needs quiet in order to flourish—not necessarily the absence of *natural* sound, but the absence of non-essential noise, people, and ideas. Creativity needs a still, peaceful environment without frantic, urgent energy. As a manager, you cannot expect creativity to "happen" if you don't create a physical atmosphere that nourishes it. You don't need to make your whole workplace quiet, but you should make a designated part of it so. I am a strong promoter of ridding oneself of the negative and irrelevant rhetoric that bombards our consciousness all day long. When you remove excess stimulation, attention can focus on the creative task at hand.

6. Adopt a true team approach. John Maxwell, the famed teacher and leadership writer, says, "Teamwork makes the dream work." The key word is team. Just because employees are assigned to work together doesn't mean they are actually a team. If they are just working together to complete an assignment but haven't taken the time to know each other authentically, then no true creativity or innovation will manifest. Territoriality will rule. Every member of the team will be more concerned with *protecting* their creative ideas than freely sharing them. But when team members truly care about one another, a sense of shared goals develops. Individual egos become less important than the success of the team and the project.

7. Establish a culture of "intrapreneurship." If you're not familiar with the term, intrapreneurship refers to the development of an entrepreneurial spirit within the structure of an existing company. Intrapreneurs are often given specific goals to accomplish and a great deal of leeway as to how they accomplish those goals. Ideally, they are able to draw on the resources of the company without being constrained by its rules and hierarchy. They operate like independent contractors. Intrapreneurship can bring a breath of fresh air into a company that needs more innovation. It can also be an appealing option for creative-minded employees. It affords them the opportunity to operate more independently while still benefiting from the infrastructure of the existing company. It's a chance to test the waters of entrepreneurship without taking the risk of immediately leaving to start one's own company.

8. Empower your employees. Even if you don't deputize any full-fledged intrapreneurs within your company, you still need to empower your existing team members. That means ensuring that they are given the time, budget, leadership, and cooperation to turn their rough concepts into sought-after products. It also means being careful not to squash their independence. Some direction from management may be necessary, but employees must be given enough breathing room so that their creative powers are allowed to shine through. Micromanagement and "having all the answers" is the wrong approach. Of course, managers should also let employees know that with freedom comes responsibility. Employees should be held accountable (but not blameworthy) for their success or failure.

9. Hire some proven innovators. Many companies *want* to become more innovative, but just don't know how to go about it. One helpful way to get there is by hiring people who have already gone through the process. Hiring key creative personnel who can helm the type of change you are trying to accomplish is the quickest way to achieve your goals.

10. Share information openly. It's crucial to encourage information sharing between groups, departments, product lines, and managers. When people operate in ignorance of the whole, they unintentionally keep their creative brakes on. However, when everyone fully understands how his/her job ties in to the big picture, surprising innovations can occur. So remove blockages in information flow. Shed the old-school delusion that *holding on* to information creates power. Embrace the Currency of Openness and Transparency.

11. Employ the carrot and stick. Reward the successes of your innovators with bonuses, a share of the profits, after-work parties, and company-wide recognition and promotions. You can also reward innovative team members by allowing them a little more freedom to be creative with their future projects.

12. Listen to your customers and try to anticipate their needs. This is perhaps the most critical ingredient in innovation. Follow the example of Nokia: constantly find new ways to get close to your customers and listen to what they want and need. Businesses that don't keep their customers close are doomed. The customers will *always* lead you to the next innovation. For it is they who have the most experience using your products and services. It is they who can fearlessly tell you exactly what is and isn't working. This point cannot be stressed enough. Every piece of customer feedback is a road map to the next innovation.

13. Reduce the red tape. According to the Bloomberg article mentioned earlier, another key trait of innovation-friendly countries is that they minimize bureaucratic roadblocks. Businesses should heed this prescription. Too many companies allow their reporting structures and procedural protocols to balloon up to truly comical proportions. Approvals, legal analyses, committee reviews, and focus groups can cripple a new idea before it has a chance to walk. An organization with too many layers is a major obstacle to innovation. So try to streamline your processes. Make your organization as flat as possible. This will speed up the time from first ideation of a new product or service to its final distribution and sale. A speedy start-to-finish time will bolster your bottom line and keep your team members excited and inspired.

14. Brainstorm regularly. Creative brainstorming is a great way to solicit unvarnished, spontaneous ideas and reactions from your team members. When brainstorming, it is critical to foster an atmosphere of "there are no stupid ideas." The point of a brainstorming session is to make sure you've left no stone unturned in your creative thinking. A few questions I find particularly helpful when brainstorming about a new product, service, or idea are:

1. Is this idea disruptive? (I hope so!)
2. Has it ever been done before? (I hope not!)
3. What local or global challenge will it help solve? How will it serve?
4. Are we thinking big enough? (Go big or go home!)

Stimulating Individual Creativity

Of course, as an individual, you cannot rely on your work environment to tease out your innovative side, nor can you blame it for failing to do so. Creativity is self-generated and must originate with you. Here are some suggestions, large and small, that can help.

1. Become master of your thoughts. An oft-noted statistic in self-help literature is that the human mind thinks about 60,000 thoughts a day, and yet the vast majority of these thoughts are repetitive— yesterday's thoughts, recycled over and over again. Most people have undisciplined minds. They do not actively shepherd their thoughts. Rather, they think in a passive, reactive way, allowing thoughts to drift aimlessly through their heads like debris floating by on a river. Creative, innovative people know better. They take full responsibility for what's going on in their heads. They continually harness their thoughts toward creative solutions to problems.

When you train your conscious mind to work on creative solutions, you also train your unconscious mind to do the same. That is why so many great "Eureka!" moments occur when the conscious mind is at rest. But these moments of sudden inspiration don't occur to passive, uninvolved minds. They come only to those who actively *work* their thoughts toward creative solutions.

If you would like to read one of the clearest, most inspiring guides to using the mind creatively and effectively, I strongly suggest *As a Man Thinketh* by James Allen. This brilliant little book was written more than a century ago, yet its words ring with the freshness of truth. You can download it online for free.

2. Learn to channel pain creatively. Perhaps the single trait that most distinguishes "creative" people from "non-creative" people is their ability to transform the pain of life into creative inspiration. Creativity, it turns out, is a much better anesthesia than drugs, alcohol, or food. Actually, it's more than anesthesia, because it *heals* pain rather than just numbing it.

Many of the great creative geniuses of history have faced enormous hardships, but instead of masking their pain, they used it as creative fuel. A recent BIO channel program, "The Tragic Side of Comedy," looks at some noteworthy comedians who followed that route. Richard Pryor, for example, used his own botched suicide attempt, which resulted in burning more than half of his body, as a source of material for the most brilliant performances of his career. When he later contracted multiple sclerosis, which would eventually rob him of his voice, he would go on stage in a wheelchair, where he turned his medical condition into further inspiration for humor. Channeling negative circumstances into positive opportunities is a liberating prescription for creativity that not only provides creative energy, but also opens up great new veins of insight and compassion.

3. Always be learning. To be innovative, you must be well educated in your field of endeavor. Otherwise you will spend your life reinventing the wheel. A deep understanding of the work that has come before you will help you see where your talents can make their most innovative contributions. It's also important, throughout your entire life, to keep expanding into *new* areas of learning. Learning new skills and disciplines actually forges new neural connections in your brain and can unleash great flurries of inventiveness. The moment we stop learning and start considering ourselves "complete" is the moment our brains start closing down and losing their creative powers.

4. Try your hand at coding. I personally found that learning to write computer code ignited my brain's creativity more powerfully than almost any other discipline. If you have the opportunity, I encourage you to give it a try.

5. Travel. Few experiences stir the mind's creative juices more than travel. Travel takes us out of our stale daily habits, awakens our senses, and exposes us to beliefs and cultures different from our own. It "forces" us to respond in new ways and move out of our comfort zones. Many artists have been inspired to create their most important works by traveling to a new country or region. I particularly recommend traveling to Africa, which is *the* emerging continent on the globe today—but any place that is fresh and new will spark your creativity.

6. Record your ideas. To make sure you are leveraging your creative genius, carry a recording mechanism with you at all times. It is all too easy to forget a great idea for a new product or service. You can buy a small, battery-operated digital recorder for a very affordable price. A notebook and pen works fine, too. Keep your device handy at night, so you can record those precious ideas that crop up near bedtime or in dreams. Leonardo da Vinci, one of the most inventive people in history, always carried a notebook in which he made quick sketches of his ideas and thoughts. It worked pretty well for him!

The Ultimate Creative Inspiration

There is one last aspect of creativity that I believe deserves special consideration—namely, its "spiritual" aspect. This is an area where Dr. King had very strong opinions. Again, this book is not intended to be religious in nature, but, when it comes to creativity, the spiritual dimension ought not be ignored.

As I've stated before, I enthusiastically share most of Dr. King's spiritual beliefs. One of these is the notion that man is created in the image and likeness of God. The following excerpt from Genesis is one that King relied on, over and over, for support and sustenance:

> Genesis 1:26. And God said, Let us make man in our image, after our likeness: and let them have dominion over the fish of the sea, and over the fowl of the air, and over the cattle, and over all the earth, and over every creeping thing that creepeth upon the earth.
>
> 27. So God created man in his own image, in the image of God created he him; male and female created he them.
>
> 28. And God blessed them, and God said unto them, Be fruitful, and multiply, and replenish the earth, and subdue it: and have dominion over the fish of the sea, and over the fowl of the air, and over every living thing that moveth upon the earth.

This biblical passage was absolutely central to King's life and work. He relied upon it as the basis for his conviction that all people are equal in the eyes of God. But he also took it much further. He believed that, since we are made in the image of the ultimate Creator, we have the right, and indeed the responsibility, to be Creators ourselves. He believed it is our birthright to use our God-given creative powers to reshape society, and the world, in a way that is consistent with God's message of love. To do less is to abdicate our divine responsibilities.

That certainly makes you think of creativity and innovation in a different way, doesn't it? Rather than being a mere business tool, the Currency of Creativity and Innovation is our *divine duty*. This is a profound idea. How would it affect *your* creativity level, for instance, if you started every day with a thought like this: "I was created in the image and likeness of God and endowed with the sacred gift of creative intelligence. I vow, today and every day, to maximize this gift by bringing forth new ideas, products, and services that benefit humanity and the world"? My guess is that it would take you to a whole new level. Why don't you give it a try?

A Final Thought

Everyone wants a piece of a vibrant, thriving, growing business. *Kingonomics* says that *service* is the route that will get us there. Solving the problems of humanity, large and small, is what will lead us to create products and services for which the world clamors. Combine the Currency of Service with the Currency of Creativity and Innovation and your company *will* become a market leader. It will also become the kind of business that makes the world a better place for all of us.

THE CURRENCY OF COURAGE

In Dr. King's "I've Been to the Mountaintop" speech, he spoke boldly about having lost all sense of personal fear because he had glimpsed the "promised land." He assured his audience that he now knew, with confidence, that the goals his people had been striving for *would* be achieved, whether he was alive to share the victory with them or not. The day after he delivered his eerily prophetic words, he was struck down by an assassin's bullet. However, his message of courage in the face of staggering adversity has lived on. Because of that courage, his legacy has thrived, and I know that Dr. King would have been ecstatic to see the election of the first black man to the office of the President of the United States.

In April of 1968, however, such a historic event must have seemed a terribly long way off. Nevertheless, Dr. King did believe that change in America was a real possibility and one worth fighting for. He also knew that, by fighting that fight, he was putting his life in danger every minute of every day. Yet the thought of giving up his mission never entered his mind as a real possibility. Every day he renewed his drive to attain equality for the downtrodden and disenfranchised. At the climactic point in King's journey when he made this famous speech, he was not afraid to risk *everything*, including his life, in order to continue the good fight. He truly was unafraid of dying.

Earlier in this final speech, King reminisced about his own brush with death in Harlem at the age of twenty-nine, when a demented woman lunged at him with a blade. She missed puncturing his aorta by only centimeters. Had he sneezed or coughed at that moment, history might have been altered. However, he knew he had been spared for a greater purpose. Perhaps this is what instilled in him the uncommon ability to rise above the common fears that plague most of us.

It was King's courage that launched a movement that spread from Atlanta to Memphis to Mumbai, and even to modern-day Egypt in its recent nonviolent revolution. King knew that in isolation we might be weak, but together we can be powerful. But in order to mobilize that power, each person has to tap the Currency of Courage in his or her own heart.

Fear Is the Real Enemy

King understood that *fear* was the main obstacle that could impede us from realizing our potential. He managed his own fear by holding steady to the principle that all men are created equal—not just anatomically, but economically. After years of nonviolent progress, King recognized that, although the communities of color had come a long way, they had a very long way to go in order to achieve upward mobility at all levels. He finally came to the conclusion that integrating into a marketplace with no seat at the table of opportunity was not progressive but, rather, counterproductive and oppressive. And he saw that fear was the enemy that lay at the root of this whole issue.

In 1958's "Stride Toward Freedom: The Montgomery Story," King remarked that people fear other people because of ignorance, and that it is *separation* that fuels this ignorance. It's time to break down these walls of separation that are holding us back from the glory that is well within our grasp. It's time to face our own fears about our fellow man, look those fears in the eye, and, for God's sake, get past them. For good. I say this: we have come far enough in our human evolution to eliminate fear as a dominant force in our interactions with one another. Fear is counterproductive and it *can* and *must* be transcended.

And we are all capable of doing this. How? Through love. Love is what gives us courage. Fear is what builds the walls of hatred and separation. Fear must be faced and kept at bay.

When you think about it, has any great feat in history ever been accomplished without first working through fear? Do you think the brave souls who stormed the beaches of Normandy on D-Day did so without first struggling with this emotion? Did Chuck Yeager not experience anxiety each time he broke the sound barrier in some new, untested aircraft? When Cinque, a Mende tribesman from Sierra Leone, sparked his famous mutiny aboard the ship *Amistad* after being illegally captured, do you think he did so without confronting fear in himself and his fellow companions?

Fearfulness Unseated

How about Rosa Parks? Exhausted after a long day's work, feet aching—do you think she was free of fear as she held her ground against the white man who insisted she give up her seat on the bus? Surely she must have known, at least in the back of her mind, that such an action would be likely to have grave consequences for her.

In fact, she *did* suffer consequences: she lost her job in a local department store and was arrested for violating Montgomery city code. Her husband, too, ended up resigning from his job when tensions resulting from his wife's act began causing issues for him there. There was a great price to pay for her and her family. But at that historic moment on Montgomery bus #2857, she called upon the Currency of Courage and acted in a way that was bigger than her isolated, individual self. Most historians today identify her signal act of defiance as the beginning of the modern civil rights movement. In her own words:

> I did not want to be mistreated, I did not want to be deprived of a seat that I had paid for. It was just time . . . there was opportunity for me to take a stand to express the way I felt about being treated

in that manner. I had not planned to get arrested. I had plenty to do without having to end up in jail. But when I had to face that decision, I didn't hesitate to do so because I felt that we had endured that too long. The more we gave in, the more we complied with that kind of treatment, the more oppressive it became.[1]

Rosa Parks had grown up with fear all around her and worried every night as a child that her family's home would be burned down by the Klan, or that a member of her family might be lynched. However, in one unanticipated moment, something inside her said, "Enough!" The rest is history. This one weary woman's personal act of rebellion against an established code of behavior set events in motion that would forever change the way America looked at race relations.

We never know how the simplest act of courage can change the world.

Rosa Parks' action led to the formation of a new black community organization in Montgomery, headed by a very young pastor of a local church named Martin Luther King, Jr. Shortly thereafter, the black community commenced a boycott of the city bus system that lasted almost a year. This, in turn, ultimately led to a U.S. Supreme Court decision that forbade laws requiring racial segregation on public transportation. This was the first of many milestones on the road to racial equality.

When the small "I" becomes the bigger "we" and we are no longer standing up just for ourselves, but for our family, our community, our nation, and our principles, we can sometimes summon up surprising courage in the face of great forces. Who can forget the photo of the lone student standing before the line of tanks in Tiananmen Square, armed only with a briefcase? What could have been running through his mind? Surely not thoughts of his own survival. At such times, Darwin's notions of biological selfishness clearly break down. The defining moments in human history often happen when ideas of justice, fairness, and principle override even our most primal survival instincts.

Courage Versus Fearlessness

"I learned that courage was not the absence of fear, but the triumph over it."

—NELSON MANDELA

In my first draft of this book, I called this final currency the Currency of Fearlessness, but I later thought better of it. I think courage is a better term. Let's briefly discuss the difference between courage and fearlessness.

Fearlessness means exactly what it says: absence of fear. This can be a good thing or a not-so-good thing. On one hand, absence of fear can be a truly noble state of mind in which a person has genuinely transcended the emotion of fear. We see evidence of this in Dr. King when he delivered his "I've Been to the Mountaintop" speech. Fearlessness of this kind is often the hallmark of a transformed person, someone who has done extraordinary inner work. Sometimes exceptional leaders and spiritual pioneers reach such a state of inner peace and confidence that they truly no longer experience fear.

Fearlessness can also arise when fear is eclipsed by a stronger emotion, such as outrage, love, or righteousness. In such cases, fear takes a back seat and is temporarily unfelt. This may have been the case with Rosa Parks or the Tiananmen Square student who stood before the tanks. Soldiers in battle often experience an eerie calm in which fear seems to be suspended; essentially they overcome the fear of death, at times even welcoming it.

Sometimes, however, fearlessness simply means a person doesn't know any better. In such cases, absence of fear is rooted in ignorance; the person is unaware of the threat he or she may be facing. This is the fearlessness of a child running into the street, or the fearlessness of a person who barges into dangerous situations blind to the potential consequences of his or her actions. This kind of fearlessness is not desirable.

But here's an important point: although we might strive for the type of fearlessness King showed the night before his death, the fact is, most of us cannot *consciously choose* to be unafraid. To tell ourselves we *shouldn't* be afraid is a very difficult exercise. Often when we claim to be unafraid, we are simply in denial.

Courage is different from fearlessness. Courage, as I use the term, means a willingness to act in the presence of fear. When we are courageous, we feel the fear, we understand the potential consequences of our actions, but we "do the right thing" anyway, understanding the risk we are taking. While fearlessness is not usually a conscious, deliberate choice, courage is. We can always *choose* to act courageously, whether we are feeling fear or not.

For that reason, courage is a currency we can always summon.

Fear Stifles Business, Courage Liberates It

One of the key factors that separates a successful business from an unsuccessful one is the courage its leaders demonstrate when the going gets tough. Courage is what empowers a businessperson to take the risks that can lead to success. It is also the quality that fortifies a leader to stay the course when there is a temptation to abandon ship or succumb to panic.

In the days since 9/11, the dot-com crash, the barrage of corporate scandals in the early 2000s, and the financial meltdown of 2008, stress has increased enormously in American business. Stakeholders of companies, boards of directors, executives, and managers have all felt the pressure of increased expectations. Some of this is due to the rapid globalization of the world economy, some is due to the fact that our communications tools have gotten so "good" that we now find ourselves flooded every day with e-mail, blogs, text messages, voice mail, and tweets, all vying for our attention. We are saturated with information pouring in at record speeds, much of it trying to influence our decision-making. There just doesn't seem to be time anymore for sitting back and thinking things through or giving our deeper intuition the space it needs to operate. We have all become victims of the clock and calendar.

And all of this, of course, increases stress and builds up fear. We fear missing something important in an e-mail or missing that big opportunity to win a new customer or project. We fear what the boss will think if we don't follow every step of established protocol for completing a task. As managers and leaders, we fear that the board or shareholders will criticize us for trying a new approach, having an unconventional idea, or taking too many risks.

In today's unforgiving business atmosphere, fear often rules the day. Instead of trying to be brilliant, we try to "not mess up." We become more concerned with covering our posteriors than unleashing our boldness and vision on the world.

Fear is an idea killer that stifles innovation, cooperation, and collaboration and fosters an atmosphere of suspicion and competitiveness. Fear can grip an organization whenever times get tough or sales drop below normal levels. Fear can become nearly palpable and, left unchecked, will infect a company like a disease and drive a business into an early grave.

Consciously and subconsciously, many dealmakers today are going into business relationships out of fear, carrying an attitude of, "I am doing business with you not because I want to, but because I have to." Both parties are suspicious of one another, convinced the other will try to take advantage of them the first chance they get. This attitude does not lay a foundation for mutual success.

I recently tried to navigate a partnership with an older businessman from a different community who had often raved enthusiastically about the possibility of our doing great things together. Yet, during all of our planning and strategizing about this new venture, he did little but advance his personal interests. It was his fear of not having direct control over the money that created our Achilles' heel. Because of the particulars of the business situation, legally, I had to be the one to collect the funds, but he could not make peace with this. And so his fears of being taken advantage of colored all of his actions. Here we had a great opportunity to generate tremendous revenue for both of us, and yet this partner defeated the venture from the start due to his groundless fears about my handling the funds. For me, this is a very present and palpable example of fear stifling mutual opportunity.

After nearly fifteen years in business, I have learned to become acutely aware of the warning signs of a one-sided deal where one party is more concerned with self-protection than mutual benefit. *Fear is a mind killer, an idea buster, and a growth retardant!* It is that little evil that eats at us from the inside out. We must learn to face it down and control it, through courage.

The truth is, if you are not taking risks, you are slowly assisting your own demise and that of your company. That is why, especially in the postmeltdown world we live in, courage is more vital than ever before. Only with courage can there be innovation, and without innovation—as we have seen before—a company dies.

Here are just a few of the dampening effects fear has on business, along with the liberating effects that courage can trigger:

FEAR INHIBITS RISK.

- Taking calculated risks is essential if we want to grow a business into a thriving enterprise. Without risk, we take only the safe, predictable actions that have proven reliable in the past, rather than look to the new possibilities that the future offers. Without risk, we never break new ground, we never unleash bold new products on the world, we never innovate, and we never become industry leaders. Fear focuses our gaze on potential loss, rather than potential gain. Ask any athlete: playing *not to lose* is a very different dynamic from playing to win. Courage, conversely, creates teams that play to win.

FEAR DESTROYS MORALE AND FAITH.

- Fear spreads like wildfire in a workplace, in a family, and in any team-based environment. It is especially destructive when it spreads from the top down. When the leader is afraid, fear ripples throughout an organization in ways both subtle and obvious, sapping the team of confidence, faith, and optimism. A team infected by fear is incapable of working courageously toward a vision. Rather, each member seeks to protect his or her own survival, often at the expense of others. A courageous leader, however, makes everyone under him feel that anything is possible.

FEAR MAKES FOR BAD DECISION-MAKING.

- Fear is often irrational. It flows from imagined outcomes that have no basis in reality. As we saw in an earlier chapter, fear literally makes us stupid by stifling the brain's most evolved thinking capacities and putting the primitive "lizard brain" in charge. Do you want a reptile running *your* business? Of course not. It is impossible to make sound business decisions when you operate out of fear. Courage, on the other hand, activates our highest and noblest faculties, such an inventiveness, optimism, love, and vision.

FEAR PRODUCES DEFENSIVE, COMPETITIVE BEHAVIOR.

- When people are defensive, they put up inner walls and shut down the Currency of Connectivity. It becomes almost impossible to collaborate with others—particularly others who look and sound different from you—when you are in a defensive posture.

The defense mechanism is often an external response to an internal pain. We put up barriers to protect ourselves from touching off a pain that we fear. Often this is a pain we have avoided our entire lives. The solution? Be courageous and *deal* with the pain—experience it, feel it, let it in, invite it to the table. Soon you will realize that the pain is not the destructive monster you feared it would be. It is just a bit of energy that wants to be acknowledged. Once you face your pain courageously, the barrier will fall. A mind without barriers creates ideas without limitations.

FEAR PUTS "SAFETY" BEFORE PEOPLE, VALUES, AND VISION.

- Fear focuses us on short-term results, rather than long-term goals. It fails to see the big picture. For example, fear tells corporations not to hire new employees because of concerns about pending tax legislation or upcoming elections, even when the company may be sitting on large cash reserves. It is this kind of fear and the defensive actions it triggers that hobble an economy. Hence, FDR's immortal prescription: "We have nothing to fear but fear itself." Courage, on the other hand, allows organizations to forge an ennobling vision and stick to it.

FEAR IS A SELF-FULFILLING PROPHECY.

- It is a strange and sobering truth that whatever we fear the most is what ultimately befalls us. That's because we create our existence with our thoughts, positive or negative. And so it is critical for us to think positive thoughts and focus on what we want to accomplish in life and business, rather than on the terrible things that *might* happen.

  I recently heard a downhill skier explain why some people have accidents on the trails and others don't. Those who focus on the upcoming rocks and roots, he said, inevitably run into those obstacles and crash. But those who look *past* the obstacles and focus on the path ahead have a smooth ride. This is a beautiful metaphor for business. Focus courageously on the path ahead, rather than the potential problems.

Common Fears In Business

In my forays into business I have encountered many common fears that seem to surface over and over again. By being aware of these, we can be better prepared to face and defeat them.

FEAR OF TECHNOLOGY.

▪ Many people in business (and all walks of life) are reluctant to change with the technological times and prefer to stick to familiar ways of doing things, even when those ways are clearly outdated. I am reminded of a woman I once knew who used her computer's word processor exactly like a typewriter, refusing to learn any of the functions that made it a superior tool.

Oddly enough, *abundance* can actually be a barrier to the adoption of new technology. A Pew Internet study demonstrates how people in underserved communities tend to adopt and adapt to new smartphone and tablet-based technologies faster than others. Why? Because they don't have *existing* desktops or laptops in the home. They have nothing to unlearn. Similarly, there has been proliferation of mobile phones versus landlines in developing regions like Africa. Many of these people didn't have landlines to start with! They have less resistance to overcome.

▪ I know of older business professionals who have been reluctant to embrace computers, e-mail, social media, and other technological trends. This is because they were fortunate enough to have secretaries and executive assistants who handled their correspondence for them. Nowadays, however, businesses are leaner and meaner. There are fewer layers of assistants in most corporations. More leaders now communicate directly. Many of these older, "privileged" executives will need to lose their fear of technology if they wish to remain employable.

FEAR OF COMPETITION.

▪ Many businesses become preoccupied with fears about what the competition is doing, rather than concentrating on the value they themselves are creating. This causes them to try to play catch-up instead of building on their own unique strengths. Forget about what others are doing! Concentrate on serving your customers and marketplace while continuing to identify ways to innovate that make sense for *your* business.

FEAR OF DIVERSITY.

▪ People who are afraid of diversity and inclusion aren't really comfortable in their own skin. Therefore, they choose— consciously or unconsciously—to isolate themselves within networks that look, think, talk, and believe as they do. Instead of embracing the great benefits of diversity, they focus on the (mostly imaginary) disadvantages and inconveniences. In doing so, they play small instead of big. They shut themselves off from vast potential resources.

FEAR OF FAILURE.

▪ Fear of failing is an almost universal issue for adults in our world. But I often wonder if people are really afraid of failing or are just afraid of what other people may think if they fail. I believe it's usually the latter. Look at children. They blissfully fail their way to success until people begin criticizing them or laughing at their stumbles. Then they become self-conscious and inhibited. But failing is a part of life and it's our greatest teacher. It's *how we handle* failure that makes all the difference. Do we grow from it? Do we learn from it? Do we build from it? As John Maxwell advises, "Fail forward."

FEAR OF SUCCESS.

▪ Almost as common as the fear of failure is the fear of success. Most human beings are resistant to change and can, therefore, be afraid of success on an unconscious level. That's why, again, many lottery winners experience their windfall as a crisis, not a blessing. This is true of many businesses as well. After all, if you are wildly successful in business, many changes may happen, fast. You might need to reorganize your company, hire more personnel, work harder, undergo public scrutiny, diversify into new areas, and/or possibly relocate your physical plant. Though every businessperson *claims* to want success, many are secretly afraid of it because it may call for sweeping and rapid change. And it may put *their* skills and performance under a bigger spotlight.

FEAR OF REJECTION.

▪ People deeply fear rejection. For many of us, this goes back to childhood when we felt that painful stab of rejection for the first time. We often spend our entire psychological lives trying to avoid having this feeling again. But learning to accept and manage rejection is a huge key to maturity and success. After all, rejection happens quite frequently in business. Customers tell you no. Investors tell you no. Partners tell you no. If you allow fear of rejection to dictate your behavior, you will never bring forth the next iPad or Velcro.

Three Major Ways to Nullify Fear and Increase Courage

For anyone looking for inspiration to overcome fear and grow in courage, it is always instructive to turn to the example and philosophy of Martin Luther King, Jr. Here are a few of the great principles he lived and preached.

▪ **Make service your main goal.** Embracing the Currency of Service is one of the most powerful ways to defeat fear and feed courage. When we focus on what we are giving to others, rather than what we are getting for ourselves, fear takes a back seat. Service not only activates the Currency of Reciprocity but also turns on our most courageous virtues. It was Dr. King's own service-mindedness toward humanity that enabled him to keep courageously fighting when it would have been much easier to give up.

■ **Adopt love as a business approach.** Dr. King continually urged his listeners to adopt love as their foremost guiding principle in life and business. If we study the most creative and innovative members of any society, love is their dominant quality, not hatred or fear. It is impossible to separate love from anything good in life. Hate and love cannot coexist in the same space; where there is love there will be no hate or fear. And vice versa.

Dr. King spoke of this in his sermon "Loving Your Enemies." He described hatred as a cancer that eats away at our core and destroys our ability to creatively respond to the challenges of life. A person who is diminished by hatred or fear cannot innovate in any meaningful way. Love, however, creates an environment where creativity and innovation can flourish. There can be no passion without love and there can be no creativity and innovation without passion.

It is worth noting that the root of the word "courage" is the French word "coeur," which means "heart." Courage and love are joined at the hip, for to have either one is to have "heart."

■ **Align your work and business with a higher purpose.** One of the surest ways to foster courage in business is to make your enterprise serve a purpose higher than mere profit. When your business adopts a purpose beyond enriching the bottom line, it becomes a "cause" and awakens in you your most heroic qualities. Each of us has a hero within us, but that hero does not stir to life unless we give it a heroic purpose. Heroism does not awaken for the sole purpose of "increasing quarterly profits," and it most certainly does not awaken for the purpose of doing shady deals or destructive activities. Nothing catalyzes courage like a noble cause. Nothing squashes courage like meaningless labor and unethical practices. Make your business and your cause one and the same.

This is the heart of social entrepreneurship. In today's fast-evolving world, society is looking more and more toward entrepreneurs to help solve its problems. Social entrepreneurship means using the spirit and principles of entrepreneurship to help nonprofit organizations do a more effective job. But it can also mean encouraging profit-making businesses to "do well by doing good." More and more, consumers are looking to spend their dollars with companies that are doing something positive to improve the world, either directly through their products and services or through their support of targeted charities.

Practically speaking, there are always two ways to do business: (1) in a way that is socially conscious and adds value to society and/or the environment, or (2) in a way that puts profits first, regardless of whether the business is exploiting people, advancing harmful values, or hurting the planet in some way. When you do business in the former way, it allows you to *believe* in what you're doing and to summon deep reserves of courage and commitment.

Take this idea one step further and align your business with a spiritual purpose. Then your business becomes, in effect, an arm of your church, synagogue, temple, or mosque. At the very least it becomes a place where you can unreservedly invest 100 percent of your energy, using not just your mental, physical, and emotional faculties, but your spiritual faculties as well.

Some Other Ways to Conquer Fear and Muster Courage in Business

Here are some additional strategies you can use to keep fear in check and become more courageous in your day-to-day actions:

- **Take action and create exposure.** The surest way to conquer any fear is to take action and expose yourself to the very thing you fear. The human mind fears the unknown more than it fears anything else. The more you place yourself in the very situations that cause you anxiety, the more these situations become "known," and the less severe your fear becomes.

- **Set goals through small, measurable steps.** Often we work ourselves into a state of panic because the goal we are trying to achieve seems huge and overwhelming. A great way to conquer this kind of fear is to break the goal down into smaller steps and focus only on the next one. Getting a Ph.D., for example, might seem an impossible goal while working a full-time job and raising a family. But you can break this large goal into small, measurable steps, such as: (1) thoroughly research six graduate programs, (2) apply to your favorite one, (3) take one evening course to "test the waters," and so on. "One day at a time" is the mantra of twelve-step programs. Why? It's a simple way of making an overwhelming goal achievable. When you break a goal down into small, measurable steps, you don't need to summon inhuman amounts of courage, just enough to take the next step.

- **Make a concrete plan.** A similar strategy is simply to make a concrete plan. Whenever you're faced with a fear-inducing problem, goal, or situation, much of the fear flows from your anxiety about how you are going to handle the situation. So make a concrete, intelligent plan. The moment you make a plan, you will feel your anxiety lessen by at least 50 percent, usually more.

- **Pray or meditate.** If you have aligned your work or business with a higher purpose, then you can, with a clear conscience, ask for spiritual help in achieving your goals whenever fear threatens to derail you. Nothing provides courage like spiritual support.

- **Practice mental rehearsal.** Anytime you're approaching a situation that is causing you anxiety—a presentation, a meeting, an interview—do as much mental rehearsal as possible. Imagine, in detail, how you'll handle tough challenges such as a difficult question or an equipment failure. The greater the sense of familiarity you can create in your mind, the less fear will have a grip on you.

- **Focus on your strengths, not your weaknesses.** As a general rule, always take a strengths-based approach to yourself, your company, and your products and services. Acknowledge your weaknesses and do what you can to correct them, but do not obsess over them. Keep 90 percent of your attention, at all times, on the things you and your business do remarkably well. This will prevent much fear from boiling up in the first place.

- **Make a fear inventory.** Make a list of the things that make you the most fearful about your job or business. What *exactly* do you fear? Next to each one, write an evaluation of the likelihood of it coming to pass. Ten percent? Twenty percent? Then imagine the worst-case scenario for each fear. Will it kill you? Will it bankrupt you? Will it destroy your family or your business? Probably not. The more you look at your fears in the daylight, the less terror they inspire.

- **Avoid too much news on TV, in print, or on the Internet.** The media learned a simple trick over a century ago: fear sells. That is why Twitter, print, and broadcast news is filled, almost from start to finish, with bad news. "If it bleeds, it leads" is literally true—car crashes, violent crimes, natural disasters, political rhetoric, and military attacks are always given top news priority (along with interviews of the tearful victims and eyewitnesses). We are told it is important for us to be kept informed about these things. But is that really true? This kind of news story wreaks havoc on our state of mind. People who start each day with the morning news and end it with the evening news are writing themselves a prescription for anxiety. It is far better to start and end each day with inspirational thoughts, words, and prayers. Feed your courage, not your fear.

- **Associate with positive people.** Avoid negative, poisonous people who wallow in the suffering of others and spread gossip, bad news, and fearful rumors. Seek out the company of those who are enthusiastic, cooperative, supportive, and goal-oriented. Nothing can put you into a fearful frame of mind faster than bad company. Nothing inspires courage like positive minds working together.

- **Listen to your heart, not just your head.** Both the head and the heart are vital in business, but it is the head that conjures up fearful thoughts, while it is the heart that is the source of courage (*coeur*-age). Literally. When it's time for courageous action, you need to get out of your head and into your heart. It is the heart that has driven every courageous act in human history.

Courage Versus Foolhardiness

Many people argue that fear is necessary, because without it, we'll do stupid things. I've sometimes heard people say, for example, "A child needs to be afraid of fire or she'll put her hand in it." But *fear* is not necessary, only knowledge and awareness; a child need not be *afraid* of fire, she need only be aware that fire can cause pain. That is enough to make the child behave cautiously. Similarly, we do not need fear to make us appropriately cautious in business. We just need awareness and knowledge.

Courage does not mean being foolhardy or being in denial about possible negative consequences. It does not mean taking stupid risks. On the contrary, it means taking full stock of the risks and making an informed decision based on the risk-to-benefit ratio. But it also means having the fortitude to stand by your decision, like Dr. King, and not let fear throw you off course.

| PARTING THOUGHTS |

I t's no secret that Dr. Martin Luther King, Jr. has been a powerful inspiration to me. On more occasions than I can count, his words and ideas have helped me persevere and push through obstacles. Without King's legacy of wisdom and courage, my life would be profoundly poorer. On every level. King was both a visionary and a tireless fighter—the most potent combination of human traits. More than any other figure in modern American history, he helped heal the wounds that have long ruptured our nation's spirit at its core. He also left us a vibrant road map for our future evolution.

King, in his day, did not have the luxury of delicacy or fine-tuning in his actions. He knew that great gulfs of injustice needed to be bridged and he did what was necessary to cover as much ground as possible in his short life. And in doing so, he brought us all closer to the Promised Land. How sad it would be if his voice were lost in the wind before we got all the way there.

That is why I've written this book. I want to do my tiny part to keep the vision and the voice of Dr. King alive in this new age, where the challenges we face are in some ways more subtle and in some ways more urgent than in King's day. On a healing level, there is still an enormous amount of work to be done. Though the most blatant and visible outrages of King's era have been addressed—American citizens are no longer forced to drink from separate water fountains or use segregated bathrooms—the inequities continue on a less obvious, but equally destructive, level. American citizens are still being targeted with junk loans, housing discrimination, legal prejudice, and cultural stereotyping because of the color of their skin. Progress has been made, but we have a long, long way to go. Look only at the statistic I noted earlier—that black Americans have an average accumulated wealth of $5,500, as compared with $115,000 for whites—to appreciate the amount of ground that still needs to be made up. And it's not just African Americans whose destinies are being molded by invisible walls. Asian Americans, gay and disabled people, Middle Eastern Americans, and many other groups suffer as well.

But even as some groups continue to struggle for equal footing, our nation as a whole faces dramatic challenges on the world stage. America is slipping. Economically. Educationally. Technologically. Manufacturing has fled our shores. Our health care system is in shambles. Our students are entering college with subpar skills and are forced to accumulate epic amounts of debt just to get entry-level jobs. Our dollar is losing value by the month. As a nation, we are in grave danger of tumbling into a ditch of malaise and mediocrity from which we might not be able to emerge. We need to make drastic changes if we want to reclaim our position of global leadership, vision, and innovation.

Kingonomics addresses both of these issues simultaneously. By making the correct efforts to heal our society internally, we will, at the same time, restore our country to greatness externally. I am absolutely convinced of this. *Kingonomics* provides a basic road map for this work.

Kingonomics is not about asking our community leaders or our government to change. It's about asking ourselves. America's journey to new greatness must begin with each one of us looking into the mirror and changing our thinking and behavior patterns. Do I believe *Kingonomics* to be a cure-all? Of course not. But I do firmly believe that these twelve simple currencies, sincerely embraced, can carry us a long, long way in the right direction.

Once again, the key is economics. King knew this. He knew there would be no true opportunity in our land, or in the world, until all of its citizens had an equal shot at financial freedom. But in his day there were so many political, legal, and institutional barriers to be toppled that he could not put the focus on economics that he knew it deserved.

We can. That is why the bulk of this book has been focused on economic justice rather than on legal, moral, or spiritual justice.

The beauty of economics is that it truly *is* in our hands, to a large degree. *We* can control how we spend our money, how we conduct business, what kinds of products and services we offer, what kinds of team members we employ, what kinds of values we want to pay for, and what kind of values we want to sell. The world has indeed become flat. That is the mind-boggling reality of the new millennium. Everyday citizens—you and I—now have access to the same worldwide sales, distribution, communication, and marketing tools that the big conglomerates enjoy. We can now shape our little corner of the market as never before. We have fresh new opportunities to make the changes *we* want to see in the world—strictly by how we buy, sell, hire, and do business. No one can tell us how to spend our money or what values our businesses can embody. *We* have the freedom to make those choices and, in so doing, to change the world, a little bit at a time. This is true democracy in action.

I read a little blurb on the web the other day. It addressed the limitations of government when it comes to erasing discrimination. It pointed out that while the law can force a white man to open his shop to black customers, it cannot force a white man to shop in a black man's store. That's a simple but profound truth. What it emphasizes, to me, is the fact that, at some point, change comes down to *us,* not the government. The law can pave the way. It can get us partway there, but it will never get us all the way. To expect the government to be able to engineer a truly color-equal society is pure self-deception. *We* have to take the reins, each and every one of us, no matter our color, culture, or creed. *We* have to be the ones who change, deep in our own hearts. And we need to carry out that change in the world by the way we leverage our checkbooks and our business plans. We must learn to make *fully conscious* economic and business choices that reflect the deepest values we believe in.

> *To expect the government to be able to engineer a truly color-equal society is pure self-deception.* We *have to take the reins, each and every one of us, no matter our color, culture, or creed.*

I humbly hope *Kingonomics* can serve as a guide in this endeavor. *Kingonomics*, I truly believe, has the power to transform our collective soul. But the work must be carried out individually. The currencies of *Kingonomics* must be accumulated, spent, and invested through personal action. It is up to each and every one of us to play a part. And so, if you connect with the truths and solutions outlined in this book, I implore you to start investing these currencies *today*. With a fierce commitment. Those of us who "get" these principles have a special responsibility. We must act with a sense of urgency. We must *be* the change we wish to see in the world. We must pressure the politicians and pundits, yes, but we must not *wait* for them.

Whether we embrace the term *Kingonomics* or not, we must starting living the values this book describes, right now, if we want to see a turnaround in our nation's trajectory and reposition America for greatness in the near future and beyond.

This work will not be simple or easy. Far from it. *Kingonomics* calls for profound changes in our hearts, minds, and professional lives. It calls for us to shake off our passivity, our blaming, our victimization, our despair, our ennui, and to make a definitive commitment for change *within ourselves*. Then it calls for us to live that commitment by consciously investing the currencies of *Kingonomics* on a day-to-day basis in our jobs, our businesses, and our purchasing patterns. It certainly will not be easy.

But as great as I know the challenge to be, the hope and excitement I feel is even greater. When I think about the power we now hold in our hands, I feel a surge of exhilaration that dwarfs all doubts. I am positively thrilled about the potential we possess at this point in our history. And I hope I have stirred up some of that same excitement in you. For without a spark of wild enthusiasm, the task may seem too daunting to tackle.

Dr. King had that spark and he never lost it. By keeping it burning in his soul, he was able to change the world.

So will you be.

This is not the conclusion of a journey, my friends. It is the beginning of one. For now is the time to stop *thinking* about these ideas and start acting on them. Will you join me in staking a claim for justice and dignity? Will you join me in sowing the seeds of service, honesty, and love back into the soil of American business?

Will you join me in reaching for the economic stars?

| NOTES |

INTRODUCTION

1   Sue Goodwin, "American Cultural History, 1940–1949," Lone Star College–Kingwood Library, http://kclibrary.lonestar.edu/decade40.html.

2   Rakesh Kochhar et al., "Wealth Gaps Rise to Record Highs Between Whites, Blacks, Hispanics: Twenty-to-One," http://www.pewsocialtrends.org/2011/07/26/wealth-gaps-rise-to-record-highs-between-whites-blacks-hispanics (July 26, 2011).

CHAPTER FOUR

1   Robert B. Cialdini, *Influence: The Psychology of Persuasion* (New York: Quill/William Morrow, Revised Edition 1993), p. 17.

2   Ibid., pp. 23–24.

3   Michael Morris, "Trust and Reciprocity in Chinese Business Networks," http://www4.gsb.columbia.edu/ideasatwork/feature/70221 (January 26, 2006).

4   Ibid.

5   "Vermont Speciality [sic] Food Producer and a New England Grocer Team Up to Feed the Hungry," http://www.pitchengine.com/bovesofvermont/vermontspecialityfoodproducerandanewenglandgrocerteamuptofeed thehungry (December 21, 2010).

6   Cynthia Bunting, "Giving Back: 36 Ways Your Small Business Can Help," http://www.businessnewsdaily.com/642-small-business-owners-giving-back-to-community.html (February 4, 2011).

7   Ibid.

8   L'Occitane Foundation, http://foundation.loccitane.com/Default.aspx?c=1&l=1&a=4919&s=166/.

9   "Eli and Edythe Broad," http://broadeducation.org/thebroads.html.

10 Rebecca Knight, "Lessons in the Art of Giving," http://www.ft.com/intl/cms/s/2/cfb646c4-90ed-11df-85a7-00144feab49a.html#axzz1fJg621AI (2010).

11   Ibid.
12   Ibid.
13   Ibid.
14   2010 U.S. Census Bureau information.
15   Caroline Wolf Harlow, "Education and Correctional Populations,"
     Bureau of Justice Statistics, http://bjs.ojp.usdoj.gov/index
     .cfm?ty=pbdetail&iid=814 (January 2003).

CHAPTER FIVE
1   Mary E. Charlson et al., "Taking Moments to Enjoy Life Helps Patients
    Make Better Health Decisions," http://weill.cornell.edu/news/releases/
    wcmc/wcmc_2012/01_23_12.shtml (January 23, 2012).
2   Marci Shimoff and Carol Kline, *Happy for No Reason: 7 Steps to Being
    Happy from the Inside Out* (New York: Simon & Schuster, 2008), p. 255.
3   Irene Lane, "Health Benefits of Hopeful Thinking," http://www.examiner
    .com/healthy-living-in-washington-dc/health-benefits-of-hopeful-thinking
    (November 4, 2009).
4   Will Marré, *Save the World and Still Be Home for Dinner* (Dulles, VA:
    Capital Books, 2009), pp. 163–69.
5   Jennifer Robison, "It Pays to Be Optimistic," http://gmj.gallup.com
    /content/28303/pays-optimistic.aspx (2007).
6   Brainy Quote, http://www.brainyquote.com/quotes/quotes/v/viktorefr
    160380. html.

CHAPTER SIX
1   "Rethinking the Social Responsibility of Business," http://reason.com
    /archives/2005/10/01/rethinking-the-social-responsi/singlepage (October
    2005).
2   "Nelson Mandela Quotes," Goodreads.com, http://www.goodreads.com
    /quotes/show/22390.

CHAPTER SEVEN
1   Donald T. Phillips, *Martin Luther King, Jr., on Leadership: Inspiration and
    Wisdom for Challenging Times* (New York: Warner Books, 2000), p. 214.
2   Thinkexist.com, http://thinkexist.com/quotation/looking-back-you-realize-
    that-a-very-special/365732.html.
3   "Oprah Winfrey Quotes," Goodreads.com, http://www.goodreads.com/
    quotes/show/119038.
4   Ibid., http://www.goodreads.com/quotes/show/236650.
5   "Oprah Quotes on Weight and Body Image," About.com, http://oprah
    .about.com/od/oprahquotes/a/oprahweightquotes.htm.
6   "Oprah Self-Esteem and Spirit Quotes," About.com, http://oprah.about
    .com/od/oprahquotes/a/esteemquotes.htm.
7   Ibid.

8   Ibid.
9   Ibid.

CHAPTER EIGHT
1   "Book Review: Leadership Is an Art," http://www.giftedleaders.com/books
     -LeadershipArt.htm.
2   Vivek Wadhwa, "We Need a Black Mark Zuckerberg," *Washington Post
     Online*, http://www.washingtonpost.com/blogs/innovations/post/we-need-a
     -black-mark-zuckerberg/2011/06/24/AGWXYHjH_blog.html (June 24, 2011).
3   Markham, Edwin, "Outwitted." *The Shoes of Happiness, and Other Poems* (1915).

CHAPTER TEN
1   Jim Loehr, *The Power of Full Engagement* (New York: Free Press, 2003), p. 9
2   Jim Loehr, *The Power of Story* (New York: Free Press, 2007) pp. 1–14
3   Loehr, *The Power of Full Engagement*, p. 48
4   Ibid., p. 96.
5   Ibid., p. 72.
6   Ibid., p. 94.
7   Loehr, *The Power of Story*, p. 204
8   Loehr, *The Power of Full Engagement*, p. 110

CHAPTER ELEVEN
1   Marguerite Reardon, "AT&T Uses Twitter During Service Outage," http://
     news.cnet.com/8301-1035_3-10216712-94.html?tag=mncol;title (April
     2009).
2   Cortney Fielding, "Eric Schmidt Explains How Google Hires," http://
     gigaom.com/2011/05/02/eric-schmidt-former-google-ceo-how-google-
     hires (May 2, 2011).
3   Clive Thompson, "The See-Through CEO," http://www.wired.com/wired
     /archive/15.04/wired40_ceo.html (March 2007).
4   Michael Marchionda, "Open for Business: Transparency in the Digital
     Age," http://www.prescientdigital.com/articles/web-2.0/open-for
     -business-transparency-in-the-digital-age.

CHAPTER TWELVE
1   Bruce Einhorn, "The 30 Most Innovation-Friendly Countries," http://
     images.businessweek.com/ss/09/03/0312_innovative_countries/1.htm.
2   Ibid.
3   Larry Huston and Nabil Sakkab, "P&G's New Innovation Model," http://
     hbswk.hbs.edu/archive/5258.html (March 20, 2006).

CHAPTER THIRTEEN
1   "Rosa Parks and the Civil Rights Movement," http://www.rosaparksfacts
     .com/rosa-parks-civil-rights-movement.php.

| ACKNOWLEDGMENTS |

To the Creator of all things—past, present and future—"I am that I am."

To Jesus, The Christ—my consummate objective is to become like you. To this end, it is my hope that I demonstrate your practical and inclusive love for all humanity in this work and in my everyday life.

To my wife and life partner—you are the greatest love of all and you demonstrate it with your endearing support through the valleys and the mountaintops.

To my children—there is great potential in you to accomplish much. Use this tool to discover and manifest your definitive purpose in ways your mother and I can only imagine.

To my team—the journey continues and we are just getting started.

To Glenn at BenBella Books—thank you for empowering me to create and fulfill the definitive purpose that *Kingonomics* will serve.

To my editors—thanks for challenging the manuscript until full clarity was achieved by all. The last two years haven't been easy, but we did it.

To Raoul—let's sell some books!

To Andy, my writer—job well done.

To Dr. Martin Luther King, Jr.—thank you for your inspiration.

To every injustice, tangible and intangible—we welcome the opportunity to overcome you.

| ABOUT THE AUTHOR |

Rodney Sampson is a social innovator, serial entrepreneur, investor, author, and consecrated bishop. Via his Episcopal affiliations with the International Bishop's Conference and Kingdom Manifestation, Sampson shapes innovative economic policy and opportunities throughout society and culture.

As a serial entrepreneur, Sampson cofounded Multicast Media Networks (Streamingfaith.com) in 2000 (sold in 2010), Intellect in 2002, Intellect Inspire in 2006, and Legacy Opportunity Fund in 2007 with private equity investments in technology, publishing, and financial services. At present, Sampson is building Opportunity Fund, a U.S.-based super crowd fund and crowdfunding platform designed to provide underserved and under-represented communities access to investment opportunities traditionally reserved for accredited and institutional investors. He also serves on the boards of a disruptive technology start-up, a New York-based merchant investment bank, a home-based business, and a community development corporation (CDC).

Sampson is regularly called upon to advise and speak to nations, businesses, universities, and bishops who employ thousands and lead millions of constituents and communities around the world.

Sampson's published works include *Kingonomics: Twelve Innovative "Currencies" for Transforming Your Business and Your Life, Inspired by Dr. Martin Luther King, Jr.*; *Your Manifest Destiny: 7.5 Words to Transform Your Future*; *Yes We Will: Solutions for Realizing Your Personal Power in an Obama Era*; and *Black Trillions: Introducing Symbiotic Economics*. His audio works include *Any Day Now: Genesis of Divine Manifestation* and *Your Manifest Destiny: 15 Audio Meditations to Transform Your Future*.

Sampson earned a Bachelor's degree in psychology from Tulane University in 1995 and a Master of Business Administration from Keller Graduate School of Management in 2001. He also studied in the Doctor of Medicine program at the Pennsylvania State University College of Medicine from 1995 to 1999. For his dedication and commitment to definitive social causes at such a young age, Sampson received an honorary Doctorate of Ministry from the I.G.F. Theological Seminary in 1998.

A strong believer in global reinvestment, Sampson has been a friend of Africa. He has worked closely with the republics of Namibia, Gabon, and Uganda in the areas of trade and development, business development, leadership development, and public affairs.

For his contributions to humanity, Sampson was awarded the Phoenix Award—the City of Atlanta's highest honor—by Mayor Shirley Franklin in 2004. In direct support of the legacy of Dr. Martin Luther King, Jr., Sampson, his wife, and a group of influencers in 2007 donated more than $50,000 to the King Papers Project, a capital campaign established to ensure that Dr. King's papers would remain in the city of Atlanta at Morehouse College for generations to come.

Sampson and his wife reside in their native home with their children.

| INDEX |